OXFORD STUDIES IN AFRICAN AFFAIRS

General Editors

JOHN D. HARGREAVES *and* GEORGE SHEPPERSON

GERMAN MISSIONS IN TANGANYIKA 1891–1941

GERMAN MISSIONS IN TANGANYIKA

1891–1941

LUTHERANS AND MORAVIANS IN THE SOUTHERN HIGHLANDS

BY

MARCIA WRIGHT

CLARENDON PRESS · OXFORD
1971

Oxford University Press, Ely House, London W.1

GLASGOW NEW YORK TORONTO MELBOURNE WELLINGTON
CAPE TOWN SALISBURY IBADAN NAIROBI DAR ES SALAAM LUSAKA ADDIS ABABA
BOMBAY CALCUTTA MADRAS KARACHI LAHORE DACCA
KUALA LUMPUR SINGAPORE HONG KONG TOKYO

PRINTED IN GREAT BRITAIN BY
RICHARD CLAY (THE CHAUCER PRESS) LTD
BUNGAY, SUFFOLK

FOR
BETTY GIBSON
IN
APPRECIATION

Preface

IN 1962 an elderly custodian of German land records, including files on the Moravian and Lutheran Missions in the Southern Highlands, gestured towards them and expressed the greatest disgust at the religious squabbling they revealed.

To a new generation bent on reassessing African history, such materials can be appreciated more broadly, as documents of primary importance for the history of the Southern Highlands of Tanzania in the early colonial period. Many more surprises awaited the researcher in those days, as the archives began to be organized in Dar es Salaam and a climate receptive to post-colonial historiography developed.

The history of the Church in the Southern Highlands touches most of the main themes and forces at work in the region before the Second World War. In some respects it is atypical. Missionary history in the half century, 1891 to 1941, normally entails a discussion of initial interaction of Africans and Europeans on a man to man basis, followed by growing integration of missionary and colonial institutions. But in Tanzania the transfer of power from Germany to Britain in 1918 arrested such a colonial synthesis and allowed many qualities of the earlier period to be carried over.

Older literature on the colonial period treated Africans and white colonials in the spirit of the 'horse and rider' image, the riders being the fit subjects of history. Recent writing has concentrated upon Africans more exclusively. While I believe the two components of the colonial situation must be treated on equal terms, the task of balancing has nevertheless been difficult. The first two chapters seek to treat the German missionaries and the peoples of the Southern Highlands separately; thereafter their stories become inseparable. Some readers may wish to begin with Chapter II, which leads directly into the narrative. Chapter I is generally concerned with the structure and perennial problems of the German actors.

Literature in English deals neither extensively nor intensively with the German missionary movement. A rather full introduction has been included because the Berlin Lutherans and the Moravians of Herrnhut reflected the debates and theories of this movement, with its predominantly conservative social outlook. As it is not enough to look at the indigenous church as viewed by the intellectuals in Germany, the social and cultural background of missionary personnel destined for the field must also be considered.

The Southern Highlands, too, are not well known. A key question, in a region of such diverse peoples, is whether it was feasible at all to develop a united church bridging and yet accommodating traditional social patterns. Missionaries continually reflected the alternative attitudes available to their parishioners, either confining themselves within a very circumscribed community or attempting to deal with elements of mobility and supra-tribal integration. The immediate pre-colonial period clearly anticipates the issues of particularism and regionalism in commercial, political, and religious affairs so evident in later times.

The missionary theme is especially useful for the study of the Southern Highlands, where it is so pervasive and continuous. Indeed, the region is in this respect an exaggerated example of a general feature of the modern history of Tanzania. A great deal is yet to be mined from the archives of the German Protestant, Roman Catholic, and Anglican Societies, not to mention those of the many smaller missions. It is to be hoped that the study presented here will stimulate the use of these documents. The German Evangelicals in the Southern Highlands provide very good illustrations of how missionaries operated as intermediates responsive to both African and imperial factors, but to some degree, all missionaries did the same.

The odyssey of a researcher wishing to uncover materials for Tanzanian history was especially challenging in the early 1960s. The beckoning horizons led from Africa to Germany, Scandinavia, England, Scotland, and America. The young National Archives of Tanzania contained an unexpected wealth of official records about missionary activities which exposed much about the general political context as well. The situation with regard to church records at the time of research was more ambiguous. Did they belong to the African churches or to the missionaries who continued to be on the scene? An inquisitive and persistent search, however, frequently brought rewards, rich ones in the case of the Nyasa Provincial files of the Moravian Church in the inter-war period, found in an attic at Rungwe Station.

The problem of digesting the past has been no easier for missionaries than for other Germans. In a few cases, records were purposefully destroyed, but in most instances, they have simply been neglected. The *Missionsrat* in Hamburg exemplifies both the tendency in the post-war period to start anew and a generosity in permitting researchers to rummage and make what they wished of the unsifted files. The disarray of records ought not to be overstated. The Moravian Archives at Herrnhut, and the archives of the Leipzig and Berlin Missions are well maintained though rarely consulted by historians.

The librarians, archivists, missionary staff members and others who have sympathetically assisted in providing materials, are too numerous to be mentioned separately. Michael Cook and the staff of the National Archives of Tanzania are owed a special appreciation. Although research depended primarily upon documentary sources, valuable insights were provided by persons with experience reaching back to the period and those who shared intimately related research. They include Dean Gustav Bernander, General-Superintendent Walter Braun, Dr. Joseph Busse, Professor Ernst Dammann, Dr. Johanna Eggert, Dr. Hans Florin, Miss B. D. Gibson, Dr. James Graham, Josephu Merinyo, Bishop Stefano Moshi, Pastor Lazarus Mwangisi, the Revd. Martin Nordfeldt, Eli Nyagava, and Dr. Richard Reusch. Professor Roland Oliver gave valuable advice as director of the thesis upon which the present work is based. I am, of course, solely responsible for factual accuracy, translations from the German, and conclusions.

M.W.

Contents

List of Maps

Abbreviations and Glossary

For details of abbreviations used in references to sources, see Bibliography.

A.A.: Auswärtiges Amt (Foreign Office)

A.A.K.A.: Auswärtiges Amt Kolonial Abteilung (Foreign Office, Colonial Section)

(*N.*)*A.M.Z.*: (*Neue*) *Allgemeine Missionszeitschrift*

B.M.B.: *Berlin Missionsberichte*

C.B.M.S.: Conference of Missionary Societies in Great Britain and Northern Ireland

C.M.S.: Church Missionary Society

C.O.: Colonial Office

C.S.: Chief Secretary *or* Church of Scotland

D.E.: Department of Education

D.E.M.R.: *Deutsche Evangelische Missionsrat* (German Evangelical Missionary Council)

D.K.B.: *Deutsches Kolonialblatt*

D.K.Z.: *Deutsche Kolonialzeitung*

D.O.: District Officer

E.M.M.: *Evangelisches Missions Magazin*

F.O.: Foreign Office

Gov.: Central Government in German East Africa and Tanganyika

H.M.B.: *Missionsblatt aus der Brüdergemeine*

I.M.C.: International Missionary Council

I.R.M.: *International Review of Missions*

J.A.H.: *Journal of African History*

P.A.: *Periodical Accounts*

P.C.: Provincial Commissioner

R.K.A.: Reichskolonialamt (Imperial Colonial Office)

T.N.R.: *Tanzania Notes and Records*

U.F.C.: United Free Church (Livingstonia)

U.M.C.A.: Universities Mission to Central Africa

Z.f.E.S.: *Zeitschrift für Eingeborenen Sprachen*

GLOSSARY

Akida	Tax Collector, District Officer
askari	soldier, policeman
ausschuss	committee
Bezirksamtmann	(Civil) District Commissioner
boma	fortified enclosure, District Office
capitao (from Portuguese)	appointed headman
jumbe	headman
Kolonialgesellschaft	Colonial Society
Kolonialrat	Colonial Advisory Council
mganga	curer or medicine man
pombe	beer or any alcoholic drink
Stationschef	(Military) District Commandant
shauri	lit. decision or consultation commonly court hearing
Volkstum	popular ethnic and cultural character

15 rupies = 20 marks = £1
Orthography generally follows that of the source, except that the prefix 'U' is preferred to 'Bu' to indicate the country of a people. Buwanji and Bundali, however, survive.

CHAPTER I

Missionary Backgrounds

Two recurrent themes in the history of the German missionary movement both at home and in Tanganyika were those of nationality and ecclesiastical character. Nationality implied no simple nationalism, for while it is true that German missionaries followed the flag to East Africa, they did so at the direction of men with well-defined, critical attitudes towards imperialism. These attitudes were the outgrowth of experiences in British, Dutch, and Danish colonies, which had been abstracted, refined, and shared in the discussions of the periodic meetings of the Continental Missionary Conference, usually held at Bremen. By 1885 when Germany embarked upon its colonial career, missionary leaders virtually in unison urged the Government to adopt their approach to Christianization as the foundation of a colonial policy. Their programme, calling for the conservation of indigenous ways of life, was hostile to both the *laissez-faire* line of the Hanseatic traders and the national chauvinism of many colonial enthusiasts.[1]

The cultural relativism that featured so prominently in the ideology of the Protestant missionary societies in the Continental Conference was related to intellectual currents in Germany in the nineteenth century. This common attitude towards culture provided a rallying point in the face of stresses inbuilt among the autonomous, 'free' sponsors of overseas evangelization. Denominational and parochial differences had caused the earlier splintering of the missionary movement, and such issues could surface again all too easily.

Nationality figured prominently in the first meetings of the Continental Conference, beginning in 1866, when the political and ecclesiastical implications of the unification of Germany were still unclear. In their view of the world situation, the assembled leaders shared a diffused feeling of antagonism against England, whose dominance in the colonized world became increasingly evident in mid century. The peculiar emotional climate of the time was reflected by the sentiments of a leader of the German–Swiss Basel Mission, who in 1869 deplored

[1] Hogg, W. R., *Ecumenical Foundations* . . . (New York, 1952), pp. 60ff. See also, Knak, Siegfried, 'The Characteristics of German Evangelical Missions in Theory and Practice', *Tambaram Reports* iii (London, 1939), 314f.

the heightened sense of antagonism between Frenchmen and Germans, and the deterioration of relations even between the Swiss and Germans. Towards the English, however, to whom Basel and other German Societies had supplied missionary personnel, his mood was different: 'Only on the day when Englishmen come to us to study here and to serve our society will the barrier be broken. But as long as the British are too proud to come to us, we will be too proud to go to them. . . . This is the right, the Godly kind of pride for Swiss and Germany.'[1] In terms of domestic developments in Germany, most members of the Continental Conference cared more for their international constituencies or their denominational identity than for the kind of nationalism represented by the convener, Friedrich Fabri, who would have been glad to see an ecclesiastical and missionary union within Germany.

The Continental Conference endeavoured to attract all Protestant missionary organizations in Europe. The Paris missionaries proved to be irregular in attendance, because of their Calvinist constitution, close co-operation with the London Missionary Society, and their reactions to the Franco-Prussian War. Lutheran ties with Scandinavia encouraged more consistent participation from that direction, but the hard core of the Continental Conference, from the start, was made up of German-speaking societies.[2] Theologically, the rigid Lutherans of the Leipzig Mission were at one extreme; the 'general' missions such as Basel, soliciting support from both Calvinists and Lutherans, were in the centre; and the pietistic splinters rejecting institutionalized church hierarchies occupied the other extreme. The spread and multiplication of independent missionary bodies came about in part because of a chain reaction started by the efforts of the Prussian Monarchy to amalgamate the Reformed (Calvinist) and Lutheran Churches as a single national church. Manoeuvres of this kind had taken place in the early eighteenth century, but the Prussian Union Church posed a more serious threat in the early nineteenth century, when its efforts prompted Lutherans and pietists to hive off on their own.[3]

Up to the beginning of the proliferation in the 1830s, the 'general' or non-denominational motive prevailed. The Moravians or

[1] Director Josenhans, quoted in Schlatter, W., *Geschichte der Basler Mission, 1815–1915*, 2 vols. (Basel, 1916), i, 283.

[2] Hogg, *Ecumenical Foundations*, p. 61.

[3] For the eighteenth century, see Deppermann, Klaus, *Der hallesche Pietismus und der preussische staat unter Friedrich III (I)*, (Göttingen, 1961).

Brüdergemeine, also called the Herrnhuters, occupied a senior position, influential because of their century of foreign evangelization and strong constitutional principles. Next in age came the Basel Mission, for many years the trainer of missionaries for 'sending' societies based in the imperial countries. In founding the newer Berlin Mission, zealous young aristocrats in Prussia were hoping that their state might also be represented in Christianizing the world. They emulated Basel by setting out to train men for other societies and by adopting the missionary and church discipline of the Moravians.[1] The general missions of this era shared a broad pietism and were free, voluntary organizations tied to no established church, soliciting support through pastors who were individually sympathetic and through auxiliaries in major centres. The process of splintering generally followed one of two courses; either missionary personnel and pastors resigned from the mother society to set up separate training and sending organizations, or auxiliaries broke away and engaged in more direct missionary activities: the need to preserve pietistic principles or orthodox Lutheran doctrine was stressed in the process. As an added undercurrent, provincial political resistance to Prussian domination often lent an extra sharpness to the 'religious' reaction to church union.

To avoid divisive issues, the basis for a uniform missionary philosophy had to be found in missiology, the science of world evangelization. The members of at least the inner circle of the Continental Conference had been able to affirm that somehow their style of work differed from that of the Anglo-Saxons. One difference was to be found in the intimate connection for the English and Americans between 'legitimate' commerce and Christianity as principal civilizing agents. Western materialism was rejected by the Continental theorists, foremost among them Gustav Warneck, who discerned a degree of decadence in Europe that required cautious distinctions to be made between what was Christian and what was 'overcultured' and destitute of Christian moral foundations: 'In the true sense of the word we have to speak of a manifold culture-war on the part of the Christian mission.'[2] A fundamental agreement, then, came from

[1] Althausen, Johannes, 'Kirchliche Gesellschaften in Berlin 1810 bis 1830', 2 vols. (unpublished diss., Halle, 1965). *A.M.Z.* ix (1882), 447.

[2] Warneck, Gustav, *Modern Missions and Culture: Their Mutual Relations*, trans. Thomas Smith, 2nd edn. (Edinburgh, 1888), p. 17. The first German edition of this most revealing book was published in 1879. Smith, its translator,

the common spiritual orientation derived from pietism, which rejected assurances of salvation in this world, and from opposition to positivism as it affected Anglo-Saxon missionary assumptions.

The transformation of this common sentiment into a full-blown ideology required time and cultivation. It was Warneck who took the lead by founding the *Allgemeine Missionszeitschrift* in 1874. In the first number, he called for a world survey to determine a method of applying universal principles. Following the semi-academic approach adopted in proceedings of the Continental Conferences, the journal was to feature anthropology, geography, and linguistics as auxiliaries to religious studies narrowly understood. Warneck in 1874 postulated that 'nations also have their individuality and the mission must treat them pedagogically'.[1] Much later in his career, he elaborated on the Christianization of cultures, which should lead to *Volkskirchen* or national churches:

> Only when Christianity has been so planted in the soil of heathen nations that it becomes naturalised there as a domestic growth, can a really independent native Christian Church be brought into being. The naturalisation required a shaping of the whole process of Christianisation of the people, of the social ties of the people. . . . Two leading dangers are specially to be avoided: the treatment of strange customs in a spirit of religious rigour and a confounding of Christianisation with Europeanisation or Americanisation. Pietistic narrowness brought with it the first of these dangers; the second lies in the cultural superiority and the national egoism of the conductors of missions: and both are favoured by lack of pedagogic skill in dealing with those who are the objects of missions. The capacity and the will to accommodate oneself to foreign peculiarities is especially a German charisma, while the English and American nature accommodates itself with difficulty. Even in respect of the cultivation of native languages, this difference asserts itself.[2]

German theorists, in judging whether indigenous churches should be autonomous or not, that is whether they were able to sustain

---

was a professor in Edinburgh who gave up writing his own book when he found so many of his thoughts effectively anticipated. Warneck found a sympathetic audience in Scotland generally, and on his part, admired and praised the work of Scottish missions. Warneck's later multivolume elaboration of theory has never been translated. See Warneck, Gustav, *Evangelische Missionslehre*, 3 vols. (Gotha, 1897–1903).

[1] *A.M.Z.* i (1874), 8.

[2] Warneck, Gustav, *Outline of a History of Protestant Missions*, 3rd edn. (Edinburgh, 1901), p. 104.

themselves in every way, accepted the criteria of the Venn–Anderson school[1] which regarded self-support, self-propagation, and self-government as the yardsticks of maturity. In addition, they stressed a standard of moral development as requisite for true independence. Warneck criticized the 'premature' independence granted by the American Board in Hawaii and generally cautioned his readers against valuing independence as a thing in itself.[2] Autonomy was the end of a long process and this gradualness fitted well with the paternalism of German missions which was at least equal to their propensity for cultural sympathy. Yet the ideal did focus strongly on the indigenous quality of the church and the ideology as a whole called for devolution as a conscious programme and some protection against excessively paternalistic field missionaries.

To achieve a pervasive influence among the Continental missions, the concept of the *Volkskirche* had to supplant certain earlier premises. When Warneck wrote of a pietistic rigour that did not tolerate indigenous customs, he referred to the ethical rigidity to which pietists were prone. This criticism came close to home, as pietism had generated missionary activities in Germany at least until the 1830s.

It can be shown that pietists were in some respects more tolerant than the stereotype suggests. Yet there can be no denying that pietism implied a rigorous distinction between those who were saved and those who were not, and that a higher standard of ethical behaviour was expected from those who had been reborn. Conversion meant an instantaneous change in one's way of life. The Moravians came to recognize that a harmonious society did not come about by gathering the saved; it required the exercise of consistent spiritual and ethical discipline throughout the community. The new missionary societies of the nineteenth century added an extra cultural load of orderliness and industry as the index of Christianity.

The idea of converting whole nations squared badly with the ethical priorities and individualism characteristic of general pietism. Warneck wished to mitigate ethical severity while retaining the element of spiritual renewal and found a solution in the 'Lutheran'

[1] Henry Venn of the Church Missionary Society and Rufus Anderson of the American Board of Commissioners for Foreign Missions, with headquarters in Boston, were leading thinkers about Protestant missionary principles in the English-speaking world. They corresponded extensively with one another in the middle years of the nineteenth century.

[2] Warneck, *Outline* (1901), p. 348.

concept of ethnic comprehensiveness.[1] By marrying the two views of the church, he came back to the idea of *ecclesiola in ecclesia* which projected a nucleus of practising Christians surrounded by the larger church coextensive with the nation or state. This idea had a long history in the Roman Catholic Church: in the Protestant version there was a distinctive concern for the layman and spiritual equality, as opposed to the Catholic reliance upon priests and monasteries as the spiritual nuclei.

The process of building a universal doctrine of missions was considerably advanced in 1885 and had succeeded in giving a common direction to the thinking of the Continental missionary movement. German colonialism offered the first real challenges to the ideology and threatened to precipitate a new series of schisms which would weaken the movement once again. Defections this time were due to the nationalistic determination to have Germans evangelizing in the German colonies, a sentiment unpopular with the established societies which objected to intruding upon fields where non-German missions were already active and which felt unable to undertake new responsibilities at a time when their existing work demanded funds in excess of revenues. Worries about the deeds of colonial adventurers and the emotions their chauvinism aroused among certain mission supporters therefore influenced the deliberations at the Bremen meeting of 1885.[2] Certain reassurances were quickly forthcoming, for the Foreign Office had become committed, through the Berlin Act of 1885, to guaranteeing religious liberty in the Congo Basin, and it extended the principle to apply to all German colonies. Having been promised that foreign societies would not be driven out, the German mission leaders took up the matter of their duty to evangelize in areas untouched by others and concluded that British societies occupied East Africa in sufficient strength. Such a judgement was warranted at that time, in view of the fact that the German protectorate formally included only Usagara where Carl Peters had made treaties, and both the Universities Mission to Central Africa, and the Church Missionary Society, were near by. Having dealt with the new colonies elsewhere by entrusting them to eventual development by specified missions, the large majority at Bremen concluded this

[1] For the theological and practical development of the 'Lutheran' theory by Carl Graul, see Krügel, S., *Hundert Jahre Graul Interpretation* (Berlin, 1965).
Peter Beyerhaus comments on the synthesis in Beyerhaus, P., and Lefever, H., *The Responsible Church and the Foreign Mission* (London, 1964), pp. 47ff.

[2] *A.M.Z.* xii (1885), 553ff.

part of the deliberations by affirming that evangelical missionaries would not become the tools of imperial nationalism.

But a small dissenting group led by Friedrich Fabri insisted upon linking missions and colonialism. Although rejected by the movement as a whole, sentiments akin to Fabri's stood behind the first German Protestant activities in German East Africa, undertaken when a few nationalistic pastors joined with leading figures in the German East Africa Company to found the Evangelical Mission for German East Africa. This organization underwent several reforms after 1890 and ultimately achieved respectability as the Bethel Mission under Friedrich von Bodelschwingh. From 1886 to 1890, however, it symbolized the dangers of splintering and bad management, and was constantly criticized in the pages of the *Allgemeine Missionszeitschrift*.[1] The East African Mission affected the Berlin Mission most directly, for Dr. Theodor Wangemann[2] seems already to have resolved privately at the time of the 1885 conference to extend the Berlin Mission into East Africa. The colonialists spoiled much by leaping first, soliciting contributions around Berlin in the very areas usually canvassed by the older Berlin Mission, and by being unwilling to accept terms Wangemann offered as the basis for a fusion.[3]

Even if the Bremen Conference could not guarantee that no new organizations would be born, it did demonstrate how easily the ideology of the movement could be adapted to questions of colonial policy. In a strong set of recommendations forwarded to the Chancellor, Bismarck was advised to oblige administrators to know vernaculars, to use them officially, and to retain them as the languages of education, rather than to introduce German. Freedom of labour and protection of native rights to the land were also stressed. The only real debate arose over whether the Government ought to institute a system of grants-in-aid to missions for their educational work. A draft resolution on this point asserted Warneck's view that missions were strictly spiritual agents and that administrators ought to set up entirely separate, religiously neutral schools for purposes of secular education. Those more in touch with field experience, however, having in mind the Cape Colony in particular, carried a substitute resolution in favour of grants, pointing out that education could not easily be separated from other aspects of missionary work.[4] This opinion became the standard one for the movement, but the

[1] e.g., *A.M.Z.* xvii (1889), 5n. [2] See below, p. 15.
[3] For the terms, see *B.M.B.* (1892), 49ff. [4] *A.M.Z.* xi (1885), 559ff.

insistence that unwelcome alien languages could not be imposed as languages of instruction remained.

Between 1885 and the second major meeting to consider the colonial situation in 1890, many issues arose concerning missionary attitudes. Gustav Warneck defended the movement's principles with a certain relish throughout this period, on one occasion responding to a conquistadore's call for more patriotism by declaring that the missionary movement would not become 'a handmaiden in the service of colonial policy, a mulch-cow to the fatherland'.[1] Unflattering comparisons in the Press, suggesting that the Roman Catholics created models of Western life in the tropics and were zealots in the anti-slavery effort whereas the Protestants were ineffectual, met with a sharp rebuttal. The editors of the *Allgemeine Missionszeitschrift* clearly labelled the anti-slavery propaganda accompanying the suppression of the Bushiri Revolt as a cover for conquest and a whitewash of the colonial methods that had really caused the resistance.[2] In a public exchange with the hero of the East African campaign, Hermann von Wissmann, Warneck defended Protestant methods, going so far as to denounce Christianization through westernization as nothing but a form of continuing slavery.[3]

The 1890 meeting took place not in Bremen, but in Halle, the symbolic home of German missions where Warneck had become a professor. By that time, the political situation had changed in several respects. The frontiers of German East Africa were fixed by the recent Anglo-German Treaty and none could ignore the fact that large parts of it were unevangelized. Aware of this and assured that no other missions were being displaced, the Berlin Mission and the Moravians of Herrnhut undertook to start work together at the north end of Lake Nyasa. The Halle meeting also made progress in organizing colonial affairs by providing regular channels of communication between missionaries and officialdom. Dr. von Jacobi, a former Minister of State, and President of the Berlin Mission, attended as the designated intermediary between the Foreign Office and the Evangelical party. He soon became a member of the Kolonialrat, the quasi-official body composed of experts and representatives of interest groups which was to advise on colonial questions. On the missionary side, a special committee with Warneck as

[1] *A.M.Z.* xii (1886), 311, 228f. [2] *A.M.Z.* xiv (1888), 497ff.

[3] Warneck, Gustav, *Zur Abwehr und Verständigung. Offener Brief an Herrn Major von Wissmann* (Gütersloh, 1890), p. 23.

Secretary was created to serve as a clearing-house and a lobby to promote the points of view of the Continental missionary movement.[1]

The decision by leaders of two well-established missions to begin work in the Nyasa region raised a whole series of practical questions that had been glossed over by the ideology of the movement in its striving for a universal formula. The organizations differed fundamentally in matters of recruitment, training, and social expectations.

The Moravians, more properly the United Brethren or Brüdergemeine, look back to John Hus and early Czech Protestants as their ecclesiastical forefathers. Husite religion had a strong element of nationalism, its protest against the Roman Church being a rebellion against Latin and sacerdotalism and an affirmation of spiritual equality based upon accessibility to vernacular Scripture. After enduring persecution at the hands of the Counter-Reformation and the Austrian imperial regime, some Husite remnants became refugees and crossed into the Oberlausitz of south-western Saxony, a frontier area where feudal prerogatives continued to prevail. There they found sanctuary under the protection of Count Zinzendorf who organized the 'pilgrims' into a community called Herrnhut and eventually became their spiritual leader as well as their temporal lord. It was from Herrnhut during the eighteenth century that a reorganized diaspora took place, for the community produced a stream of missionaries who ventured overseas, at first to the colonies of Denmark, Holland, and Great Britain in the Western Hemisphere, and later to other parts of the world. Another kind of evangelization also emanated from Herrnhut, aiming to renew the Christian spirit within the established churches of Europe. This European missionary activity deserves some comment before the major features of the communal life of the Herrnhuters are treated.[2]

Count Zinzendorf was a Lutheran of pietistic bent, which meant that he was a low churchman and apt to be out of place in the formal, high Lutheran state church of Saxony. His education under August Hermann Francke, the Professor of Biblical Studies at Halle University, had confirmed the sense of belonging to a freer, more cosmopolitan order.[3] Whatever his conflicts in Leipzig with Saxon

[1] *A.M.Z.* xviii (1891), 256f.

[2] The major history of the Moravian missionary work is Schulze, Adolf, and Karl Müller, *200 Jahre Brüdermission*, 2 vols. (Herrnhut, 1931-2).

[3] See Benz, Ernst, 'Pietist and Puritan Sources of Early Protestant World Missions', *Church History* xx (1951), 30ff., and Maleng, F., *et al.*, *Zum Gedächtnis August Hermann Franckes* (Halle, 1927).

officials, Zinzendorf on his own estates could be the kind of Lutheran he wanted, and in settling the Brethren he sought to bring them into a relationship with the surrounding Lutheran congregations. The meeting-house in Herrnhut at first served as a place of supplementary prayers, not as a parish church. In time, the special character of the community tended to foster distinctive religious practices and a new church was born, but the ideal of ecumenical reconciliation remained a fundamental one for the Moravian Church and in its 'diaspora' preaching in Europe and overseas, the Gospel of love and spiritual reunion formed the central message. The utter simplicity both of this message and of the faith practised in Herrnhut and similar communities allowed the Moravians, when outside their own communities, to merge into an established church, whether Calvinist or Lutheran. In this respect they could be described as ecclesiastical chameleons. Herrnhut itself had a Lutheran shade while the colony at Zeist in Holland reflected Calvinist practices. These efforts to minimize structural differences and to revive Christendom were widespread and influential in stimulating missionary zeal. Moravian evangelists operating through established churches in Berlin played a part in the revival of the early nineteenth century which among other things prompted the founding of the Berlin Mission.[1]

The Moravians abroad had a distinctive way of life, the outcome of several stages of development in the mother community. The pilgrims from Bohemia and Moravia, and pietists attracted from other parts of Europe, all submitted to temporal control by the Overseers, a group of wealthy aristocrats of like sentiments who joined with Zinzendorf in the Utopian project of sponsoring a perfectly Christian community. The common Herrnhuters came mostly from artisan backgrounds and through their skills communal industries became possible. It has been suggested that this specialization in non-agricultural enterprise had economic reasons, for Herrnhut thereby complemented rather than competed with the peasantry of Zinzendorf's estates.[2] Weavers' villages are typical of that part of the Oberlausitz, however, and the degree of innovation due to the Herrnhut arrangements deserves further study. Nevertheless, the Herrnhuters did produce on a scale which exceeded both cottage industry and village weaving in the degree of its organization.

Herrnhut became more and more unique during the eighteenth

[1] Althausen, 'Kirchliche Gesellschaften', p. 26.

[2] Golin, G. L., *Moravians in Two Worlds* (New York, 1967), pp. 166ff.

century as its economy developed and pietism continued to be actively expressed. As pietism retreated in the face of rationalism in the world at large, a steady trickle of skilled townsmen gravitated towards Herrnhut to share its way of life and spiritual milieu. Such a small community could accommodate the newcomers partly because room was made by the movement outward of missionaries and colonists. For those entering Herrnhut, the process of assimilation to the values of the Brethren had already begun with the religious commitment to join. The real indoctrination of the values of the society began with the first experiences of the village, laid out as it was around a central square containing the meeting-house, a handsome unadorned structure whose architecture was reflected in the surrounding buildings. To the east lay the Herrnhaus, from which Zinzendorf and his friends, and the successor bodies, managed external relations. Large buildings on other sides housed the various 'choirs', the social and economic units of the community, segregated by sex, marital status, and age. At one extreme stage of collectivization, children were surrendered at an early age to the mature bachelors and spinsters for upbringing. The family soon reasserted itself as a dominant institution in the community, but the emphasis upon the quality and uniformity of common education remained a feature of the Brüdergemeine.

A new member would be immediately incorporated into a choir, where he or she would work, live, and participate in special prayers. No shirkers were tolerated and the system of spiritual counselling and confession re-enforced the work ethic as much as it nurtured the soul.[1] Segregation by sex seems to have encouraged the rise of women to roles of leadership unusual in the patriarchal society outside the community and this functional equality was supported by the premise of the spiritual equality of all souls. Notwithstanding the democracy of the community, specialization took place, and the young men's choir naturally became the reservoir and training ground for the first missionaries. By the later eighteenth century, the missionary vocation was honoured and frequently inescapable for men and women, for by drawing lots or collective decisions, members were

[1] In the various daughter Provinces, Moravians ultimately became integrated into the surrounding society. In the home Province with its seat at Herrnhut, the insistence that all must pull their full weight economically in the still discreet communities remained in force to the end of the nineteenth century. See Brüdergemeine, *Die Kirchenordnung der evangelischen Brüder-Unität in Deutschland* (Herrnhut, 1897), pp. 42, 122ff.

called or drafted according to the needs for their skills. Very few of the Brethren undertook university theological studies, relying upon their indoctrination from birth or by long exposure to the values of church and society and sustaining the conviction that laymen could assume ecclesiastical responsibility. Their training, therefore, coincided with life in the community and was completed by apprenticeship as teachers in the Moravian educational system or as artisans. As a consequence, missionaries tended to carry with them the model of Herrnhut as the ideal of a Christian community and to transplant its physical and social features as well as its spiritual zeal and ethics.

Inevitably, the institutional mood of Herrnhut shaped its church, within which questions of authority and government had to be solved. The temporal rule of the aristocratic patrons gave way as the community developed and although Zinzendorf and other leaders were ordained bishops in an apostolic succession derived from an Eastern church, the bishophood was not cloaked in great spiritual authority. Christ alone was recognized as Head of the Church. The theocracy operated through the drawing of lots, a practice which in time diminished as Synods comprised of elected representatives assumed more formal legislative functions.[1] The Moravians moved from forms of paternalism and authoritarianism towards democracy in their church-society. By the nineteenth century, the executive body in missionary matters was a Mission Board situated in Herrnhut and responsible to the General Synod of the Church. The Board included representatives of the American, English, and Continental Provinces of the Church, a highly international collection bound together by many shared values, even though the provinces had necessarily lost some of their original cultural uniformity. The Church as a whole undertook new responsibilities, even if they were then entrusted to the special care of one Province. For example, the German–Swiss Home Province supplied field staff and inspectors for German East Africa.[2]

The great demands for missionary personnel in the later nineteenth century led to the establishment of a special seminary at Niesky, Prussia, for young men, some of them accepted from outside the community.[3] At the seminary and through contacts in Continental

[1] Golin, *Two Worlds*, p. 60.

[2] *P.A.* (1896), 162f. For an American Moravian perspective, see Hamilton, J. Taylor, *History of the Missions of the Moravian Church* . . . (Bethlehem, Pa., 1901).

[3] *P.A.* (1895), 579.

Conferences, the ideology of the general missionary movement gained some influence. Yet on the other side, the fact that many men and women were still called from the community and that the Board members frequently had long field experience tended to retard the impact of the *Volkskirche* theory. German East Africa was one of the first areas where such a goal was contemplated at a formative stage. The Mission Board concurred in this departure, but it was 1909 before the General Synod conceded that the unity of the Church could be limited by cultural heterogeneity:

> We have to deal with races forming distinct and original nationalities (e.g. in South Africa–East, East Central Africa, and the Himalayas) though in working among these races we maintain the doctrine and principles of the Moravian Church, and seek to keep our converts in close connection with our Church, yet the future will probably see the development of National Churches quite independent of our own or any other European denominations.[1]

Long before this capitulation, the Moravians had made an enduring contribution to the constitutions of the nineteenth-century missionary organizations. In particular, the employment of church discipline as an instrument of social control came from them.[2] The coincidence of church and community at Herrnhut, and its theocracy, had led to a system of penalties, the greatest of which was exclusion from the Church. Such an expulsion represented a total sanction in that economic and social relationships depended upon religious good standing. It is not difficult to see that the missionary situation in frontier areas might be very like that at Herrnhut, forming as it did a nearly self-sufficient economic and social unit. The Berlin Mission based its missionary church discipline upon that of the Herrnhuters but administered it without the gentleness and concern for the individual which remained the hall-mark of the Brethren. In the hands of outright paternalists, discipline of this sort seemed 'medieval' to progressives.[3]

In describing the Berlin Mission, the word paternalism must come to the fore. Patriotism and pietism had been merged in the motives

[1] *P.A.* (1909), 356.

[2] Steinborn, Erwin, *Die Kirchenzucht in der Geschichte der deutschen evangelischen Mission* (Leipzig, 1928), p. 1.

[3] According to Capt. Ernst Nigmann, an administrator in Iringa District, G.E.A., see pp. 80ff below. For a liberal theological polemic, see Langhans, Ernst, *Pietismus und Christenthum im Spiegel der äusseren Mission* (Leipzig, 1864).

of the aristocratic young men who formed the first Committee of the Berlin Mission. The Gerhards and the rest of the Berlin Committee knew they were destined for high places in the Prussian state. Their value system accommodated the glorification of the state and the maintenance of the social *status quo* with missionary zeal.[1] Although indebted to the Moravians for elements of missionary regulation, the mood and relationships in the Seminary at Berlin, and in the field in South Africa, reflected the hierarchical and authoritarian milieu of Prussia. To be sure, the founders alone did not instill the characteristic paternalism of the society; it was re-enforced at several turns and survived far-reaching reforms in the first decade of the twentieth century.

As the Berlin Mission expanded its scope from the mere conduct of a training seminary to direct responsibility for fields in South Africa, an ever greater degree of professionalism was called for. Just what principles should be followed became a controversial matter during the religious turmoils of the 1830s and 1840s. The founders had declared that they intended to develop a non-denominational mission, but when the Prussian Union Church came into being, the Berlin Mission was forced to take up a position, and defined itself as a voluntary association within the union, adopting the 'symbolic books' of the Lutheran Church, the Augustana Confession and Luther's smaller catechism. This mild Lutheranism incited defections on two sides, from some orthodox Lutheran seminarians, who objected to employment on Anglican fields contingent upon their subscribing to the Thirty-Nine Articles, and from the pietists led by Gossner, who objected to the degree of institutionalization and Lutheran doctrine imposed in the Seminary.[2] Both Gossner's rival Seminary and the Leipzig Mission of the orthodox Lutherans solicited funds in the regions formerly monopolized by the Berlin Mission.

One response by the Berlin Mission to its confessional dilemma was to employ an orthodox Lutheran in 1857 as head of the Seminary and Inspector of the South African fields. Under Johann Christian Wallmann, the organization reached an apogee of Lutheranism and centralization. Wallmann exacted filial obedience in the Seminary and through the Superintendencies instituted in South Africa. He also subordinated the Committee to a function of merely approving his

[1] Althausen, 'Kirchliche Gesellschaften', pp. 44, 180.

[2] Richter, Julius, *Geschichte der Berliner Mission* (Berlin, 1924), pp. 25f., 67f. Fleisch, Paul, *Hundert Jahre Lutherischer Mission* (Leipzig, 1936), p. 3.

policy initiatives. Altogether, the Berlin Mission in these years, headed by a 'monarchical' Director, became a hierarchical structure which responded badly when called upon to surrender authority to African churchmen.[1] The picture might have been different had Wallmann been able, as he wished, to emulate the Leipzig Mission, which under the leadership of Carl Graul in its field in India, had implemented a policy of Christianization within existing social institutions. Graul employed university men with theological training as missionaries and asserted that the best men in Germany were none too good for the task of planting Lutheranism in non-German cultures.[2] From 1850 to 1853, before the Wallmann era, the Berlin Seminary had attempted without success to attract qualified teachers and students of theology to supplant the normal intake of youths with elementary and artisan education. As a fundamental change in personnel had proved to be impossible, Wallmann's only option was to urge his missionaries to take a broader, more sympathetic view of tribal customs.[3]

Theodor Wangemann, the successor to Wallmann who remained Director of the Berlin Mission down to the close of the nineteenth century, was aware of the weaknesses of missionary recruitment and training. Yet he would not have agreed with the criticism of the liberal theologian Ernst Langhans that the Seminary was cloistered and despotic and bound to turn out pharisaic missionaries.[4] As a man of pietistic bent he worried about spiritual quality, and in his view difficulties arose because ambitious boys who lacked the resources to study beyond the free church-related *Volkschule* tended to apply for seminary training, especially as it became evident that missionaries enjoyed a respected position in the middle classes, and life in South Africa grew less perilous than it had been in the early years. The seminarians were articled much as apprentices in the crafts, and during their five years in the Seminary ascended a ladder of privilege and material dependence. In their studies, they spent one half of the academic week on Biblical studies and the other half on church, dogmatic, world and mission history, geography, ethics, liturgy, catechism, singing, Latin, Greek, Hebrew, English, Dutch, and industrial skills. As Wangemann admitted, they learned mainly about

[1] Axenfeld, Karl, 'Johann Christian Wallmann', *A.M.Z.* xxxviii (1911), 574, 577.
[2] Fleisch, *Hundert Jahre*, p. 26.
[3] Richter, *Berliner Mission*, pp. 36f., 175.
[4] Langhans, *Pietismus und Christenthum*, pp. 331f., 339ff.

the Bible.[1] The regime of the Seminary, with its stress upon obedience and humility, easily became the regime of the mission field, with the missionaries assuming the role of the paternalists over converts. Even the Superintendents, however, were never allowed to forget the superiority of the authorities at home whom they addressed as 'Hochverehrte Herrn und Väter' (Most Reverend Masters and Fathers). The contrast between the formal brotherhood of the Moravians and the hierarchical paternalism of the Berliners symbolized a world of difference in social values and concepts of authority.

During Wangemann's long tenure as Director, from 1866 to 1894, the Society made some new departures in its geographical range, taking up fields first in China and then in East Africa. The China venture created demands for highly educated missionary personnel and, as a result, university men in the field became less of a rarity. Only a few went to Africa before 1900 and they were a source of embarrassment, in one notorious case for defying paternalistic convention and by a readiness to take self-directed action, and more generally because the university training qualified men as Pastors in Germany, whereas the Seminary certificate gained ordination only for work overseas. The coming of Pastors into missionary ranks blurred the clear-cut social-educational stratification evident in the backgrounds of upper-middle class university teachers and inspectors on the one hand, and lower-class artisan seminarians and working missionaries on the other. Some seminary-trained men at first evinced anxiety about their proper role when their 'betters' became co-workers rather than occasional visitors.[2] The admixture of missionaries who were less indoctrinated through Seminary training in the long run helped to reduce the extreme paternalism of the Berlin Mission regime.

But before this adjustment took place, a model of Berlin missionary rule in Africa had been established in the Transvaal, on the Botschebelo Station pioneered and developed by the energetic Alexander Merensky. Merensky dramatised the heights to which a gifted, impoverished youth could rise through a missionary career, given the frontier situation in South Africa and the flowering of colonialism

[1] Wangemann, Theodor, *Motive und Erläuterung zu der Missionsordnung . . .* (Berlin, 1882), pp. 14f., 18. Conditions for admission to the Seminary were printed each year in the *Jahresbericht*.

[2] For an East African example, see pp. 81f below. Warneck's views were expressed in *A.M.Z.* xviii (1891), 124, 257ff.

in Germany.[1] After finishing his seminary studies under the stern tutelage of Wallmann, Merensky became a missionary in the Transvaal. In 1859, at the age of twenty-two, he went beyond colonized lands to still independent African peoples and in 1861 settled near the paramount chief Sekwati of the Bapedi. A new chief, Sekukuni, soon followed and Merensky's success in preaching seemed a threat to chiefly authority. In 1864 Sekukuni began to persecute Christian adherents. Presented with the alternative of renunciation of the new faith, extermination, or exile, some eighty-five Bapedi fled under Merensky's leadership.[2] Upon retiring within the pale of Boer power, an accommodation with colonialism had to be made. Merensky developed a *modus vivendi* which permitted him nearly autocratic authority on mission lands, while in Berlin his superiors had already ceased their earlier echoes of the London Missionary Society's criticism of the Boers. The rationale of the new attitude was that the evils of colonial rule were less than the evils of despotic chiefs:

> Missionary work in colonial territory, it is true, has many perils. The loss of political independence of the natives, the greater expense of the mission, the whole colonial spirit with its dangerous influences on natives and missionaries—all are certainly drawbacks. The advantages are nevertheless overwhelming. Political independence of the natives ought not to be too highly rated. It raises many and large difficulties for the mission and it is only too frequently the vehicle of unbroken paganism working in opposition to the missionaries. From the time of Paul's work, also amongst politically subordinated nations, up to the most recent times, it is certain that in a country where God's judgement has broken the people politically, the seed of evangelism is most conveniently sowed; that is, where the missionaries enjoy the legal protection of the colonial government.[3]

Merensky gathered his Bapedi and remnants from another destroyed station to establish the Botschabelo (Refuge) Station. His civil rule was confirmed by collaboration with both the Boers and the British, and the lands of Botschabelo reached an extent of about 28,000 acres in his time.[4] The instrument for regulating the life of tenants on these estates was the *Platzordnung*, which laid down a

[1] See Petrich, Hermann, *Alexander Merensky—Ein Lebensbild* (Berlin, 1919).

[2] This saga was often featured in Berlin Mission literature. For a recent view of the era, see Smith, K. W., 'The Fall of the Bapedi of the North-Eastern Transvaal', *J.A.H.* x, 2 (1969), 239ff.

[3] *B.M.B.* (1861), 174f.

[4] It later expanded to over 40,000 acres. Richter, *Berliner Mission*, p. 241.

code of cleanliness, morality, orderliness, and Godliness. Church discipline gave the missionary landlord another element of power, and it is not surprising that the fusion of spiritual and temporal functions and control excited the jealousy of neighbouring African chiefs.[1] Beyond exercising quasi-chiefly prerogatives, Merensky developed industrial and educational complexes and generally made Botschebelo the showplace of the Berlin Mission up to the 1880s.

Director Wangemann on his 1866–7 Visitation in South Africa had applauded the start made at Botschebelo. Not long thereafter Merensky was promoted to the Superintendency of the Transvaal Synod; this post carried with it a formative influence upon new Seminary graduates who served an apprenticeship in the field before being granted full missionary status. When Wangemann, influenced by the metropolitan discussion of devolving responsibilities to the *Volkskirchen*, undertook to reform missionary practice in South Africa, Merensky resigned, preferring rather to return to Germany than to participate in what he foresaw would be a dull and routine life under the new orders.

The *Missionsordnung* of 1882 had been submitted to the Moravian Mission Board for criticism and was accompanied by a thoughtful evaluation of the Berlin Mission practices which admitted that the prevailing style was autocratic.[2] Missionaries were instructed to encourage African initiatives and personnel, an improved training-centre for African church workers was called for, and the eventual ordination of native pastors foreseen. This programme heralded a profound change in white–black relations, but the most portentous acts came in 1883–4 when the Director visited South Africa again and revolutionized the missionary scene by proceeding immediately to ordain two of the leading African evangelists. This leap of faith was not followed by the rank and file of missionaries, however, and their reactionary spirit may have helped to produce the chain of events which halted further implementation of the *Missionsordnung*.

The unreconstructed views of the South African missionaries received a reprieve due to the 1890 Bapedi secession in the Northern Transvaal, where one of the African pastors ordained by Wangemann declared the independence of the 'Bapedi National Church'. Succour

[1] Merensky, Alexander, *Erinnerungen aus dem Missionsleben in Transvaal 1859–1882* (Berlin, 1899), pp. 409ff. Richter, *Berliner Mission*, pp. 234ff.

[2] Wangemann, *Motive*, pp. 7, 33, 69.

for this African church was given by Johannes Winter, a university man who had been placed in charge of pastor training. Winter's commitment to the ideal of an autonomous church led him to officiate at the ordination of former mission helpers as pastors in the Bapedi Church. This self-declared national church has been described as a thorn in the flesh of the Berlin Mission. It certainly drained the life of the movement for devolution. In terms of advanced education for African leaders in the Transvaal, the reaction was disastrous; the Botschabelo Seminary closed and station paternalists succeeded in their demand that helper training revert to the control of the individual missionaries.[1] The cloud of disillusionment and the stress upon control necessarily affected the expectations and ideals of the young seminarians in this ebb-tide of leadership in the Berlin Mission which coincided with the pioneering of the East African fields.

Alexander Merensky, after returning to Germany, assumed the position of Metropolitan Inspector. This job entailed much contact with the public in the course of the speaking and fund-raising rounds of Berlin and the Prussian countryside. Almost inevitably, he became deeply involved with the circle of colonialists whose enthusiasm far exceeded their knowledge and who looked to Merensky as an authority with the right blend of nationalism and experience. A sample of his public combination of religion and patriotism is available:

> Many are of the opinion that the Africans think 'now the dear Germans have come to free us from the Boers and the English'. But that is not so. On the whole they do not view us favourably at all. 25 years ago Germany was still entirely unknown in South Africa. Now, since more German missionaries have come . . . and since the victory of 1870 this has changed. It pleases them that the Germans are brave; on the other hand they are not pleased that the Germans are poor; German thrift they call meanness. The German is also too diligent for them; the clock, order and punctuality do not please them at all. Nor do they like the certain disregard and openness . . . especially if beating is involved. The English are on the whole more respected because they have more money and do less work. The English let the Africans have their independence earlier, allow them to live in laziness and scarcely ever punish sins by church discipline. Also the German Mission Institutes [landed stations] are not beloved . . . because the people there pay fees and work for nothing. Nevertheless, the German mission works more in the sense of Jesus than the missions of other people, by introducing the correct discipline and upholding it.[2]

[1] Richter, *Berliner Mission*, pp. 241, 267f.

[2] *B.M.B.* (1885), 248f.

Beyond this assertion of the German qualifications for colonialism, Merensky participated in his first years back from South Africa in more adventurous, covert activities, such as advising Carl Peters about ways to seize a colony.[1] Gradually, however, the weight of opinion among mission leaders in Germany against imperialism and the manifestly disastrous performance of the late 1880s which sobered even the colonialist Fabri, also had an influence on Merensky.[2] More and more he entered the circle of contributors to the *Allgemeine Missionszeitschrift* and came into full contact with the Continental ideology. Yet the hankering of a pioneer for personal ascendancy survived and was demonstrated again when he led the Berlin Missionary Expedition to East Africa in 1891 and supervised the first year of activities on the new field. In succeeding years, Merensky occupied a position of prestige both among the colonialists and in missionary circles. He also became a power on the Berlin Committee with particular effectiveness in matters of strategy for East Africa.

In sum, the German missionary backgrounds included some very strong and potentially conflicting lines of development. The experience of the Berlin Mission in South Africa demonstrated the imperviousness of conventional missionary practice to certain dictates of the *Volkskirche* ideology. The constitutional principles of the Herrnhuters contained an ingredient of individualism liable to be in tension with organic views of the church community. East Africa provided opportunities for new departures both in ideology and missionary structure. Colonial and African affairs in the Southern Highlands were such, however, that in the course of their fifty-year occupation, 1891–1941, the German missionaries were never able to reconcile theory and practice.

[1] Mueller, F. F., *Deutschland–Zanzibar–Ostafrika* (Berlin, 1959), pp. 111f.

[2] In 1887, Merensky won the prize offered by the German East Africa Company for a treatise on economic development. The piece actually outlined an administration very close to the one eventually evolved. See Merensky, Alexander, *Wie erzieht man am besten den Neger zur Plantagen-Arbeit* (Berlin, 1887).

CHAPTER II

The Southern Highlands to 1891

THE nineteenth century in the Southern Highlands was far from placid. Nothing less than a revolution took place in mid century, when commercial penetration by coastal traders, and the disciplined military organization of the invading Ngoni, offered new elements of power to local leaders. These men consolidated their own people and sought a wider dominance. The commercial, military, and political scale became enlarged to such a degree that it becomes possible for the first time to regard the region as a whole. The Sangu people, led by the Merere dynasty, were at the hub of regional integration and remained so even when their ascendancy was rivalled and exceeded by the Hehe. The missionaries at first had often to deal with the consequences of the regional power struggle. By championing the aspirations of peoples whose autonomy was lost or threatened, they contributed to the dismantling of the spheres of influence claimed by the strong Sangu, Hehe, and Ngoni states. The revolution and enlargement of scale after 1850 was carried through against natural conditions which encouraged limited and localized contacts. A description of the region and its subregions is therefore necessary before we recount the political background prior to the missionaries' arrival.

The topography of the Southern Highlands is extremely varied.[1] To understand the historical implication of these physical features, it is useful to distinguish three major subregions, each of which served as an area of local affairs both before and during the era of regional integration. These three subregions include the eastern plain, the western or Nyiha plateau, and the area to the north of Lake Nyasa called Rungwe.[2]

[1] The best description of the region is to be found in Moffett, J. P., ed., *Handbook of Tanganyika*, 2nd edn. (Dar es Salaam, 1958), pp. 233ff. Southern Highlands as understood above generally means the area of some 45,000 square miles defined as a province by the British for purposes of administration. From time to time neighbouring areas, Ufipa, Songea, and Mahenge, become intimately connected with the Southern Highlands as more narrowly understood, but the missionary activities remained primarily within the area of the province.

[2] Rungwe is a name in current usage which has the advantages of a certain

The eastern plain is flatter and lower in the north-west than in the south-east, where hills develop. Along the south side, the hills drop off precipitously into the Rufiji River system. Part of the plain, known as the Sangu or Bororo flats, once formed the bed of a lake, and even in the past century has been a swampy area. South and west of the Sangu flats, mountains rise abruptly from the plain, the Mbeya massif in the west being severed by a trough of the Rift Valley from the southward-lying Livingstone Range, and connected ridges. Through the gap created by the rift, a corridor passes from the eastern plain to the western plateau. The strategic advantages of dominating this bottleneck, the obvious route for traffic to Zambia, especially in a time of increasing commercial activity, need not be elaborated.

On the western side of the corridor, the Nyiha plateau opens out and merges with the flat country of north-eastern Zambia. Part of the

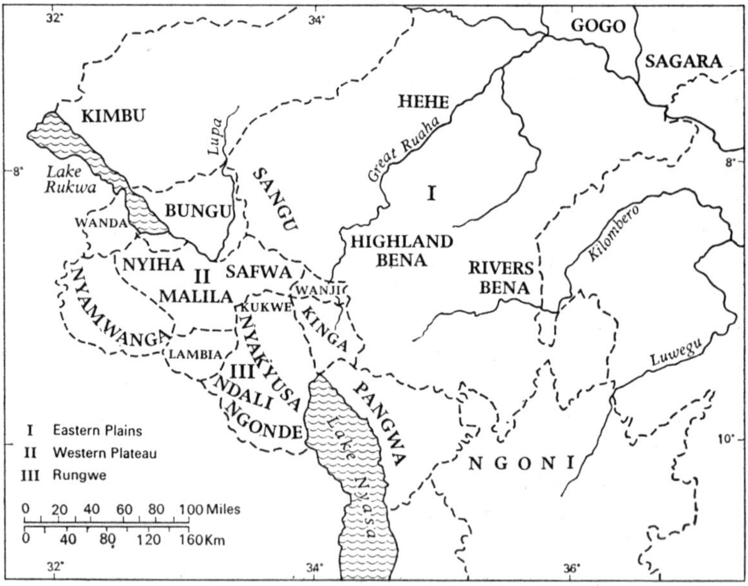

Map I Ethnographic Map of the Southern Highlands

historical neutrality. The Germans called the area Kondeland and the Berlin Mission adopted the name Konde Synod for purposes of church organization. Due to the confusion of the Ngonde of Malawi with Konde as applied by the Germans, however, Rungwe is much to be preferred as a subregional designation and will be so employed.

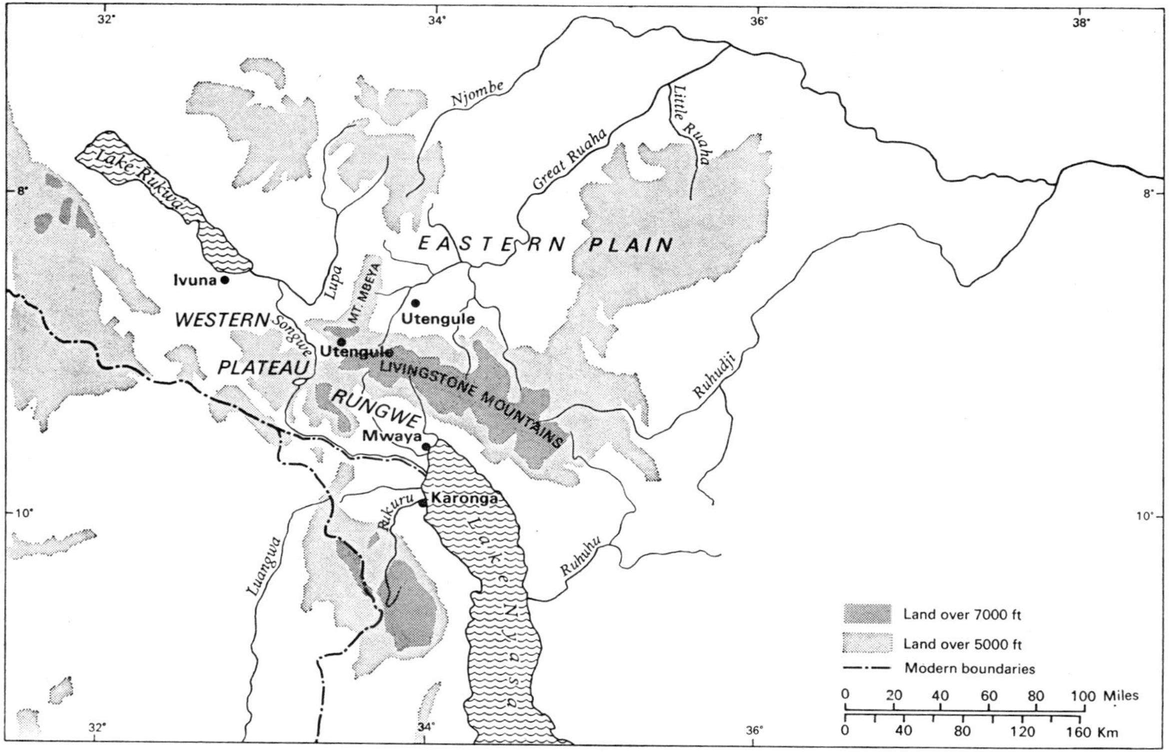

Map II Topographical Map of the Southern Highlands

northern boundary of this subregion is formed by Lake Rukwa, a brackish reservoir without an outlet that has played a paradoxical role in the history of the entire region. On the other side of the Nyiha plateau, to the south, rugged hills offered a degree of protection to peoples who might have been periodically raided, but were not under continuous pressure during the nineteenth century, as were the Nyiha and Safwa in the exposed plateau and corridor.

Rungwe, the remaining subregion, contained a variety of zones, including a level lake plain, ascending valleys, and a highland plateau ruptured by Mount Rungwe, and other volcanic peaks. Enclosing the area as a whole are the Bundali hills in the west, the Poroto hills in the north overlooking the corridor, and the Livingstone Mountains in the east. Within this protective embrace, with its particularly rich environment, Rungwe enjoyed a degree of isolation and prosperity unrivalled in the rest of the Southern Highlands.

An ethnographic map reveals that a large number of 'tribes' occupy the Southern Highlands.[1] To accept, however, that these designations represent, either today or in the nineteenth century, exclusive cultural or political units would lead to a serious misjudgement of the social situation. Under the name 'Nyakyusa' on modern maps, for example, are actually included at least five dialect groups whose common identity as Nyakyusa has been fostered since the 1880s. Monica Wilson has commented on this fusion as follows: 'The fact that more dialect groups are listed under the Nyakyusa than under any other people is largely because more detailed information is available on them than on any of the others, but also because they have been expanding for three centuries and absorbing smaller peoples.'[2] Such a statement represents in part an apology for the tendency in her own extensive work on the Nyakyusa to neglect these 'smaller peoples'. Unfortunately, such a theory of absorption badly errs in assuming that the pattern of outward colonization from Rungwe so evident in the 1930s had prevailed for centuries rather than for decades, as appears to have been the case.

In dealing with the nineteenth century and earlier times, especial caution is required to avoid making uncritical inferences from later ethnographic data. In the case of the Nyakyusa and related peoples,

[1] See p. 23.

[2] Wilson, M., *The Peoples of the Nyasa–Tanganyika Corridor* (Cape Town, 1958), p. 9, n. 4. Notwithstanding certain misconstructions of history, this survey of the Southern Highlands and Ufipa is of great value and has earned a place in the literature for its stimulus to anthropologists to study a neglected area.

the Ngonde, Ndali, and Nyakyusa have always been recognized as discrete, albeit related tribes. In the last century, the Kukwe, who are now regarded as Nyakyusa, had the same sovereignty, and the peoples of eastern Rungwe (in the Lugulu, Selya, and Saku areas) also acted with virtual autonomy, extending their identity only under outside pressure.[1]

To retain the flexibility which the historical situation requires, it is useful to think in terms of clusters of peoples with linguistic similarities and shared cultural values. The peoples of Rungwe–Ngonde form one such cluster. On the western plateau, another cluster, composed of the Nyiha, Safwa, and Malila peoples, may be discerned. The peoples of this group offer their own examples of varying degrees of orientation towards tribal unity. Among the Safwa, one anthropologist has described a condition of political fragmentation with many distinct chiefly lines, each the focus of a different political unit.[2] The possibility of genealogical connection between these lines cannot be precluded, but in contrast to centralized tribal polities, there has not been enough external pressure or internal consolidation to make such kinship politically useful. Likewise among the Nyiha, who are of very heterogeneous origins, the tendency is to reconstruct the past in order to explain the present, and the present is one of social and political fragmentation. For both the Safwa and the Nyiha, then, history has not been employed for the purpose of reinforcing a broad tribal identity. In their dispersed settlements, a narrow focus on neighbourhood and kinship prevails, to the frustration of the historian who has archaeological data going back to about 1300 to suggest a larger canvas for Nyiha history in particular.[3]

The eastern plain, too, has its cluster of peoples, including the Bena, Hehe, and Sangu.[4] Again there are broadly-shared cultural values and institutions. Political fluidity in this area was greater in pre-colonial times than later, when administrative arrangements allowed for appeals from, and recognition of, weaker peoples who

[1] See pp. 55ff below.

[2] Harwood, A., 'Witchcraft, Sorcery, and Social Classification in a Bantu-speaking Tribe of South-western Tanzania' (unpublished Ph.D. diss., Columbia, 1967), p. 4. Harwood adopts Evans-Pritchard's usage, understanding tribe to be the largest recognized political unit.

[3] See Brock, B., 'The Nyiha', in A. Roberts, ed., *Tanzania Before 1900* (Nairobi, 1968), pp. 59ff. See also Fagan, B. M., and Yellen, J. E., 'Ivuna: Ancient Salt-Working in Southern Tanzania', *Azania* iii (1969), 11f.

[4] The Kinga, Wanji, and Pangwa, peoples of the Livingstone Mountains, form a special group with affinities to both the Rungwe and eastern plains clusters.

might have become submerged had Sangu-Hehe power politics continued to prevail.

The three subregions again prove useful foci for the examination of perennial features affecting economic activities. The related factors of rainfall and water supply have most influenced the style of life and standard of living in these areas. Oskar Gemuseus, the leader of the Moravians in the inter-war years, went so far as to suggest a kind of climatic determinism in analysing the two distinctive areas, Rungwe and the western plain, which the Brethren tried to integrate into a united church. He contrasted the gushing streams and fruitful gardens, banana groves and prosperous herds of Rungwe, with the poorer, more arid country immediately on the other side of the mountains to the west. This watershed, he was forced to recognize, formed

> an important cultural divide separating our whole missionary field into two entirely different units. To the west is a dry steppe with decidedly marked dry and rainy seasons, to the east and south much damp fog, [with] torrential tropical rains lasting for weeks. . . . In the west the tribes of the Safwa, Nyika, Inamwanga, cautious of manner and speech, cling to the old and are not easily influenced. In the east and south the Nyakyusa and their relatives, the Ndali, are lively in manner and speech, open to innovation and admittedly subject to evil [as well as good] influences.[1]

Water supply may come from direct rains or from run-off. The Rungwe peoples, with their mean rainfall of 100 inches well distributed through the year, rarely experienced drought. The Sangu were favoured by a large catchment area and a high water-table, so that sufficient grass for their herds was generally available despite the meagre rainfall of 15 to 24 inches annually.[2] Because of the considerable fluctuations in rainfall in the corridor lowlands, the Safwa in modern times farm also at higher altitudes where rains are more plentiful and occur in different patterns from those below.[3] It is not therefore surprising that the Sangu relied predominantly upon cattle herding, and the Rungwe peoples could afford both to cultivate land and keep cattle. There is no entirely satisfactory explanation for the fact that the Safwa did not traditionally keep cattle, but like

[1] Gemuseus, O., *Sakalija Mwakasungula* (Hamburg, 1953), p. 12.
[2] Moffett, *Handbook*, pp. 234f.
[3] Harwood, A., 'A Case of Sociocultural Adaptation to Food Scarcity in a Safwa Community', *Proceedings of the E.A.I.S.R. Conference*, Jan. 1964.

the Nyiha, confined themselves to small stock and devoted their energies to their fields. It is possible that just as the upland cultivation may have represented a prudent anticipation of the need for flight, the exposed position of the Safwa in the corridor may have discouraged the keeping of cattle.

The most complex economy in the Southern Highlands before the nineteenth century, existed in the western area. The centuries-old salt works at Ivuna near Lake Rukwa supplied regional trade with an important raw material, even though the industry does not appear always to have been operated at high productivity. Rukwa also attracted hunters of ivory. Elephant watered there and ivory was undoubtedly relatively easy to come by. Of the peoples in the western area, the Nyiha and Nyamwanga seem to have been most affected by economic specialization. Both peoples produced cloth, smelted iron, and worked metal. The Nyiha were known also for their skills as hunters and regional traders.[1] Such a diversified economy compensated for the precariousness of agricultural conditions. The rains were irregular, and there was the perpetual likelihood, as Lake Rukwa expanded and contracted over the long cycles of wetness and dryness, that the red locusts bred in its basin would erupt in plague proportions, to consume all vegetation.[2] Before the Ngoni and Sangu forced them into barricaded concentrations, the Nyiha had a very varied economy. They were still quite enterprising in the early colonial period, although in later colonial times they became more withdrawn and relied almost exclusively upon agriculture for subsistence.[3]

For the political history of the Southern Highlands we may take the widespread tradition of the reception of new chiefs, probably in the seventeenth century, as a starting-point. It was at one time supposed that migrants from the interlacustrine region made up this cadre of organizers, but closer examination has indicated that the newcomers came from a variety of places.[4] A useful distinction may be made between the dynasties with historical founders and those going back to legendary heroes. Legendary founders were frequently credited with creative powers and reputedly brought with them fire,

[1] Fülleborn, F., *Das deutsche Njassa und Ruwuna-Gebiet* (Berlin, 1906), pp. 167, 506f., 518f. See also St. John, C., 'Indigenous and Long-distance Trade in the late pre-colonial period', unpublished M.A. essay, London, 1968.

[2] Gunn, D. L., 'A History of Lake Rukwa and the Red Locust', *T.N.R.* 42 (1956), 1, 15.

[3] No satisfactory analysis of this transformation is available.

[4] *Tanzania Zamani*, 2 (Jan. 1968), 11.

iron, and cattle. Chiefs descended from these almost supernatural beings continued to perform ritual functions which varied depending upon local custom, but they all had a sacred aura and were broadly responsible for the spiritual and the material well-being of their people. Certain Nyiha, Safwa, and Rungwe chiefs and the Nyamwanga paramount, had this character.[1]

On the other hand, the chiefs of the new paramountcies of the nineteenth century, including those of the Sangu, Bungu, and Hehe dynasties, had historical origins and relied upon less supernatural attributes to maintain their positions. The rise of the Sangu, Kimbu and Bungu power was linked with the development of trade,[2] being aided by commercial activity along the Unyanyembi-Tabora to Zanzibar route in the early nineteenth century, when the route passed through the northern part of Usangu. A realignment of this route later caused traffic to pass further north through Ugogo, and further development had to await the establishment of a new route traversing the Southern Highlands. The motive for developing this new thoroughfare came from the desire for a quick and cheap route from Central Africa to Bagamoyo and Zanzibar; these commercial activities influenced power relationships throughout the region.[3]

In contrast to these long-distance trading connections were the activities of the Ngoni in the 1840s. After their settlement in Ufipa, while searching for a place to live, the Ngoni made forays into the western plateau. Upon the death of Zwangendaba, they split up and dispersed in various directions, a northern column taking the opportunity to serve as mercenaries in a local conflict in Ukimbu, while the south- and south-eastward-moving bands were remembered, much as plagues of locusts are remembered, as transient but devastating.[4] The permanent settlement of Ngoni in Songea opened a new chapter in their relations with the Southern Highlands, for dominance could no longer be easily established. The Sangu had learned much from their clashes with Zwangendaba's impis and employed the new techniques against the Hehe who in turn mobilized themselves along the same lines. By the time the Ngoni became involved

[1] Wilson, *Peoples*, pp. 12f., 26.

[2] The most extensive reconstruction of commercial–political events in the earlier nineteenth century has been made by Aylward Shorter. See his 'Ukimbu and the Kimbu Chiefdoms of Southern Unyambezi' (Oxford University Ph.D. thesis, 1968), ch. VIII.

[3] Wright, M., 'Chief Merere and the Germans', *T.N.R.* 69 (1968).

[4] Kootz-Kretschmer, E., *Die Safwa*, 3 vols. (Berlin, 1926–9), ii, 191.

in affairs from their lands in Songea, therefore, their comparative advantage in military affairs had been overtaken.

Trade gave the Sangu an early impetus, after which they sustained losses, and then consolidated their position against the Ngoni, finally embarking upon aggressive expansion.[1] Co-ordination in this effort took place under the command of the paramount who was selected as the most effective candidate, from the family that had fought its way to supremacy in the early part of the century. Given the recency of its status, the Merere dynasty did not have the kind of institutionalized political structure and ritual functions that may develop around chiefly lineages through many generations. Sangu women married strangers from the coast and from Buwanji, who had magical powers ascribed to them, and women continued to be conspicuous in rituals. Their sons, not having a role *vis-à-vis* ancestral spirits, became known for their war medicine, their ability to declaim martial rhetoric, and their generalship. A ceremony at the grave of Merere Towelamahamba, observed by the Moravians in 1895, summarized the history of the dynasty to date, as the new Merere presided over mock warfare and then shared out the sacrifice among the royal family, with the women in the forefront.[2]

The political structure of the Sangu paramountcy was similar to that of the Hehe.[3] A large number of people lived in a concentration at the capital, usually designated Utengule by the Sangu. The capital also served as the enclosure sheltering royal herds of cattle. The chief's councillors, called *wafumo* by the Sangu and *wasagira* by the Hehe, resided at court unless appointed to administer a district or conquered province. Among the Sangu, other officers led parties to collect tribute from peoples who were under the Mereres' sway, without being subject to direct rule by resident governors. Where resistance occurred, or on the outskirts of the Sangu sphere of influence where contact was irregular, raids and booty-taking replaced regular terms of tribute. The commissary requirements of the Sangu regiments led to demands for grain upon the Wanji and later upon the Kukwe, while pasturing of cattle seems to have been required of the Bena and Safwa. Merere Towelamahamba claimed

[1] For corroborating studies, see Shorter, A., 'Nyungu-ya-Mawe and the "Empire of the Ruga-rugas" ', *J.A.H.* ix, 2 (1968), 235ff., and Redmayne, A., 'Mkwawa and the Hehe Wars', *J.A.H.* ix, 3 (1968), 409ff.

[2] *H.M.B.* (1896), 15ff.

[3] Fülleborn gives ample evidence of constitutional and other similarities between the two related powers. *Das deutsche Njassa*, ch. 4.

in 1877 that he had formerly used fifty carved ivory staffs as insignia for his officials.[1] The situation had at that time made such settled authority impossible and it is a difficult task to assess the exact proportion of diplomacy to force, at any point in the Sangu empire.

The wealth accumulated by the Sangu was displayed by the beads, pearls, metal body ornaments, and later the cloth worn by the chief and aristocrats. The principal form of capital, and the pride of the state, lay in its herds of cattle. The identification of the paramounts with prosperity in cattle was evident in the custom of the Mereres' riding astride an ox and receiving the reverent praise-name 'Ox'.[2] In spite of the long-standing relations of the Sangu with Muslim traders, the essentially regional priorities of a cattle ethos and the related struggle with the Hehe for control of grazing, seem to have greatly exceeded interest in the accumulation of exportable products. When forced out of their homeland, the Mereres turned to more commercial exploitation, but this was in order to strengthen the tribe so as to renew the struggle with the Hehe.[3]

Although the Sangu form the linchpin of many developments in the Southern Highlands, the new paramountcy of the Mereres did not represent the only kind of centralized chiefship in the region. Nyamwanga had a much older and more stable state, ruled over by a chief called Mkoma in the later nineteenth century. Mkoma's court had the usual complement of councillors (*wasongo*), but since the Nyamwanga raided without seeking to administer surrounding areas, a system of control through appointed governors did not prevail. The only deputy of the paramount was a female relative, either an aunt or sister of the ruling chief. This sub-chief, called the Waituika, had responsibility for the southern part of the country.[4]

Demand for ivory and slaves led to an institutionalized procedure for hunting and raiding. The ground tusk belonged to the chief, as did all captives. Some slaves might be returned to the captor later, offering an inducement to turn them in, and an efficient intelligence system militated against cheating. The combination of rewards and sanctions appears to have worked effectively to channel wealth into

[1] Elton, J. F., ed. H. B. Cotterill, *Travels and Researches among the Lakes and Mountains of Eastern and Central Africa* (London, 1879), p. 364.

[2] Fülleborn, *Das deutsche Njassa*, p. 216.

[3] See pp. 34ff below.

[4] Mwashitete, M., *Wege, die ich gegangen bin* (Herrnhut, 1936), pp. 11ff. See also Coxhead, J. C. C., *The Native Tribes of North-Eastern Rhodesia* (London, 1914).

the hands of the chief. In comparison with the Merere dynasty, the Nyamwanga chiefs were surrounded by terrifying rituals, duties, and prerogatives. Under pressure from missionaries in later years, Mkoma repeatedly asserted that as the spiritual guardian of the tribe he was obliged to guarantee the proper observance of its rituals and customs. The human sacrifice involved in the burying alive of a wife and slaves at a chief's funeral represented the considerable fusion of ritual and secular power in Nyamwanga government.

Centralized rule was by no means the only political mode in the Southern Highlands. The Nyiha, Safwa, Nyakyusa and other peoples of the region had no supreme chief at all, although leaders with the greatest religious significance sometimes played conspicuous roles. The possibility that a spiritual figurehead could become a secularized paramount was exemplified by the Kyungu of the Ngonde.[1] But in the absence of pressure to concentrate power, such state-formation did not take place in Rungwe, notwithstanding the similarity of the mythical character of certain princes. The 'divine kings' in Rungwe, Lwembe foremost among them, tended to remain secluded, priests more than chiefs. According to the mythical charter, all princes were descended from heroic individuals who had come down from the mountains of Ukinga. One prince of a lineage was selected to become the living representative of this hero, whose spirit became embodied in the chosen successor. Great concern for the well-being of the living representative led to the ritual practice, at the time when the health of the incumbent began to fail, of suffocating him so that the spirit would not become blemished.[2] The princes serving as spiritual figureheads, acted with kinsmen and princes of other lineages as arbitrators of secular affairs. Instead of consolidating in the pre-colonial era, independent princes in Rungwe proliferated.[3]

The complexity of religious beliefs matched the intricacy of politics. While it is impossible to offer a complete reconstruction of the various alternatives, 'divine kingship' ought not to be regarded as the focus of spiritual life. An extremely interesting hint of heterodoxy in ritual slaying suggests that it may not have been applied to the living representative alone. Before the First World War, there were occasions when a powerful commoner or the child of such a personage

[1] Wilson, G., *The Constitution of Ngonde*, Rhodes–Livingstone Papers, No. 3 1930), 39ff.

[2] Wilson, M., *Communal Rituals of the Nyakyusa* (London, 1959), ch. 3.

[3] Charsley, S. R., *The Princes of Nyakyusa* (Nairobi, 1969), undertakes a detailed analysis of princes and politics.

disappeared and would be found dead, having been deprived of certain parts of the body which when mixed with other ingredients became the medicine to be strewn in the countryside in the rite of 'sprinkling the homesteads' to assure prosperity.[1] Fear and rumour of liability to this fate, however, were seen to be more common than evidence for its occurrence, and it may have been a positive inducement to some men to lease out their cattle so as to avoid the appearance of great wealth and power. It must be admitted, however, that the reinforcement of kinship obligations is the more obvious reason for distribution of cattle.

In Rungwe, variations on the theme of sacrifice to maintain the goodwill of the spirits and to assure their favourable intercession in nature also included cults which celebrated certain of the heroes from Ukinga whose lineages did not survive. The cult of Kyala at a centre called Pali-Kyala near the lake in the Saku division was presided over by a priest who inherited his office. Mbasi was another hero who like Kyala had been endowed with the powers to breathe life into figurines of cattle. Both Kyala and Mbasi remained immanent as spiritual forces even though their will had to be interpreted through mediums rather than by such living representatives as a Lwembe or a Kyungu. It is important to note that some of the strength of the cults came from the fact that Mbasi, Kyala, and Lwembe all had Kinga priests although situated in Rungwe. This relationship was strengthened economically, for the intertribal rituals facilitated the exchange of iron goods from the mountains of Ukinga for meat and other products of the Rungwe area. Without the ritual connection, Kinga coming to trade in the vicinity of the Berlin missionaries at Wangemannshöh in the early 1890s encountered considerable derision. Iron wares may have been highly prized by the valley peoples, but that fact did not automatically lead to great respect for the producers.[2] The relative prestige of the Nyakyusa showed itself in the initial utility of their language as a lingua franca for evangelization in Ukinga. The fuller implications of this spiritual and economic interdependence have not, however, been analysed and deserve to be explored.[3]

A more pervasive type of religious figure in the Southern Highlands

[1] Gemuseus, O., 'Über Zaubermedizin' (Herrnhut, Nachlass Gemuseus, *c.* 1931). See also Wilson, *Communal Rituals*, pp. 120ff.

[2] Merensky, A., *Deutsche Arbeit am Njassa* (Berlin, 1894), p. 290.

[3] *B.M.B.* (1896), 220.

was the priest-doctor or *mganga*, whose activities might include witch-finding, prescription for atonement in cases of misfortune caused by bad social relations, and physical medicine. Local practice reflected local concerns. In Rungwe and among the Safwa, sensitivity to opinion and illwill made the diviner a particularly important person. Rain-making was associated with princely cults in Rungwe, with certain chiefs among the Safwa, and priest-headmen among the Bena. The Sangu and Hehe *waganga*, by contrast, were known principally for their skills in herbal medicine.[1] At least during the later nineteenth century, the strengths of one school of medicine and magic could also be valued by peoples predominantly served by another school. The Sangu exported war medicine and certain other compounds and in turn kept close watch over Safwa rain-makers and priests during their occupation of Usafwa, where indigenous mediators alone, so it was believed, could assure the balance of nature.[2]

The emergence of peripatetic practitioners may be linked with the integration of the region and the spread of cultures along commercial routes. Elise Kootz-Kretschmer has recorded aspects of the career of one such Sangu *mganga*, a woman named Namesa. As the daughter of a famous doctor known as Mesa, who had served many chiefs and grew wealthy in cattle accumulated from fees, Namesa had a thorough apprenticeship. She took up practice on her own after she and her father had become trapped with other Sangu refugees in the palisaded village of Nzova, surrounded by Ngoni. Fleeing by night with her father's satchel of medicines as her inheritance, she began a wandering life, going as far as the coast and mastering many tongues including Swahili.[3] By reckoning backward from the time Namesa came into contact with the Moravians, it seems probable that she began her career in the 1850s. The biography reveals the facility of movement for a *mganga* in the later nineteenth century which in turn indicates the diminished importance of ethnic frontiers. Given this freedom of movement of certain individuals, the spread of the Maji-Maji Rebellion through common oaths is not so remarkable as it has appeared to be to scholars postulating that tribal and ritual exclusivity prevailed in the pre-colonial period.

A narrative of events leading up to the colonial intrusion can

[1] Fülleborn, *Das deutsche Njassa*, p. 218.
[2] Kootz-Kretschmer, *Die Safwa*, ii, 237f.
[3] Kootz-Kretschmer, E., 'Die alte Zauberin' (Herrnhut, Nachlass Kootz-Kretschmer).

justifiably begin in about 1870, when the young Merere Towelamahamba beat off the challenges of pretenders, one of whom had been supported by the coastal traders who used Utengule as a staging point and may well have hoped to gain greater influence over the policies of the Sangu state.[1] Having consolidated his political position and re-established amicable relations with the traders, the chief turned to the regulation of the extended sphere of influence created by his grandfather. Defence of this sphere proved to be a difficult and indeed impossible task as the Hehe became increasingly effective in fighting back and then penetrated Usangu itself. The reign of Merere Towelamahamba was to be noted not for successes on the plain but rather for concentration upon areas to the west. While this reorientation was forced by Hehe victories which obliged the Sangu to leave their homeland, it also made sense in terms of the commercial activities and the modifications in the caravan routes of south-western Tanzania taking place in that time. Continuing collaboration with traders, together with sheer will and determination not to admit defeat, kept the Sangu as resilient as they were in the face of the Hehe, whom they always strove to dislodge from Usangu.[2]

Merere suffered serious reversals in the mid 1870s at the hands of Munyigumbi, the Hehe paramount who as a young man had experienced the encroachments of the Sangu. Against the Hehe, an alliance was formed between Merere, Mtengere who was the most formidable Bena chief, and Chipeta of the Mbonane Ngoni. The Hehe campaigned into Ubena, a part of which was controlled by the Sangu, with the apparent purpose of eliminating Mtengere and driving a wedge between the Sangu and Ngoni. A decisive loss in 1874–5 caused Mtengere to opt out of the power struggle and retreat with his section of the Bena to the riverine lowlands, thus giving up the pastoral occupation which had complemented cultivation in the highlands.[3] Merere himself sustained a major defeat, probably in 1875, which brought about the first evacuation of the Sangu, cattle and all, into Usafwa. When the enemy retired, one column of the Sangu returned to their former settlements, while Merere set out to the north-west to stay with his Kimbu ally Nyungu. At Nyungu's the Sangu army reassembled but sustained serious losses due to famine. In spite of this weakened condition, Merere's force remained large

[1] Livingstone, D., *Last Journals* (New York, 1875), p. 355.
[2] See Wright, 'Chief Merere'.
[3] Culwick, A. T. and G. M., *Ubena of the Rivers* (London, 1935), pp. 23f.

enough for Nyungu to give him a daughter as a wife, a symbol of peace, and probably, subservience.[1]

After an unsuccessful effort to construct an intertribal alliance against Merere, the Bungu were brought under the sway of the Sangu. It was probably at this point that the Baluchi advisors to the Bungu chiefs transferred their allegiance and attached themselves to the Sangu. Several years before 1875, the Bungu chief, Shilange, had attacked Usangu on the advice of his Baluchi councillor and, in the ensuing disastrous defeat, had lost his life. The superiority of the Sangu in 1875–6 was still more compelling, since they had subjugated Ubungu itself. After the northern sojourn of the Sangu forces, during which they had claimed the commercial sphere formerly worked by the Bungu, they returned to Usangu. From this time (1876), a Baluchi officer known as Jemedari became prominent among the elements at the court of the Mereres.[2]

The Hehe did not let the renewed Sangu challenge make much headway and by late 1877, when the British Consul Elton passed through the Southern Highlands, he found Merere in a temporary fort pressed up against the hills rising to Buwanji.[3] Having benefited from the support of Elton's caravan, which raised the Hehe siege, Merere immediately set off in pursuit of the retiring enemy. The advantage could not be sustained, however, and the Sangu once more started on an odyssey that was to be at once a retreat and a campaign of conquest. This time they ascended the Livingstone Mountains and raided the Wanji, northern Kinga, and the Kukwe. Merere seems to have camped on a flank of Mount Rungwe for some time and acquainted himself with the Kukwe language.[4] Before long, however, he complained of the dampness and headed west through Malila into the country of Mwashambwa where he occupied a village and undertook foraging raids into Usafwa and Unyiha, in 1878–9. Tactics used to gain a footing in these lands were not only military in a direct sense, but also included 'non-aggression pacts', whereby Merere gained recognition without conflict. Nzowa of the Nyiha and Malema and Mwalyego of the Safwa concluded such a pact and their friendship proved to be very helpful during the first round of punitive

[1] Shorter, 'Nyungu-ya-Mawe', pp. 244f.

[2] Ilonga II, M., 'The Story of Wawungu', trans. F. G. Finch, *T.N.R.* 52 (1959).

[3] Elton, *Travels and Researches*, pp. 337–68 *passim*.

[4] Kootz-Kretschmer, E., 'Abriss einer Landesgeschichte von Usafwa in Ostafrika', *Koloniale Rundschau* 4–6 (1929), 14. The page reference is to a consecutively paged offprint.

expeditions against the resisters.[1] An extensive sphere was thus established in the western plateau and was maintained so long as the Sangu remained convincingly powerful. The sparks of resistance never died, however, and when the occupiers showed signs of weakness, assertions of independence came quickly.

The Baluchi may have influenced the choice of a site for a new Utengule in Usafwa. The location, with its back to the walls of Mount Mbeya, was strategic in being at once deep in Usafwa, away from the country the Hehe would contend, near the caravan route to Central Africa, and well situated for access to the economic resources of the western plateau. A formidable fortress was constructed with labour levies from the Safwa, many of whom were virtually enserfed. Provisioning of the concentrated populace at Utengule, especially grain for beer, was arranged through tribute paid by the Wanji and Kukwe, and cultivation by slaves and others in the more immediate environs. Ivory from the Rukwa–Bungu area, foodstuffs from the southern mountains, and manpower in slaves from every direction, supplemented the pastoral economy and provided support for the regiments.

Sangu military strength could not have been rebuilt so many times without a good deal of assimilation. A remarkable narrative of the life of a Penja man, Kilindu, illustrates how the process of foraging and taking of slaves might be followed by the captives' adopting Sangu ways.[2] Kilindu had been seized with his mother and two of her other children early one morning in about 1880 when the Sangu fell upon their village. The captives were all obliged to carry vessels filled with grain, the other fruit of the plundering expedition. After going to Utengule, Kilindu's mother died and a sister was sold to coastal traders. The boy himself joined a household with other boys and began to serve as a cattle herder. Next, he became part of a group directly under one of the chief's sons, who treated him so badly that he attempted to escape. After reaching the Igale Pass leading into Rungwe, some Safwa discovered his status and returned him to Utengule: 'Then I accustomed myself to live with Merere. I changed my language and spoke only "Ki-Merere", as now his slave, and grew up as such.'[3] Kilindu eventually had the good fortune to become

[1] Harwood, A., 'The Safwa before 1900' (unpublished paper presented at Columbia University, February 1969).

[2] Gemuseus, O., and Busse, J., *Ein Gebundener Jesu Christi, Fiwombe Malakilindu* (Hamburg, 1950), pp. 7ff.

[3] ibid., p. 15.

the friend of his overseer and graduated from spear-bearer to warrior in the ranks of one of the twelve Sangu regiments, the 'Amanjambwani' or 'Coastmen'. He came to know Merere himself and took care especially to emulate the famous Safwa slave captain, Mwatangala.[1] Such a process of absorption must have occurred again and again, so long as Sangu prestige remained high.

Besides making forays to acquire booty of commercial or domestic value, warriors also undertook expeditions against the Hehe. The opportunity to regain control of Usangu seemed to be offered by the succession difficulties of the Hehe after the death of Munyigumbi in 1879. During the short civil war that took place before Mkwawa became firmly established, a tentative reoccupation of Usangu did take place. Once the Hehe solved their internal difficulties, however, they returned to the attack. Furthermore, owing to a truce between the Hehe and the Ngoni negotiated in 1881, the possibility of renewing the anti-Hehe alliance became a mere dream.[2] To punish Merere for his persistent harassment and encroachments on the Hehe sphere, Mkwawa launched at least two major expeditions, in 1883 and again in 1886, which besieged Utengule and rallied Safwa to resist the Sangu. The stone fortifications of Utengule withstood these trials, however, and the Safwa paid dearly for their collaboration.[3]

The great period of struggle in the Southern Highlands was over by 1883, by which time Mkwawa dominated the central plain, Merere the western plateau, and the Ngoni the southern hills descending towards Songea. Notwithstanding the Hehe ascendancy, the Sangu era had not been forgotten by the highland Bena, and this recognition was exploited later, when Sangu restoration was attempted under German auspices.[4] Right of conquest and spheres of influence had been so well established as principles in the precolonial period, indeed, that the task of defining colonial administrative units and devising a method to take advantage of African leadership was relatively easy in this area. The unhappy fate of such a people as the Bena must be brought out, however, for they more than any other people suffered a political partition as a consequence of the power balance and its colonial perpetuation. Mtengere, it will be recalled, removed himself from the plains, and the 'Bena of the Rivers' continued under his dynasty to be governed by a paramountcy.

[1] ibid., pp. 16, 19. [2] Redmayne, 'Mkwawa', pp. 413f.
[3] Wright, 'Chief Merere', p. 43. [4] *D.K.B.* (1899), 13.

The Bena of the highlands, however, inside the power triangle, had no centralized political authority, recognizing that of the Ngoni in the south and of the Sangu and Hehe in the north and north-east.[1]

Division into spheres also affected the Livingstone Mountains, if more mildly because of their natural defensibility. The Pangwa in the south, nevertheless, deferred to the Ngoni, the Kinga feared both the Ngoni and the Sangu, and the Wanji in the north were regarded by the Sangu as their vassals. Likewise in Rungwe, the Kukwe paid tribute under duress to the Sangu, and the Nyakyusa of the lake plains feared cattle raids by the Ngoni. The expression 'sphere of influence' seems most apt for these relations partly because of their irregularity. Although formal arrangements sometimes existed between chiefs, the areas were more often those raided habitually or occasionally, or used as outposts to spy on rivals in the power game. The avoidance of treaty relations by the Sangu in particular seems to have been based on expediency, for a curtailment of plunder would have required a much more elaborate administration, another method of recruitment into the warrior grade, and different commercial practices.

In 1886, Merere's forces undertook an unusual expedition into Rungwe. Normally, the Sangu crossed the northern passes, controlled by 'loyal' Safwa, in order to exact tribute from the Lugulu or Kukwe. On this occasion, however, the objective was entirely different. At the invitation of the Ngoni, who wished to arrange a successful initial command for a new chief, it was agreed that the Sangu would send a regiment to participate jointly in a raid on the Nyakyusa lakeshore. Merere entrusted command of this Sangu contingent to Mwatangala, whose reputation for invincibility had achieved such a peak that he epitomized to many Africans the whole might of the Sangu.[2] In the face of this invasion, the Nyakyusa overcame their normal division by making a temporary defensive alliance. The great battle of Mwaya ensued. The Sangu and Ngoni each functioned under their own commanders and the Sangu fared far better than the Ngoni, who were so badly mauled that the Sangu had to come to their aid. Then both went under.[3] It was a calamity for the Sangu and a fillip to Nyakyusa

[1] The highland Bena were described in 1879 as 'of servile character, who submit themselves without a murmur to whosoever happens to be master of the field'. Thomson, J., *To the Central African Lakes and Back* . . . , 2 vols. (London, 1881), i, 246f.

[2] *H.M.B.* (1893), 276.

[3] Gemuseus and Busse, *Ein Gebundener*, pp. 20ff.

prestige that the great Mwatangala was killed in this battle. The remnant of the Sangu returned home to find that Utengule had been besieged by the Hehe, who according to one version had been informed of the absence of Mwatangala by the Safwa who hoped to see the Sangu defeated. After a siege of several months, the encounter had been declared a stalemate and the Hehe retired just too soon to hear of the events in Nyakyusa country.[1]

The Battle of Mwaya had several consequences. It emboldened the Kukwe to greater resistance to levies of food, and to identify themselves with the Nyakyusa.[2] At the lakeshore, the three strongest princes, Mwakyusa, Mwanjabara, and Mwankenja, who naturally feared renewed attacks, agreed to a defensive alliance with the African Lakes Company at Karonga.[3] The A.L.C. sought the alliance because it was too weak alone to contend effectively with the opposition offered by the Muslim trader Mlozi. While the Ngoni seem to have been too chastened to attempt to raid Unyakyusa again, Mlozi took the offensive. The alliance was activated in November 1887 when Karonga was besieged. Although they turned up to aid the Europeans, the Nyakyusa followed their customary practice of distributing the booty and disbanding immediately upon securing the victory, rather than pursuing the enemy as the A.L.C. men had hoped. The white residents of Karonga, instead of having auxiliaries to use for their own purposes, were obliged to accompany their defenders back to Unyakyusa in order to retain their protection. The alliance thereafter fell into abeyance because the British Vice-Consul ordered Captain Lugard not to call out the Nyakyusa, who from 1888 were regarded as within the German sphere.[4]

In spite of these provisional European political arrangements, the Livingstonia Mission continued its extension into the north. The Revd. Bain and Dr. Kerr-Cross in August 1888 established a station at Kararamuka's in Ukukwe. The outpost was only sporadically occupied owing to the renewed hostilities around Karonga. Bain's death and the general shortage of mission staff arrested further development, but the Kararamuka project nevertheless played a part in the mild form of scramble that occurred in 1889, when

[1] Kootz-Kretschmer, *Die Safwa*, ii, 238, 276f.

[2] *P.A.* (1893), 45.

[3] Merensky to von Soden, 15 Oct. 1891 (T.N.A. IX A 6).

[4] Lugard, F. D., *The Rise of Our East African Empire*, 2 vols. (London, 1893), i, 49, 57.

Ukukwe became disputed territory.[1] Consul Harry Johnston, who had a record of fighting for every possible inch, authorized an official of the A.L.C., Montieth Fotheringham, to make treaties with the Kukwe. This commission conveniently coincided with the desire to promote the Company's trade above the north end of Lake Nyasa and Fotheringham found the princes of Ukukwe, although acutely disunited politically, agreed on the advantages of friendship with the 'great lady across the sea'. For the Kukwe, these treaties represented a means of acquiring support for their resistance to the Sangu. Specifically, the chiefs asked the white men to 'smash' Merere.[2]

Johnston was not the only man determined to retain Rungwe. Dr. Kerr-Cross returned to Scotland in 1890 to contribute to the campaign to acquire the whole area between Lakes Nyasa, Rukwa, and Tanganyika.[3] Scottish feeling did not suffice in this instance to sway negotiations, however, and when Bundali and Ukukwe went to the Germans by the terms of the 1890 Anglo-German Treaty, the Livingstonia Committee discussed whether to fight for a boundary revision, to continue in German territory, trusting in the guarantees of religious liberty contained in the Berlin Act, or to withdraw. The situation altered when the British Moravians notified the Scots of the intention of their German brethren, backed by Chancellor Caprivi, to establish a field in German Nyasaland. With this news, the Scots decided to expand in other directions while retaining Kararamuka as a centre of evangelization and observation.[4]

Because the Livingstonia Mission had knowledge relating to their prospective fields, the German missions soon dispatched men to Glasgow to learn what they could. Kerr-Cross proved to be especially helpful and the general spirit of co-operation showed no trace of the recent protest against the legitimacy of German claims. The Livingstonia Committee wrote to Dr. Robert Laws, leader of the work in Nyasaland, that 'the German Societies are likely to work well near us'.[5] Merensky, to demonstrate the 'unity of belief and principles of the evangelical communion', took the instructions of

[1] Free Church of Scotland, *The Livingstonia Mission: Third Quinquennial Narrative* (Glasgow, 1891), pp. 6, 20f., 24.

[2] Fotheringham, L. M., *Adventures in Nyasaland*... (London, 1891), pp. 288, 290.

[3] Kerr-Cross, D., 'Geographical Notes on the Country between Lakes Nyassa Rukwa, and Tanganyika', *The Scottish Geographical Magazine*, vi (1890), 281 ff.

[4] Minutes of the Livingstonia Committee, 19 Dec. 1890 (N.L.S. 7912).

[5] Smith to Laws, 25 Mar. 1891 (N.L.S. 9712).

the Berlin Mission Expedition of 1891 largely from the 1875 General Instructions to the Livingstonia missionaries.[1] The Moravians did likewise.

Co-operation between the Lutherans and Moravians extended to the parcelling out of fields following supposed ethnic lines. By a provisional agreement, the work was separated at 23°E., with the Moravians on the west expanding to the north and the Berliners on the east. According to information provided by Kerr-Cross, it appeared that the Livingstonia Mission would be active among the Ngonde and Ndali peoples, the Moravians among the Nyakyusa and Kukwe, and the Berliners among the Kinga. Notwithstanding the discovery that the Nyakyusa rather than the Kinga occupied the Lufilio Valley beneath the Livingstone Mountains, the line remained in effect.[2]

Even before they had any first-hand experience, the Germans began to think of Rungwe as a prize for missionaries. Using the authority of Johnston and Lugard to describe its peoples as untainted and arcadian, supporters were urged to help preserve the area from Arab slave commerce. The epic qualities of the situation were especially stressed by the Moravians, who extolled the luxuriance and perennial rivers of their newly acquired field and anticipated only one serious adversary, Merere, 'an Arab': 'Crafty, audacious and powerful, he may give our missionaries much trouble.'[3]

[1] Merensky, *Deutsche Arbeit*, pp. 35f.
[2] *H.M.B.* (1891), 86.
[3] P.A. (1891), 218.

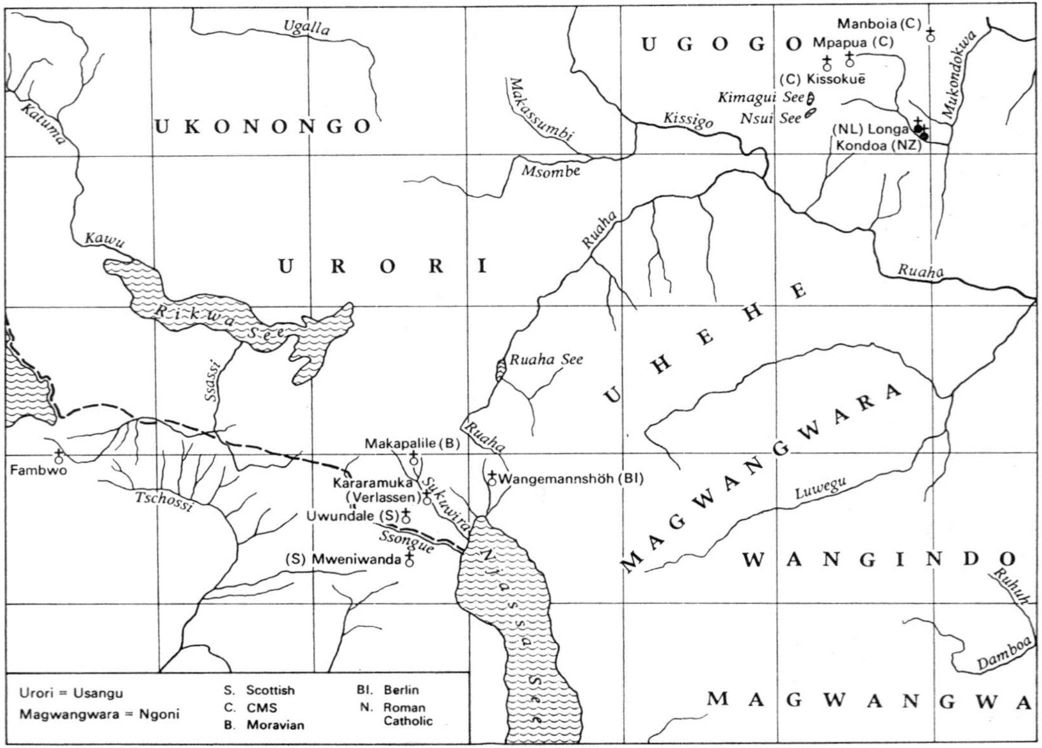

Map III South-western German East Africa—from an early colonial map [Deutsches Kolonialblatt 1892]

CHAPTER III

North of Lake Nyasa

THE four young men of the Moravian party sent to establish the field north of Lake Nyasa had no previous experience as missionaries. They were typical of their church, however, in having all acquired some handicraft along with various degrees of literary education, and in reflecting the geographical mobility of the Brethren. Theodor Meyer, the leader of the party and subsequently head of the Nyasa Province until the First World War, had been called to the foreign mission from his post as a school-teacher in the Moravian community of Neuwied in western Germany. Alone of the men of the party, he had been in Africa before, as a boy on his father's frontier mission station in Cape Province. Theophil Richard, a gifted linguist and second in command, was the son of a Bishop of the Church in French Switzerland, and with Georg Martin had attended the Niesky Seminary. Richard had special influence during the formative period as the chief communicator in English, and later in the vernacular. Johannes Häfner, the fourth member, had been a missionary child in Surinam before becoming an artisan in a home community.

The plans worked out before embarkation called for close co-operation with the Scottish missionaries of Livingstonia who had experience of the north end of the lake, and the African Lakes Company, the agency for supply and transport. In their courtesy calls upon Governor von Soden at Dar es Salaam, the Moravians first encountered official pressure to sever relations with Nyasaland in favour of overland communications direct to the German controlled coast. Although the Nyasa connection continued for some years to be convenient and desirable for its encouragement of missionary co-operation, the southern orientation inevitably underwent a relative decline as colonialism matured. In May 1891, however, the Governor could offer neither concrete information about, nor protection in, the south-western parts of German East Africa. Pending reports from the Moravians and Berliners, indeed, he remained ignorant of the political and social conditions prevailing in the regions beyond the powerful and resisting Hehe.[1]

The long trip to their destination which took the Moravians via Quilimane, Blantyre, Bandawe, and Karonga may have had its hazards in fever and bad communications, but it proved also to be instructive to the novice missionaries. At Blantyre, the lush plantations and large European-style buildings of the Church of Scotland Mission could not fail to make an impression. At Bandawe, still the headquarters of the Livingstonia Mission, the more African appearance of the place fulfilled better the expectations of Theophil Richard.

Bandawe station had far more than neatly thatched roofs; its clinic, carpentry shop, and press represented the beginnings of industrial activities. In the directly religious sphere, the Moravians observed the sequence of Sunday church and out-station services and noted details of the school system. Dr. Laws revealed that his priorities were plainly focused upon the centralized facilities of the Mission, while his colleagues spoke more directly of problems of frontier conditions to be anticipated at the north end. The Revd. Gossip, for example, warned against settling Africans on mission land for fear that the missionary would become a *de facto* chief liable to friction with surrounding authorities. Altogether, the Moravians left Bandawe assured of the continuing friendship of the Scots and impressed with Livingstonia as a missionary enterprise worth emulating.[2]

Business with the African Lakes Company came next. Supply lines were not cheap to maintain and freight forwarded from Karonga to Ukukwe in 1891 cost £12 per ton.[3] Karonga in 1891 was like an armed fort, with three cannon and a garrison of over a hundred men, its stockade being guarded by watches of four men each night to warn of attacks from Mlozi, the Swahili trader with whom the African Lakes Company had a protracted commercial feud. The effects of this struggle were apparent as the party moved off to the north-east across the lake plain, passing through deserted villages. As the travellers turned northward, the swamps and rivers they encountered revealed the physical barriers which had kept active long-distance trading or slave-raiding from penetrating the Nyakyusa–Kukwe area.

[1] Von Soden to Caprivi, 12 May 1891 (T.N.A. IX A 6). *H.M.B.* (1891), 269.

[2] Richard, T., *Von Katunga nach Makapalile* (Herrnhut, 1892), pp. 27ff.

[3] ibid., p. 34.

In the uplands, the Brethren used the abandoned Scottish station at Kararamuka's as a staging point in their journey to the slopes of Mount Rungwe, the station site preselected on the recommendation of Kerr-Cross. As an established friend of Europeans, Kararamuka co-operated fully. In contrast, some of the princes encountered by Meyer and Richard on an exploratory journey displayed their endemic jealousy and quickness to threaten violence. Furthermore, the shifting political calculations of the Sangu made the situation uncertain. Makumbaki, supposedly Merere's ally and unfriendly to white men, proved to be hospitable.[1] After this first taste of Rungwe politics the explorers retired in some bewilderment to Kararamuka, where they remained stationary for several weeks, weakened by the death of Martin and the departure of their colourful interpreter, Lewis, who returned to the service of the A.L.C.

Fortunately, the Kukwe chiefs to the west of Mount Rungwe still wanted white men to settle with them as a deterrent to Merere. As the local authority over land use, Mwakapalile attended the negotiations. He came veiled, for although only an adolescent, he was already the ritual prince for the region. After picking a well-watered site on a slope of the mountain near a village of a hundred dwellings, the three missionaries settled down with a fraction of their Nyasa porters and six people from the Scottish mission at Chirengi, to begin the slow process of acquiring a command of the language and building a station. For more than a year villagers and missionaries remained in a state of quiet coexistence, the latter forced by linguistic barriers merely to observe Kukwe customs and to maintain polite but distant relations with the surrounding princes. A few village people were taken on as workmen, but contact in general remained minimal. The fortunes of the 'Arab War' around Karonga contributed to changes of feeling towards the missionaries, which were expressed in pressure upon Mwakapalile as their sponsor.[2]

The progress and settlement of the Berliners contrasted dramatically with the modest début made by the Brethren. The Expedition, as it was called, assembled at Durban, Natal, in June 1891 under the command of Alexander Merensky. Besides Merensky, who would remain only one year, three young men went as future missionaries for a longer term. Carl Nauhaus had already served his apprenticeship in South Africa, where his father was a Berlin Mission Superintendent. The other two, C. Schumann and C. Bunk, were recent

[1] *H.M.B.* (1892), 101 ff. [2] *H.M.B.* (1893), 10.

graduates of the Seminary, Schumann being also the son of a missionary in South Africa. The Expedition as it departed from Natal was completed by three European artisans and two Zulu Christians.[1]

Dr. Laws was absent from Bandawe when the Expedition passed, but it is doubtful in any case whether the Berliners would have regarded it as a 'model' at this point. The foundations of a firm personal relationship with Carl Nauhaus, the English spokesman and African linguist among the Berliners, were none the less laid. A further six men were enlisted at Bandawe to serve in the new field, so that Nauhaus came away with linguistic materials and helpers commanding Swahili, Ngonde–Nyakyusa, and Ngoni dialects. With his excellent Xhosa, the chain of translation required for initial communication at the north end might be long, but it could all be in forms of Bantu. A most significant addition to personnel came at Karonga, when the African Lakes Company released Kumoga, its chief messenger to the eastern Nyakyusa, to act as chief interpreter. Kumoga remained permanently with the Berliners, conducting diplomatic negotiations and thereby wielding substantial influence. In representing the white men, he was obviously guided by his previous experiences and by the apparent nature of the powerful expedition under Merensky. Kumoga himself commented in retrospect upon his changing perspectives: 'Had I then known what I now understand about you as missionaries, it would have been very different. But directly after your arrival you began to [sit in judgement in] every kind of complaint. How could we recognize that you were not like the A. L. Co.?'[2]

The political instability of the Nyakyusa had become apparent as soon as the Expedition passed through the lake plain. Chief Mwapoeri, predicted to be an independent prince 'craving missionaries', had just been defeated by Mwankenja to whom he had perforce to refer matters of external relations.[3] As they turned northward up the Lufilio Valley in search of an altitude free from malaria, the Berliners entered a mixed political area where some local princes had ties with Selya in the north-west and others were refugees from defeats in the plains. The intrigues rife in this area soon involved the missionaries as naïve participants, but at the moment of their arrival, the complexity of the situation was masked by the unanimity with which

[1] *B.M.B.* (1891), 409ff.
[2] Nauhaus to Committee, 26 Dec. 1893 (Berlin IV 1 86).
[3] *B.M.B.* (1892), 359. Merensky, *Deutsche Arbeit*, p. 91.

the princes welcomed the white men as a reinforcement to their defences against the Ngoni.

The Berlin Expedition, being numerous, self-confident, and armed, had an immediate effect on the local balance of politics: though Merensky counted on his patriarchal appearance to engender respect, no special action was required to encourage the welcoming gift of cattle sent to the Mission by the surrounding chiefs during October 1891. Kinga chiefs also sent greetings, and a party of Sangu under a Swahili spokesman paid Merere's respects and hinted that the chief wished to be visited. The local chief, Mwaihojo, sent a representative to say 'my land, my people, my cattle, all belong to the white men.'[1] Merensky was quite prepared to exploit superstition about his powers and to become the court of appeal to the whole area. He had been more impressed than his experience warranted by Henry Drummond's transient experience and anti-slavery journalism, when Drummond stated: 'let a single European settle, with fifty square miles of heathen round him, and in a short time he will be their king, their lawgiver, and their judge.'[2] Supernatural attributes did not in the long run promote mission influence, however, and backfired to such a degree that Kumoga, for the sake of Merensky's safety, had virtually to smuggle him out of the country when he departed in mid 1892.[3]

With Wangemannshöh well advanced by Christmas 1891, after the construction of the first station, and his year in the field half gone, Merensky became impatient to explore the wider hinterland from which Merere issued repeated and urgent calls. At the turn of the year, he and Nauhaus set off under the guidance of Sangu emissaries, hiking through the Elton Pass, into and across the Rift to Utengule to meet Merere Towelamahamba, the notorious 'Sultan'. Here was a tribal ruler to fill South African expectations. In the first tediously formal reception, the words of the strangers were repeated down a whole line of *wafumo* before being acknowledged by the chief. Subsequent meetings dispensed with this ritual and on the second day Merere revealed his real interest in the Europeans: that they were Germans and could serve his political purposes.[4]

[1] *B.M.B.* (1892), 356.

[2] Drummond, Henry, *Tropical Africa* (London, 1888), p. 105.

[3] Merensky, *Deutsche Arbeit*, pp. 203, 317f.

[4] Merensky, A., 'Die deutschen Missionsunternehmungen im Njassa-Gebiet' *Petermanns Mitteilungen* (1892), pp. 252ff. See also Wright, 'Chief Merere and the Germans', p. 45.

Merere had heard rumours of German action against the Hehe, but not of the fiasco resulting from Mkwawa's ambush of the detachment under Zelewski. Merere's scribe produced a letter from Rochus Schmidt, the Commander at Bagamoyo, which Merensky read and interpreted. At the chief's insistence, he wrote a letter to the Governor introducing Merere and conveying the chief's desire for an alliance against the Hehe. Merere dictated a similar letter in Swahili to his Muslim scribe, then immediately dispatched messengers to take both letters to the coast. The alliance seemed natural, since Schmidt had promised that recognition of the German flag with his letter would be reciprocated by German protection. Merensky, though he paid lip-service to his non-political office as a missionary, was obviously in sympathy with the beleaguered Sangu and wished to see German influence spread.[1]

The Berliners took an opportunity also to prepare the ground for the Moravians, whose sphere was to include Usafwa and Utengule. When Merere proved very appreciative of medical treatment for his inflamed eyes and wanted war-charms too, Merensky took the opportunity to recommend a peaceable way of life. To the obvious disconsolation of the leader of the Muslim community, he also extracted a vague promise to sponsor a resident missionary. Merere seems to have been at that time quite oblivious of the possible religious conflicts, wishing mainly to enlist all possible forces in support of his cause.[2] In returning to Wangemannshöh, Merensky and Nauhaus passed by Rungwe to tell Meyer, as head of the Moravian mission, that Merere had promised to exempt the country occupied by the missionaries from his raids. Although gladdened by this news, Meyer hastened to write to the Governor to counter Merensky's optimism about a Sangu alliance:

> The name 'Merere' is hated and feared here. Our station is on part of a village that has been laid waste by him. The people can well describe Merere's atrocities. It is to be hoped that Merere's wishes communicated at his request through Superintendent Merensky's letter are just and the petition about military force for common battle against the Wahingi [Hehe] will not have the effect of fastening the German troops in a snare.[3]

[1] Merensky to von Soden, 15 Oct. 1891 and 5 Jan. 1892 (T.N.A. IX A 6). *B.M.B.* (1892), 362. Merensky, *Deutsche Arbeit*, pp. 243f.

[2] *B.M.B.* (1892), 405.

[3] Meyer to von Soden, 12 Feb. 1892 (T.N.A. IX A 6).

The Southern Highlands beyond the Hehe were very remote, nine months being required for the return journey to Dar es Salaam. Pending the Governor's reply, the Berliners remained in frequent contact with Merere through his emissaries. When, during the summer of 1892, *rinderpest* spread from the north and killed the Sangu herds, Merere was sorely tempted to recoup at the expense of the Kukwe. Anxious not to offend the Germans, he sent a message to Wangemannshöh in mid August giving notice of measures to punish the Kukwe for their disobedience. The action took the form of a raid at the end of the month. At the rumour of the approaching Sangu, the local people assembled on a hill-top near the mission station, cattle were driven into the vicinity, and a chief asked the missionaries to lend their fire-power to the defence. The pacifistic Moravians declined and quietly observed through a telescope as five to six hundred Sangu warriors marched into the valley below their station with many captured cattle, mustered as the booty was paraded before them, then attacked one of Masioge's villages.[1]

The raid proved that the missionaries could not and would not deter Merere. The people could not comprehend the reasons for their refusal to fire on the Sangu, just as the missionaries were astounded at the Kukwe disunity which left single villages within the same chiefdom to fend for themselves. Although the raiders did not enter Mwakapalili's country where the Rungwe Station was situated, Meyer was conscious of a need to vindicate the trust of the people. He therefore protested to the Berliners at Merere's breach of the promise not to disturb the countryside near the missionaries.[2] Just as the Moravians lodged their complaint, Merere's Swahili ambassador, Muintschande, was at Wangemannshöh with the Governor's letter. Nauhaus refused to interpret the letter because of Merere's bad faith in raiding Ukukwe. Muintschande explained that the Kukwe were disobedient vassals. Furthermore, as overlord, Merere was offended that the Moravians had never called upon him. Following this exchange, both Muintschande and the Moravians returned home to organize their respective briefs. Meyer called together the Kukwe princes who claimed that they had never been subjects, but had given gifts voluntarily in order to avoid raids. Admittedly, one of their number had rendered regular quantities of meal until the Nyakyusa victory of 1886, the arrival of the Europeans in 1887, and the treaties

[1] *B.M.B.* (1893), 159. *H.M.B.* (1893), 15f.
[2] *B.M.B.* (1893), 16f. *P.A.* (1892), 620.

with Montieth Fotheringham of 1889, had emboldened him to cease. With a deputation of princes, Meyer met Muintschande in November 1892 at Wangemannshöh, to learn that Merere claimed even more land than before 'by right of conquest' and alleged that the Kukwe stopped paying tribute only when the missionaries settled with them.[1]

As no clear judgement could be made, the Moravians resolved to go to Utengule to negotiate directly. Ten African delegates from the neighbourhood of Rungwe and ten from that of Wangemannshöh travelled with Meyer and Richard to Utengule, where again a ceremonious reception preceded the real discussions. Withdrawal of the Muslims indicated the essentially domestic nature of the issue. Surrounded by his Sangu *wafumo*, Merere offered the Moravians a bargain; he would concede Kukwe independence in return for promises by the Moravians to write on his behalf to von Soden, whenever a messenger came to request the service. Merere further attempted without success to extract a promise that the Moravians would come to his defence if he was attacked by the Hehe. Meyer's reactions to the meeting were pleasure at the Kukwe concession, mistrust of any 'external guarantees' by the wily chief, and sympathy with his precarious position—'one or two lost battles and his empire dissolves into small disintegrated areas'.[2]

Merere gambled more and more on alliance with the Germans, even though the Governor's letter had not been encouraging in its assurance that troops would reach him via Kalenga, i.e. after peace with the Hehe. At the same time, von Soden had underlined the importance of the missionaries, advising Merere to listen to Merensky. Von Soden also wrote to the Berliners, to state his conviction that Mkwawa wanted peace but did not know how to open negotiations. While urging the missionaries to take initiatives towards the Hehe, von Soden was combating the project of the Anti-Slavery Association to send an expedition under von Wissmann to place a steamer on Lake Tanganyika or Nyasa. Armed force loosed in the south-western interior, he predicted, would menace the good relations with the Tabora Arabs and increase the 'mistrust' of the Hehe. Again the governor urged the Berlin Mission to penetrate Uhehe to make peaceful contact: 'If the Berlin Mission will take this course, they can be certain of every support on my part. The post at Merere's has no

[1] Meyer to von Soden, 4 Apr. 1893. (T.N.A. IX A 6). *P.A.* (1893), 45. *H.M.B.* (1893), 51f.

[2] *H.M.B.* (1893), 274, 286.

instructions to proceed militarily against Kalenga and the Hehe, on the contrary, its task is thoroughly peaceful . . . to win the trust of these people and thereby to gain passage through their country.'[1]

Carl Nauhaus, left in charge of the Berlin endeavours after Merensky's departure, shied away from the commission. In any case von Wissmann was on his way via Lake Nyasa and the Muslims at Utengule were well aware of his approach as early as February 1893 when they asked the visiting Moravians when 'Bissmann' would arrive. The instructions to the Anti-Slavery Expedition referred only to opening the country for commerce by floating the steamer and founding stations, but an expedition with von Wissmann in charge could not be anything but an effort to secure German influence on the frontiers, especially among the slaving Bemba he had met in his 1887 journey. Von Wissmann appreciated that obtaining recognition of suzerainty by a show of force was only a preliminary to political and judicial control, and although his position was unofficial, he represented the beginning of German administration and armed force in the Nyasa–Tanganyika corridor.[2]

Merere was the key to military action in the south-western region of German East Africa, as any strategist could see; but the Moravians remained non-aggressive. Meyer did not want a military station either in his mission field or at Utengule where it was most likely to stir up the war lust of the Sangu. Although no stations were in fact established except on the lake, an alliance between Merere and von Wissmann could not be prevented, and he went so far as attempting to revive the Ngoni–Sangu alliance against Mkwawa. The alert Hehe, however, cut off the Sangu messengers and forced the Germans to tackle projects more within their power, such as an expedition to Lake Rukwa against a hunter and self-styled chief who had slipped from Merere's control, and who, as an independent supplier of ivory, disrupted the trading pattern of the coastmen based at Utengule.[3]

The joint Sangu–German–Arab foray towards Lake Rukwa was

[1] Von Soden to Nauhaus, 21 Aug. 1892 (Kidugala 1), von Soden to Merere (draft), 28 Apr. 1892, and von Soden to Berlin Station Kondeland, 28 Apr. 1892 T.N.A. IX A 6).

[2] Instructions in Antisklaverei-Lotterie to von Wissmann, 31 May 1892. A.A.K.A. to von Schele, 1 May 1893, enclosing von Wissmann's plan of action, 30 Jan. 1893 (T.N.A. IV B 26).

[3] Meyer to von Soden, 4 Apr. 1893 (T.N.A. IX A 6). Von Wissmann to Antisklaverei Kommission, 20 Apr. 1893 (T.N.A. VI B 26). Selim bin Abakari, in Velten, C., *Schilderungen der Suaheli* (Göttingen, 1901), p. 74.

greeted as an attack by the Nyiha who inflicted great damage upon the force under Captain Bumiller before it was relieved at the last minute by von Wissmann. When Captain Tom von Prince arrived in Kondeland as a special commissioner to receive the transfer of the lake station, Langenburg, and the steamer 'Wissmann' from the Anti-Slavery Association, he had no formal powers to negotiate with the Sangu. Nevertheless, his former assignment to establish German influence on the periphery of Uhehe had engaged him in a duel with Mkwawa and he felt that the opportunity to secure the back door to Uhehe could not be allowed to slip. He found Merere disillusioned with German power, however, and unwilling to volunteer assistance. But, having literally hired Sangu auxiliaries, von Prince gained a notable victory near Lake Rukwa where Bumiller had failed. This transformed the prospects for an alliance, which was sealed by promising to restore to the Sangu their homeland and provinces.[1]

When Langenburg became an administrative post in October 1893, Baron von Eltz of the Anti-Slavery Expedition was selected as *Stationschef* or military administrator. His first duty was to secure the Sangu alliance by guaranteeing that a competent chief succeeded Merere Towelamahamba who died late in 1893. Recognizing that the immediate heir was mentally unfit, von Eltz urged a new election and then officially confirmed Merere Mugandilwa as chief. As part of the ceremony, von Eltz received 100 pounds of ivory as tribute and had the Sangu pledge to raid only against the Hehe renewed. This promise was almost immediately broken by a Sangu party, probably a ritual command for the new chief, which raided Unyiha, whereupon von Eltz overtook the raiders and ordered them back to Utengule, where he fined Merere Mugandilwa heavily for his unauthorized action.[2] The penalty was accepted without trouble because co-operation was a pre-condition for the prospective restoration of Usangu. For their part, the Germans also wished to keep up friendly relations, looking forward to the joint offensive against the Hehe planned for mid 1894. Moravian settlement near Utengule was postponed because Merere's reluctance caused Eltz to advise the missionaries to await the successful completion of the Hehe operation.[3]

[1] Von Wissmann to Antisklaverei Kommission, 26 Apr. 1893 (T.N.A. VI B 26). Von Prince, T., *Gegen Araber und Wahehe* (Berlin, 1914), pp. 229, 245, 258f.

[2] *D.K.B.* (1894), 547. For raiding, a Sangu sub-chief was in 1894 fined 1 tusk, 15 cattle, and 100 goats and sheep. *H.M.B.* (1894), 368.

[3] *H.M.B.* (1894), 280.

Within the confines of the north end—Rungwe area, both sets of missionaries found plenty to do. During their first three years, the Berliners established a series of stations, running from Ikombe on the Lake, near Langenburg, up the Lufilio past Wangemannshöh to Manow in Selya and Mwakaleli in Lugulu country. Being well staffed and fairly concentrated, they were able to make an intensive study of dialect groups, local religious beliefs and ritual centres. With regard to traditional religious forms, they anticipated that the peoples of the area, in common with other Bantu, would have some idea of an abstract creative force or high god and that this conception could be used by them to interpret Christianity. The results of inquiry indicated that a high deity variously known as Mbambe, Kyala, and Mbasi, was widely acknowledged and worshipped in many places. The missionaries recognized the special importance of the grove of Lubaga near Manow, but did not analyse it. Other holy places noted at the time, generally associated with water, included the head-waters of the Kibira River where they emerged on Mount Kieyo from an underground stream, the grotto of Pali Kyala on the lakeshore near Ikombe, and the lagoon known as Lubasi at the outlet of the Mbaka River.[1]

Confusion among the missionaries as to the hierarchy of spirits is revealed in a short paper by Theodor Meyer, written in June 1893. While he understood quite accurately the relationship of the *baganga* or doctors and defenders to the *barosi* or wizards who could make themselves invisible in order to do malicious acts, a major difficulty arose in the higher orders of supernatural mediation and personification. According to Meyer, Mbasi stood above other spirits and was feared as the source of many ills, especially disease in men and cattle.[2] From this simple reversal of the attributes of creativity in the founding hero, Meyer concluded that Mbasi was the Devil and this connotation has been perpetuated in venacular translations of Scripture. More immediately, the erroneous identification of Mbasi affected the attitude of the Berliners, who became engaged in a spiritual conflict with a cult of Mbasi in the neighbourhood of Wangemannshöh.

Wangemannshöh, it will be remembered, was erected in an area of accentuated political instability. In the first months of the settlement

[1] Merensky, *Deutsche Arbeit*, pp. 110ff.

[2] Meyer, 'Something of the Religion of our People', June 1893 (Herrnhut R15 MI A6).

when the princes outdid themselves in welcoming the foreigners, the one dissonant factor had been the herdsman-priest of the cult of Mbasi who attempted to exchange gifts and claimed that Mbasi, manifest as an 'unseen voice', had called the white men into the country. Concerned to assess the influence of the cult, the missionaries observed that the powerful lakeshore chief Mwanjabara went directly from Wangemannshöh to call upon the priest. After 15 November 1891, when Merensky's prophecy of an eclipse was fulfilled, religious tension had mounted. A failure of the rains gave the Mbasi priest the opportunity to seek retribution for the rude denial of his powers by the missionaries by blaming them for the drought. Although his order to kill the white men was not carried out, they were shunned and, until the rains resumed, supplied with no provisions except by their immediate sponsor, Mwakatungile.[1]

Mwakatungile had taken on the missionaries with the agreement of the neighbouring chief Mwaihojo, but in time it became evident that the two princes were at odds. Mwakatungile had declared effusively that as his other fathers were dead, the Berliners would serve in their place. Thereafter, the Mbasi priest became aligned with Mwaihojo, and the missionaries were caught in the snares of local religious politics.[2] According to the state of public opinion, the priest alternated between claiming the missionaries as spiritual allies or denouncing them as enemies. His conflict with the missionaries arose when they sought to arbitrate in a case affecting his ability to acquire wives and cattle in the name of Mbasi. It was claimed that a woman, Kinjorobo, was a wife of Mbasi although she was living as Mwakatungile's wife. With the missionaries as his protectors, the prince went against the generally held opinion that she should be given up to the priest. A confrontation between the two in April 1892 provided the missionaries with an opportunity to convene a local council to decide the case. Merensky addressed Mwaihojo and Mwakatungile and deputies of four other princes on the fraudulent divinity of Mbasi, offering them instead 'one God' and the Bible. The case went against the priest and Mwaihojo, now appearing to capitulate to the Christians, led the way in repudiating the cult and in asking to be taught by the missionaries. Others expressed a general scepticism about the oracle but commented that it was accepted by

[1] *B.M.B.* (1892), 360. Merensky, *Deutsche Arbeit*, pp. 212ff.

[2] Merensky, *Deutsche Arbeit*, pp. 212, 221. *B.M.B.* (1892), 152. For a more detailed narrative, see Charsley, *Princes*, pp. 5ff.

the majority. Mwakiambo, the leading chief of the area, sent word affirming the justice of the decision and branded Mwaihojo as a political mischief-maker using the cult to his own ends. The missionaries urged all chiefs to withdraw their shares of the cattle deposited with the priest as an evidence of real rejection, but only Mwakatungile, now riding high, reclaimed his stock and severed with the cult.[1]

The *rinderpest*, reaching the lake plain in May and June 1892, revived the importance of traditional rituals for the restoration of prosperity and drew together chiefs who in normal times would have observed few common rites. Mwanjabara sent a tusk to the priest of Mbasi, asking that the hero resurrect a cow in acknowledgement. A council, assembled in the presence of Bunk and Nauhaus, explained the plague by declaring that the dispute over the woman Kinjorobo had angered Mbasi and that she must be restored to the priest. An armed party of Mwanjabara's men came from the plains to force Mwaihojo to appease the god and when Mwaihojo side-stepped personal responsibility by calling the missionaries to book, Mwanjabara's spokesman blamed them for the disturbance: 'I find, white man, that you who wanted to bring us peace have brought us war. You stand by Mwakatungile, who has brought misfortune to our people.'[2] Nauhaus denied the charges of spiritual causation, explained the plague in natural terms, and affected a peaceful withdrawal. The Mbasi priest, who was not attached to any fixed ritual centre, then decamped to Lubaga, where he persuaded the Selya chiefs that the woman was the source of divine displeasure. The missionaries at Manow shared the blame, and when swarms of locusts added to the holocaust, Mwaipopo, the leading prince of Selya, declared that the woman must be returned.[3]

The process of generalizing relationships in terms of religious symbols had begun. It is reasonable to conclude that among the Selya and Lakeshore Nyakyusa the uniformity of missionary doctrine and presence helped induce a co-ordinated response. At the outset, Kumoga had been sent ahead to assuage the suspicions of the chiefs surrounding the question of mission occupation of land, and Nauhaus and Schumann then selected the site for a station. In great haste to secure a large tract of land before he left the territory, Merensky

[1] Merensky, *Deutsche Arbeit*, pp. 217ff., 222.
[2] Merensky, *Deutsche Arbeit*, pp. 223f. *B.M.B.* (1893), 158.
[3] *B.M.B.* (1893), 546.

had quickly negotiated with a prince, Mwakarobo, for the purchase of 3,000 acres. Mwaipopo subsequently charged that Mwakarobo was an illegitimate chief and that he, Mwaipopo, should have received the payment for the land. Again the Berlin missionaries owing to unpopular sponsors were faced with a political dilemma. In hard times when chiefs seized pretexts for raids to build up their devastated herds, Mwakarobo became the object of continual robbery. Arbitration by missionaries was unacceptable, they were abused behind their backs for their pacifism, and they could not even persuade the neutral chief Lwembe to settle the dispute between Mwakarobo and Mwaipopo. Antagonism towards the white men mounted, and only months after Merensky had requested forty flags and treaty forms in order to accept the chiefs' submission to German overrule, the illusion of missionary influence lay shattered and both Moravians and Berliners complained of their inability to mitigate lawlessness.[1]

At this juncture von Wissmann's force arrived and imposed a general if transient recognition of German power. Von Wissmann received Mwanjabara's pledge of loyalty, askaris were drilled in the vicinity of Wangemannshöh as a public display, and courts or *shauris* were held. At the behest of the Berliners, von Wissmann decided a case between the Nyakyusa and the Kinga, and it was in the sphere of intertribal arbitration that the colonial authorities continued to enjoy success.[2] Regulation of internal affairs, on the other hand, proved to be much more difficult. The missionaries' role as mediators gained for them popular trust as protectors against the new alien power. Chief Mwankenja, for example, refused to accept the German flag or to hand over a man wanted in Nyasaland for theft, and accused locally of murder. Von Wissmann was preparing to use force against Mwankenja when Carl Nauhaus succeeded in persuading the chief to co-operate.[3]

The new German administration would have been sorely strained had all the quarrels of the contentious Nyakyusa been submitted to it. The reactions of the people to askari police patrols emanating from Langenburg to deal with such complaints as were lodged, put the missionaries under great pressure to show their primary loyalties.

[1] Merensky to von Soden, 7 Mar. 1892 and 16 June 1892 (T.N.A. IX A 6). Merensky, *Deutsche Arbeit*, pp. 210, 255, 264f.

[2] Von Wissmann to Antisklaverie Kommission, 20 Apr. 1893 (T.N.A. VI B 26).

[3] *B.M.B.* (1893), 453, 527. *H.M.B.* (1895), 56. For the princes' function in providing sanctuary, see Mackenzie, D. R., *The Spirit-Ridden Konde* (London, 1925), pp. 87ff.

It was normal when a patrol came to fetch an accused person, for the whole village to decamp, assuming that the traditional legal principle of collective responsibility still obtained. As the askaris often confiscated cattle or burnt huts, they were also equated with raiders and general resentment fanned anti-European sentiments.

Von Eltz did his best to minimize the use of force and won the praise of the Berliners and Moravians for his patience and fairness. He authorized Meyer to arbitrate between the Safwa and Kukwe in one dispute, but when capital cases arose, he had to assert his own authority. A punitive expedition against a prince protecting an accused murderer occurred in 1894 in the neighbourhood of Ipiana, a new Moravian station developed by Richard on the Nyakyusa lake plain. Sergeant Bauer's lack of restraint in commanding the action caused Richard to complain, and the local princes began to talk among themselves of armed resistance to Langenburg. Von Eltz declared that he regretted the necessity of force but saw no alternative way to impress the princes. When some refused the order of the *Bezirkschef* to attend a conference, Richard stepped in to persuade Mwakalinga and Mwakatundu not to provoke the authorities at Langenburg. Mwakatundu, a senior and respected prince, revealed the political thinking of his peers. As he explained, he had sent a sheep to Langenburg with an apology for not coming himself because of the fever in the lowlands, and receiving no reciprocal gift, assumed that he was in bad standing. If troops came to fetch him he would not resist, in order to demonstrate clearly that the white men, not he, disturbed the peace. Against Richard's reasoning that the administration had stopped wars between chiefdoms, Mwakatundu protested that his fights were personal; some were merely self-defence, others were for recovery of property: there was no cause for subjugation. After a protracted session on the civics of colonial rule, the chief agreed to send a deputy. On the day, he appeared in person to go to Langenburg, where his intelligent arguments won the respect of von Eltz.[1]

Fear of askaris at times caused the people to turn in a flattering way to missionaries as arbitrators. The Berliners cultivated this political reaction and were rewarded with declarations of loyalty: 'Do we recognize the Germans [Langenburg]? You are our father, you give us peace.'[2] In an effort to ameliorate the interaction between the Government and the people, the missionaries jointly proposed an

[1] *H.M.B.* (1895), 150ff. [2] *B.M.B.* (1896), 223.

official court circuit, allowing cases beyond the competence of local chiefs to be heard at mission stations every three or four months. Officials would then be able to gather evidence immediately and the people would be relieved of their anxiety over implications of distant proceedings at Langenburg. Regular assessors from among the people were also recommended. These resolutions as a whole were favourably received by von Eltz and the Governor.[1]

While Europeans sought administrative solutions, Africans contended with colonial pressures by unifying the ritual leadership of the Selya and Nyakyusa princes. In this episode, the Mbasi priest and the disputed woman were again principal characters, for through Kinjorobo's testimony that the priest hid himself and projected the voice of Mbasi, the spiritual powers of the cult were brought into disrepute. A quarrel between Lwembe and the priest, resolved by the *mwafi* ordeal,[2] finally saw the Mbasi cult vanquished by traditional judicial means. Immediately after the fall of the priest of Mbasi, many Nyakyusa declared that as all their other priests had been in league with him, the people were left without spiritual protection.[3] Missionary hopes for a breakthrough for Christianity were disappointed, however, for spiritual and ritual leadership was transferred and reconstructed around the Lubaga–Lwembe cult.

Affairs quietened in 1895 and 1896. Von Eltz went on leave and returned for a second tour in early 1896 as 'Bezirksamtmann' because the district seemed ready for civil administration. The Moravians, wishing to keep temporal responsibility to a minimum, agreed upon a formula in October 1896:

> Disputes among the people living on station land are looked into and, as far as possible, settled by the missionaries themselves. All others that are brought to their notice are referred, in the first instance, to the native chiefs and if they fail to affect a settlement, to the Government officials at Langenburg. For the purposes of the Government, our Brethren are only interpreters and reporters.[4]

This procedure was intended both to teach respect for missionaries

[1] *B.M.B.* (1896), 220f. Von Elpons (personal statement), 25 Feb. 1899 (T.N.A. IX A 6).

[2] In the *mwafi* ordeal, individuals drink a poisonous concoction. If they vomit, they are innocent. In this case, the deputy of the priest of the Mbasi cult retained the liquid, 'proving' guilt.

[3] *B.M.B.* (1894), 206. *B.M.B.* (1895), 199ff., 389f.

[4] *P.A.* (1897), 277.

on their own property and to encourage general obedience to princes as part of a hierarchy of government.

Von Eltz died in June and was succeeded by one of the most experienced administrators and military officers in the territory, von Elpons.[1] Calling at Rungwe on his first tour of the district in November 1896, the new *Bezirksamtmann* spoke of his aspirations to avoid military action during his administration. Later the same day, however, an incident aroused his suspicion that the district was not in proper order. At a *shauri*, a woman appealed to him on account of mistreatment by her husband. Unprepared to delay his departure, von Elpons placed her in the official caravan to go to Langenburg for further hearing, only to encounter Meyer's protest that the local people would claim she had been stolen. This protest symbolized to the ruffled officer Meyer's culpable disloyalty in putting the native sense of justice above trust in German impartiality.

Annoyance turned to anger as the Nyakyusa sense of independence became increasingly evident. At Mwaya on the lake shore, an old scene of resistance, von Elpons was greeted neither by chiefs paying respects nor by the provisioning gifts normally given to visiting officials. Returning to Langenburg, he sat through the rains of December and January waiting for local chiefs to acknowledge his existence and power. The dearth of cases for his judgement indicated a lack of submissiveness for which he blamed the missionary influence and von Eltz's methods, concluding that his predecessor had been too weak in not asserting official prerogatives, in delegating judicial powers to the missionaries, and in apologizing for his occasional resorts to force.[2]

In February Makiembe and his people were the first to suffer, following von Elpon's decision to teach the Nyakyusa the meaning of subjugation. Askaris reported that the people had refused to sell them food, not for lack of it but from the desire to disobey. After two askaris were killed in a preliminary skirmish, von Elpons personally led an expedition to capture Makiembe, who fled to a neighbouring chief. Häfner, who had succeeded Richard at Ipiana, pleaded for negotiation and although von Elpons would not change his punitive methods, he did compromise by issuing only three bullets to each of

[1] Von Elpons was *Stationschef* at Mpwapwa in 1891–2 and later participated in expeditions against the Chagga and the Hehe.

[2] Von Elpons to Gov., 31 Oct. 1898. Von Elpons (personal statement), 25 Feb. 1899 (T.N.A. IX A 6).

his askaris. The ensuing engagement chastened the western Nyakyusa and cases submitted to the court at Langenburg increased markedly. Von Elpons continued to be dissatisfied because the Berliners in the east still handled cases in a 'dilatory' way, influenced by the political or domestic situation of the convicted party. They were unprepared to employ force to exact a penalty. This ineffective pacifism and the attitude of his askaris, who were bitter at restraints such as the three bullet limit which caused the death of some of their comrades at Makiembe's, drove von Elpons to reject all half measures.[1]

The subjugation of the Nyakyusa occurred in the second half of 1897, and the missionaries shared the responsibility for their resistance. Nauhaus, the senior missionary at Ikombe near Langenburg, enjoyed good relations both with officials and with the local people of Saku-Kisi background, and the Moravians too had won the confidence of von Elpons, but in the troublesome areas near Wangemannshöh and Manow, Schumann and Bunk appeared to be engaged in active opposition to the Government. After Nauhaus went on leave in mid 1897, everything seemed to degenerate.[2] A punitive expedition against the princes near Wangemannshöh in August 1897 set the tone for relations between the officials and the Mission for the next year and more. The missionaries claimed that the cause, an alleged murder, was twelve years old and that the death had been due to a fatality in a raid, not to homicide. Zenkewitz, the officer commanding the foray, accused the missionaries of forewarning the people, thereby diminishing its effect. Captives taken to Langenburg seemed to confirm this by naming as allies all the missionaries in Unyakyusa, including Häfner, the Moravian at Ipiana. The Berliners protested their innocence, at the same time deploring the unwarranted devastation, the death of several princes, and the removal of women and cattle.[3]

Criticism of military methods had little chance of a hearing so long as Governor von Liebert gave his officers his unquestioning support. Von Liebert, a soldier himself, fully sympathized with the complaints of von Elpons against the political activities of the missionaries, and their other acts of presumption such as insistence on priority in the use of the Government steamer. In October, the

[1] Von Elpons to Gov., 31 Oct. and 10 Nov. 1898 (T.N.A. IX A 6).

[2] Von Elpons to Gov., 13 Jan. 1897 (T.N.A. IX A 6).

[3] Von Elpons to Gov., 31 Oct. 1898. A.A.K.A. to Gov., 17 May 1899 (T.N.A. IX A 6). *Afrika* (1898), 100. *B.M.B.* (1898), 189ff.

Governor ordered von Elpons to prosecute missionaries for any further obstruction of justice or for aid to rebellious chiefs. Nerves became frayed as the Nyakyusa opposition stiffened rather than diminished. Von Elpons believed that missionaries identified themselves as 'ingleza' as opposed to the official 'ndaki' (Deutsche). And indeed, when askari movements in Ukinga aroused hostility to all Europeans, the Berlin missionary Hübner at Bulongwa redoubled his efforts to distinguish between the Mission and the Government, hoping to restore the confidence of the chief who had initially wanted to give away his whole country—'so that he could live as our man—protected from Langenburg'.[1]

There is no evidence of one leader having called together the Nyakyusa alliance formed in the autumn of 1897. The ground was well prepared by public outrage at the police and punitive expeditions, at the threatened extinction of princely prerogatives, and at the prospect of a regime of German force symbolized by the unsympathetic von Elpons. The division between officials and missionaries must have helped, but possibly the direct inspiration was the order of early November that all Nyakyusa chiefs should assemble at Mwankenja's village to proceed to von Elpons at Langenburg.[2]

At the holy grove of Lubaga on 24 November, amid much spear-shaking and the sacrifice of animals sent by many chiefs, the alliance was formed. In typical Nyakyusa fashion, the prospective booty was distributed in principle; the white man's horse was a prime item, but even mission pigs were claimed. Reports of the ceremonies reaching the Berliners indicated that no white men should be spared. Near Ipiana there were rumours of the alliance, but Häfner's intelligence indicated that the purpose was defensive only, against the 'ndaki' and not against the Mission.[3]

It became a prime charge against the missionaries that Bunk, who knew of the proceedings and was in charge of the Berlin Mission, did not report them to Langenburg. Arabs informed von Elpons of the mobilization. His scouting party with orders to propose negotiation

[1] Von Elpons to von Liebert, 9 June 1897. Von Liebert to von Elpons, 25 Oct. 1897. Von Elpons to Gov., 31 Oct. 1898 (T.N.A. IX A 6). *B.M.B.* (1897), 198.

[2] The prime movers were thought by the Berliners to be the chiefs of the lake plain, who prophesied that 'after the sacrifice, all white men . . . without exception will vanish.' *B.M.B.* (1898), 195. Von Elpons to Gov., 31 Oct. 1898 (T.N.A. IX A 6).

[3] *B.M.B.* (1898), 195. *H.M.B.* (1898), 182.

was rebuffed, and at the report of four hundred Kinga warriors in league with the Nyakyusa camped within an hour of the station, von Elpons seized the initiative, precipitated a battle by attacking Mwanjabara, and thus activated the alliance. Two neighbouring chiefs, Mwakalinga and Masurama, came to Mwaya, again a field of combat. The Germans' Maxim guns wreaked havoc with their first blasts and, lacking discipline, the Nyakyusa quickly dispersed, giving the Germans a decisive military victory. Among others, the revered Mwakalinga (Kirota) was killed. The people, aquiver with fear of further reprisals, fled into the bush at the sight of Meyer, who, *en route* to Ipiana station, the next day travelled near the scene of the rout. When he obtained a hearing, the Moravian Superintendent admonished the people for their folly in supposing that they could overpower the Germans.[1]

The Moravians were temperate in their reflections on the causes of the rebellion. On the political side, Meyer commented:[2]

> Self-respect is to be admired, when coupled with humility. But the latter is, as a rule, lacking in the Baniakyusa. Above all, they will brook no authority. If anything crosses them, they throw submission to the winds. They obey only so long as they can gain anything by it. They want to be free; alas! too free. Only too easily does a Government commit some mistake, even while trying to respect this love of freedom; the chiefs are irritated, they rebel, carried away by the will of the people, whose hatred is aroused by what they consider the oppression of the foreigner.

Kretschmer's report from the Rutenganio station contributed a religious explanation, for he believed that *waganga* (doctors) and *wagogo* (diviners), especially the old women among them, had encouraged popular resentment.[3]

The continuing feud between the Berlin missionaries and von Elpons allowed the Nyakyusa a considerable voice because each European party all too willingly accepted embroidered evidence against the other. The most serious accusation was that Bunk and another Berliner had given support behind the African lines in the December encounter. Bunk denied the specific charge and also the general one that the mission was overtly and covertly anti-Government, replying that on the contrary, its services to the colonial

[1] Von Elpons to Gov., 31 Oct. 1898 (T.N.A. IX A 6). *H.M.B.* (1898), 182.
[2] *P.A.* (1898), 623.
[3] *P.A.* (1898), 624f.

government had been generously acknowledged by von Eltz and visiting dignitaries.[1]

The official charges of disloyalty determined Merensky in Berlin to carry the defence of his men to the highest authorities, whereas in East Africa, Governor von Liebert unquestioningly accepted von Elpons's version of the causes of unrest. Merensky's twofold strategy consisted first in giving publicity to African justifications for resistance through *Afrika* and then in using Dr. von Jacobi to reach the Foreign Office and the Kolonialrat. Askari brutality, the malevolence of Muslim agents, and German officers inclined to talk with powder and shot were described in *Afrika*. An article published in April 1898 suggested that unnecessary violence had been employed in Kondeland from the beginning of 1897 when the villagers were forced to seek refuge from marauding askaris by crossing to the English side of the border. The demand for a full investigation was taken up by the colonial circle, obliging the Foreign Office to instruct von Liebert to explore the whole sequence of events. While the report was outstanding, the Berlin Mission presented its interpretation, which idealized the era of von Eltz as a time when chiefs gradually and peacefully grew accustomed to colonial rule and the court circuit promised to solve the judicial problem.[2]

The political atmosphere in Kondeland remained disturbed. During 1898 a number of punishments were meted out to leading rebels, following which tax collections began. The Moravian area of Rutenganio showed early signs of obedience to instructions to undertake road construction, but the Berlin parts of Unyakyusa remained disorderly. Missionaries inundated Langenburg with complaints; von Elpons reported that almost every official act in the uplands evoked letters expressing missionary 'animosity' against the administration: 'To them the very existence of askaris is an excess.' Bunk seemed to him too ready to tolerate fights between individual citizens while at the same time preaching of 'robbery' and 'atrocities' by askaris.[3]

A protracted correspondence between and within the mission and

[1] Bunk to Gov., 4 Feb. 1898 (T.N.A. IX A 6). Von Liebert to Bunk, 28 May 1898 (Kidugala 1). As both Schumann and Nauhaus were on leave, Bunk was in charge of the field.

[2] Von Liebert to A.A.K.A., 1 July 1898. A.A.K.A. to von Liebert, 4 July 1898. Berlin Committee to von Jacobi, 18 Oct. 1898 (T.N.A. IX A 6). *Afrika* (1898), pp. 98ff., 217ff.

[3] Von Elpons to Gov., 30 May and 31 July 1898 (T.N.A. IX A 6).

official hierarchies went on until mid 1899 with certain concrete results. On the mission side, instructions were given to avoid even hints of political partiality, except in favour of the administration. Mediation between the people and the colonial government was to cease. It was agreed that Bunk would not be allowed to live or work in Kondeland, although the mission successfully protested against his total exclusion from the colony, because of their shortage of men and his knowledge of local vernaculars. On the other side, officials from Governor down to *Bezirksamtmann*, while they resented the troublesome missionaries, were compelled to acknowledge the power of the humanitarian lobby to censure official behaviour. Wilhelm Solf, the later Colonial Secretary, in 1898 and 1899 had the specific task, as a political adviser in German East Africa, of restraining the military mind. His drafting of instructions to Langenburg showed the new sensitivity: 'In consideration of the influence of the evangelical mission in the pro-colonial circles in Germany, I expect you to further the work of the mission in your District.'[1]

Beginning in 1899 with the tax posts set up in the highlands of Rungwe, and increasingly as the new district headquarters developed at New Langenburg (Tukuyu), colonial control closed in upon the area. Hans Zache as *Bezirksamtmann* wished for a company of troops to deal with sporadic Kukwe resistance, and regretted that the German military presence had never been as impressive in Langenburg as it was in areas of military rule. He recognized, however, that the tendency of colonial policy led away from such methods, and resigned himself to wearing down recalcitrants by a system of warranty, capturing herds to be returned upon pledges of loyalty. Constant investigations into the conduct of his police, of Sudanese and other nationalities, continued to harm their morale. His ambitious plans for the economic development of the Langenburg District faltered owing, so he asserted, to his critics' defence of the 'right' to unemployment. The readiness of humanitarians to leap to the side of the Rungwe peoples as martyrs persecuted by scoundrel askaris, caused the exacerbated official to see in the situation a *Kulturkampf* between the administration's progressive programme and askari agents on the one hand and the humanitarians and idle, backward tribesmen on the other.[2]

[1] Von Liebert to Langenburg, 23 July 1898 (T.N.A. IX A 6). See also von Vietsch, E., *Wilhelm Solf, Botschafter zwischen den Zeiten* (Tübingen, 1961), p. 37.

[2] Zache to Gov., 30 Jan. 1901 (D.Z.A.P. B.A. 1a/19).

The conflict between the administrative tradition of primary reliance upon alien élites, and the missionaries who bid for influence among indigenous peoples, was nowhere more classically exemplified than in the Rungwe area from 1896 to 1901.[1] The sense of immediate confrontation receded, but the *Kulturkampf* did not cease to smoulder until the German administration came to an end.

[1] For a discussion of the development of the administrative tradition, see Wright, M., 'Local Roots of Policy in German East Africa', *J.A.H.* ix, 4 (1968), 623ff.

CHAPTER IV

Expansion beyond Rungwe

THE missionaries in 1895 established footholds beyond Rungwe, the Moravians moving towards the north, to Utengule and the Safwa–Sangu country, while the Berliners looked towards the east and built Bulongwa in Ukinga. Further expansion in both directions was contingent upon the fortunes of the Hehe Wars. By a supplementary agreement, the Berlin Society relinquished the rights to Usangu so that the Moravians might follow Merere and his people when they were repatriated.[1] But this agreement did not finally determine who would evangelize in the Sangu flats; political conditions and the mutual dislike of the Moravians and Merere kept the Protestants at arm's length. The Roman Catholic presence, too, entered more and more into calculations of strategy because the Benedictines had by 1895 established themselves in Iringa and the White Fathers approached from the north-west.

The immediate steps forward came easiest to the Berliners, who had explored Ukinga in 1893 and found the way open because of their charity towards the Kinga traders in the vicinity of Wangemannshöh. At the time of the 1893 survey of Ukinga, Nauhaus had looked upon stations there as part of a series which might continue to Ngoni country. Rather than enter Uhehe, where troubles abounded and the Roman Catholics would be encountered, he preferred the then unoccupied Songea area, where his own command of Xhosa could be used to advantage.[2] In this early effort to rearrange the commitments of his Society as conceived in Berlin, Nauhaus displayed the independent disposition which later brought about serious clashes with the home committee. In the matter of Uhehe, however, Merensky and the Committee stood firmly in control and intended to take full advantage of the publicity generated by the Hehe Wars to gain popularity for their East African work. In 1895 when local missionaries again suggested a deflection from the route into Uhehe,

[1] *H.M.B.* (1895), 37.
[2] Minutes of Conference, 22–5 May 1893 (Berlin IX 1 8b).

the Berlin Committee reaffirmed its intention to follow up the military occupation of Uhehe, and Merensky went further to emphasize that the mission would spread further, 'to the sea'.[1]

The vicissitudes of the Hehe resistance and guerrilla warfare had a more direct effect upon the Moravians in the mid 1890s, for they became involved with the allies of the German forces, the Sangu. The Mission Board in Herrnhut had been anxious to advance into Usafwa and to follow the Sangu. Again local missionary opinion preferred alternative courses. Meyer as Superintendent wished to capitalize on the withdrawal of the Livingstonia Mission from Bundali, where the people were related to the Kukwe and Nyakyusa, but like Nauhaus in the east, he dutifully postponed his own projects.[2] Usafwa thereafter became the real linchpin of expansion.

By their preliminary agreement with Merere Mugandilwa in 1894, the Moravians had been able to stipulate that the chief would never ask them for armed assistance and they in turn could not oblige him to listen to Christian preaching. The *modus vivendi* came to a test when in 1895 von Eltz finally approved the missionary settlement at Utengule and presented Theophil Richard and Johannes Kootz, a young recruit, with a letter to the paramount chief indicating that they had the blessings of Langenburg in their presence at the Sangu capital. After an amicable reintroduction to Merere, it was not long before the missionaries received demands conflicting with their conscience and the preliminary agreement. Exploiting his licence to raid Mkwawa's lands at will, Merere observed that the swollen Ruaha River had cut off a group of Hehe subjects and gathered his forces to attack the vulnerable settlement. Richard would not be persuaded to join this expedition and treated the chief to a sermon on the sinfulness of his warfare and the fiery fate that would be his if he fell in action. Merere's petition for prayer in support of the expedition was likewise rejected, and later when the Sangu were menaced by a reciprocal Hehe attack, Richard refused the protection of the walls of Utengule and continued from his independent and exposed homestead to declaim against Sangu robbery and plunder.[3]

The feud between missionary and chief flourished as Merere denied Richard the right of itinerant preaching in his villages and Richard in turn lost his temper and publicly damned the Sangu, Arabs, and all other hardened sinners. Although careful not to

[1] *B.M.B.* (1896), 224f. [2] *H.M.B.* (1894), 245.
[3] *H.M.B.* (1895), 276ff. *H.M.B.* (1896), 9f.

endanger his standing with the Langenburg authorities by acting directly against the evangelical white men, Merere did his best to obstruct them. His people were instructed to refuse to work and a sudden shortage of food amounted to a boycott, though the chief would not admit having sanctioned it. Supplies carried from Rungwe to the Utengule outpost proved that the missionaries could not be starved out, at which point Merere resorted to a direct invitation that Richard take his message elsewhere, as he made no apparent contribution to the Sangu state.[1] The ruling aristocracy adhered to its dynastic rituals, such as those carried out in June 1895 at the grave of Merere Towelamahamba. Richard and Kootz observed at a distance as Merere presided, surrounded by his female relatives, the *wafumo*, and warriors. At the general festival following this celebration, a spirit of conciliation prevailed as Merere delivered one of his typical rallying speeches and even Richard was permitted to make a short sermon. No breakthrough had been achieved, however, and the renewed hostility of the Sangu élite soon proved that this concession was a courtesy for the occasion.[2] After Richard returned to Rungwe, leaving Kootz and his wife in Usafwa, the Sangu made no secret of their derision by refusing to describe the young missionary as 'white', a synonym for powerful, but labelled him instead 'woman', one unable to fight and therefore not worth hearing. In reaction, the Moravians tended to invest their energies in Merere's alien subjects, especially the itinerant Nyiha who as labourers formed the core of the station community. Once again, local missionaries began to look in a different direction than their home authorities had anticipated, in this case because Unyiha beckoned far more hopefully than the restored Usangu.[3]

When it came to the missionary occupation of the former Hehe empire, the Berliners proved to be far more aggressive than the Moravians, who had been chastened by their proximity to the Sangu. A factor in the Iringa District new to the Protestants was that they were a secondary rather than the primary wave of colonialism. In the later 1890s, the German administration undoubtedly superseded tribal states as the source of political initiative. Yet Tom von Prince, the *Chef* of the Iringa District, ruled very much in the indirect

[1] *H.M.B.* (1896), 18f.
[2] ibid., 13ff.
[3] *H.M.B.* (1897), 23f. Kootz-Kretschmer, *Die Safwa*, ii, 193. Meyer to von Wissmann, 9 Nov. 1895 (T.N.A. IX A 6).

style, employing traditional African authorities and parts of the old superstructure of power, leaving it to the Berliners either to co-operate or to work through submerged peoples. In their unerring, naïve way, the missionaries soon became aligned with dissidents.

The colonial history of the Iringa District had begun with a fiasco for the Germans when the Zelewski Expedition was wiped out by Mkwawa in 1891. Two punitive expeditions in 1894 and 1896 preceded the administrative occupation of the area by a party of Roman Catholics, Swahilis, askaris, von Prince and his extraordinary wife, Magdelene. Mkwawa was still at large when Iringa was founded as district headquarters, but many of the Hehe *wasagira* or councillors seemed to accept German authority. Von Prince planned to rule the Hehe domains by recognizing three paramount chiefs, Merere in the west, Kiwanga in the south, and Mpangire as the heir to Mkwawa in Uhehe proper.[1]

The stability of this arrangement was uppermost in von Prince's mind when Bunk and Maass called at Iringa to lay claim to Uhehe as the religious sphere of the Berlin Mission. To their disappointment, they found that the Roman Catholics had already pre-empted a large part of the region, leaving only the unpacified South to the Lutherans. In parcelling out the North to the Catholics, von Prince had taken into account the dislike of Merere for evangelical missionaries, and Bunk's presentation of the case for separate treatment of Kahamele, a brother of Merere, giving practical evidence of his willingness to undermine the Sangu hierarchy, confirmed the political wisdom in keeping the Berliners away from Merere.[2]

Eighteen months elapsed between the missionaries' visit to Iringa and their active penetration of the Hehe–Bena area. That year and a half was full of stress in the German–Sangu alliance, for the initial indications that the *wasagira* would recognize Mkwawa's brother Mpangire as paramount chief proved to be false. After Mpangire had been ceremoniously installed by von Prince in December 1896, the *wasagira* began to rally to the fugitive Mkwawa. At the end of January Mpangire himself became suspect and was then convicted and executed for supporting Mkwawa. The rest of the royal clan was sent into exile, ending paramountcy by an African authority in

[1] Von Prince, M., *Eine deutsche Frau im Innern Deutsch-Ostafrika* (Berlin, 1908), p. 62. See also Redmayne, 'Mkwawa', pp. 434ff.

[2] Von Prince to Gov., 18 Jan. and 5 July 1899 (T.N.A. IX A 6). *B.M.B.* (1897), 746. *B.M.B.* (1898), 47.

Uhehe proper. Conscious of the insecurity of his position, von Prince upon receipt of reports that the southern Bena and Ngoni contemplated joining arms against him, called on Merere to garrison Iringa and provide irregulars for the continuing struggle with Mkwawa.[1]

After hesitation, Merere agreed to go with the officer from Iringa who came to persuade him, and he was retained in German service by the payment of maintenance for himself and his men as well as by hints that he might be installed as paramount chief over the Hehe. The idea of promoting Merere faded, however, after the death of Mkwawa when the *wasagira* finally pledged their loyalty to von Prince who assumed the paramountcy himself and ruled through traditional sub-chiefs.[2]

The area of the Iringa District in which Merere continued to be paramount included Usangu, a small part of western Uhehe and north-west Ubena. Von Prince believed that residual respect for the Sangu as former overlords legitimized this restoration, but the instance of Ngera II of the Bena proved that not all leaders acquiesced.[3] Learning of the intended missionary occupation of Ubena and having heard of their opposition to officials, Ngera II sent messengers to Bunk at Ikombe in early 1898 to complain against Merere and ask that 'men of peace' should settle in his war-fatigued country. Having established this contact, he recalled the local Bena warriors serving Merere as auxiliaries and withdrew other forms of recognition. In a a more aggressive spirit, he pressed the local Sangu *mfumo* with harassing skirmishes. Von Prince sent a company of *Schutztruppe* to intimidate the errant Bena leader, but Ngera II soon returned to the attack, and then evaded Merere, who had been ordered to arrest him, and fled to the mountains, purportedly to the protection of the missionaries.[4]

A second embassy from Ngera II brought a gift of four sheep to the missionaries and received their promise to come if the Bena supplied porters. With the assistance of over a hundred men from Ngera, a mission party headed by Bunk and including the probationary missionaries Neuberg, Priebusch and Groeschel, reached the western hills of Ubena on 14 July 1898. Quickly picking the site for the Kidugala Station because of its location between areas controlled by Ngera

[1] Von Prince, *Eine deutsche Frau*, p. 75. *H.M.B.* (1897).

[2] Von Prince, *Eine deutsche Frau*, pp. 84f. [3] *D.K.B.* (1899), 13.

[4] Von Prince to Gov., 5 July 1899 (T.N.A. IX A 6). *B.M.B.* (1899), 347. Ngera II enters the literature before Ngera I. Further inquiry into local history would doubtless result in a more satisfactory identification.

in the north, Kisuaga in the south and south-west, and Mbejela in the south-east, the Berliners assumed a central position for dealing with the Bena as a separate people. Ngera kept up his complaints against the tyranny of Merere and supplied men to build temporary houses for the missionaries at Kidugala. Bunk made no promises to obtain recognition of Ngera as an autonomous chief, but encouraged his hopes by agreeing to put the matter before the authorities.[1] Bunk and Neuberg then hurried off to the east, answering the call of von Prince to fill the vacuum in the southern part of the district as his troops withdrew. The shrewd commander did not scruple at hinting that the Catholics wanted Muhanga in the far east and that the rule of first come first served would obtain if the Protestants did not hasten, even though he gave assurances that he still preferred the general separation of the missions: 'I hold the partition to be politically correct: the north half of the district with the Wahehe and Wassangu for the one mission, the south half of the district with the Wabena and Wazungwa for the other mission.'[2] Bunk fulfilled the assigned role as an adjunct to German authority in directing the occupation of far-flung posts, personally escorting Zumba-Yamba, a brother of Mkwawa, to Iringa and receiving the arms of other surrendering leaders.[3]

A more complex situation prevailed in August 1898, when Bunk was called to a *shauri* at the official sub-station at Malangali, and was instructed to bring with him Ngera II who had reverted to an actively anti-Sangu policy. Ngera had attacked Merere's *wafumo* and occupied new areas 'in the name of Bunk'. When a patrol came to arrest him, he had fled to Kidugala and was there taken into custody. Bena–Sangu animosities flared again after the *shauri* when, while Lt. von der Marwitz was absent from Malangali, Merere decided on his own authority to punish the rebellious Ngera clans, which retaliated by calling together the people again for a campaign in the name of Bunk.[4] All this time Groeschel lived at Kidugala without comprehending the events occurring around him, having neither a command of the language nor prior experience of frontier politics.[5] Von der Marwitz forced his way through to Kidugala in December

[1] Groeschel, P., *Zehn Jahre christlicher Kulturarbeit in Deut ch-Ostafrika* (Berlin, 1911), pp. 13ff.

[2] Von Prince to Bunk, 5 Sept. 1898 (Berlin IX 1 8b).

[3] Bunk to Berlin Com., 12 Nov. 1898 (Berlin IX 1 8b).

[4] Von Prince to Gov., 5 July 1899 (T.N.A. IX A 6).

[5] Groeschel, *Christlicher Kulturarbeit*, p. 23.

to persuade Ngera's people to leave their war camp near Kidugala and their mountain retreats, to return to their old homelands. That the Mission would not support them against Merere and that the administration would not tolerate this manner of liberating Ubena from Sangu overrule at last became clear. Von Prince avoided making a scapegoat of the Mission as his Langenburg colleague had: 'I am far from concluding that Herr Bunk is directly to be blamed for the unrest . . . [but] he has been incautious and it is necessary in the future that pressure be exercised from above in the Berlin mission so that individual missionaries will be more soundly instructed in political matters.'[1] In spite of his patience, von Prince watched with concern the continuing communication between the dissident Kahamele and the Mission, for although the Ngera area and adjoining parts of Ubena were detached and assigned to the Jumbe Kisuaga, he had no intention of generally curtailing the extent of Merere's sphere.[2]

At Kidugala, following the decisive German official action, the Ngera clan in disappointment turned against the resident missionary, Groeschel. They first refused to sell food and then moved away, depriving the Mission of the very people who had called it in. A new basis for prestige was established in October 1899 when the administration enlisted the missionaries to vaccinate during a smallpox plague. This provided the ideal opportunity for direct contact with thousands of people, and identified Christianity with public welfare and medicine, frequently associated with spiritual power in the minds of Africans.[3] Von Prince continued his patronage of the Berliners in Ubena and for pragmatic reasons encouraged the establishment of stations near Chiefs Lupembe and Ngosingosi. The fillip of prestige derived from the vaccination campaign helped the missionaries to be well received, although Chief Lupembe did not allow officials to use missionaries as an extension of administration to the degree the *Stationschef* had hoped.[4] By the end of 1900, through combined official expediency and missionary brashness, the heartland of the future Bena-Hehe Synod had been claimed.

The Berliners, with their hands full in Ubena, seemed to acquiesce in the allotment of Usangu to the Catholics. The Moravians were supposed to take the initiative and as a preliminary the Utengule

[1] Von Prince to Gov., 5 July 1899 (T.N.A. IX A 6).

[2] Von Prince to Gov., 18 Jan. 1899 (T.N.A. IX A 6).

[3] Groeschel, *Christlicher Kulturarbeit*, pp. 25, 41. By October 1899, 20,000 people had been vaccinated in Ubena.

[4] *B.M.B.* (1900), 74. Nauhaus to Berlin Com., 6 July 1900 (Berlin IX 1 8b).

missionaries maintained a close watch over the comings and goings of the Chief. A confrontation between von Elpons and one of von Prince's subordinates on the occasion of Merere's departure for Iringa in early 1897 had made it clear that the Langenburg *Bezirksamtmann* did not take kindly to the removal of his most important paramount. While Merere was absent, the atmosphere of suspense was accompanied by a cessation of cultivation. The Sangu began to look to their homeland and Utengule became dependent upon supplies sent from the east. The cost was high, for von Elpons's irritation at the unauthorized absence of the Chief led him to fine the Sangu 147 head of cattle per day for one month.[1] In May, Merere returned to conduct sacrifices at the grave of his father. Whereas this memorial ritual remained entirely traditional, the civil celebrations revealed a transformation. Only a few months earlier, Merere had arrived at Iringa astride an ox representing his chiefly dignity, full of prejudices against European food and drink, and to the mind of his hostess, Frau von Prince, altogether a 'shensi'. Her efforts to reform his manners succeeded in part because Kiwanga, the other official protégé and his rival, was already advanced in westernization.[2] On his return to Utengule, he wore a full military outfit, from fine leather boots to tropical helmet. That the depth of his allegiance remained open to some doubt, however, was apparent to the missionaries who spoke with the Iringa official who accompanied him.[3]

The last insult by von Prince to the authority of the Langenburg *Bezirksamtmann* was administered through the installation of an adolescent boy to govern as Merere's deputy in Usafwa. Thereafter, to the delight of the Moravians, von Elpons concluded that all Sangu and Arabs should follow Merere out of Langenburg District, and resolved to appoint Safwa chiefs in their place.[4] When the boundaries between the Langenburg and Iringa Districts were drawn at the end of 1898, Merere was therefore confined to Iringa, an exodus of Sangu and others took place, a Safwa became paramount chief in that part of Langenburg, and the Sangu citadel at Utengule near Mbeya was left in ruins. Langenburg won territory from Iringa when it was decided to grant Kahamele autonomous authority in a subdistrict of Usangu near Usafwa, and to incorporate it into the Langenburg District.

[1] Meyer Tour Report, Dec. 1897 (Herrnhut R15 MI A4).
[2] Von Prince, *Eine deutsche Frau*, p. 87. *H.M.B.* (1897), 345ff.
[3] Meyer Tour Report, Dec. 1897 (Herrnhut R15 MI A4). [4] ibid.

From the reports by Meyer related to the 'Merere question' it is clear that the Moravians did not wish to follow the departed Sangu. In June 1898, after a conference in which the Berliners expressed the concern of their home committee lest the Catholics settle at the new Sangu capital, Meyer made a tour through the decaying villages of eastern Usafwa from which the Sangu had moved. His comments upon the migration noted that Merere Mugandilwa's mother with other old people held back from the body of people following the chief. Merere himself had become established at Ngabilo two days to the east of the Ruaha, but Meyer would go no further than Old Utengule, as he had undertaken, and did not fail to notice the unattractive aspects of the Sangu country and people. In conclusion, the Moravian Superintendent advised against expansion into Usangu because of the long-standing difficulties with the court, the closed door to Christian preaching and the anticipated political difficulties should Merere resent the loss of his western provinces. Ngabilo, so far as Meyer was concerned, lay in Ubena and with Merere's influence spreading much further east into Uhehe, occupation ought to be left to the Berliners.[1] The consequent inaction on the part of the Moravians meant that the Sangu court never again had to contend with a continuous Protestant presence.

It was 1901 before the Berliners called at Utengule-Usangu. By that time, the Chief had built a two-storeyed house and wore a uniform on appropriate occasions. Priebusch from Ilembula in Ubena and Källner from Magoje in Buwanji paid a visit to prepare the way for evangelization and present the grievances of the Wanji, who would not speak for themselves because they feared Merere both on traditional grounds and because of his powers as a 'white man' due to his adoption of alien ways. Displaying good-humoured obstructiveness, the Chief declared that he would continue to levy labour from Buwanji in spite of the fact that it had become part of the Langenburg District, and only an order from the Iringa Chief could effectively deprive him of this traditional tribute. To Priebusch, the missionary from Ubena, he made it clear that the Ngera incidents had not been forgotten.[2] Indeed, the old animosity against Protestants flourished through the continuing friction with *wafumo* near Ilembula, and the Berliners never received permission to establish a station in Usangu during the lifetime of Merere Mugandilwa.

[1] Meyer Tour Report, 22 June 1898 (Herrnhut R15 MI A4).
[2] *B.M.B.* (1902), 22ff.

The Berlin Mission had spread rapidly over an extensive area, causing the Society to decide on a separation of their sphere into two Synods, Konde and Bena-Hehe. Christian Schumann became Superintendent of the Bena-Hehe Synod in 1902 after several years of acting as such in relations with the Iringa and Songea District officials. Relations with a multiplicity of district officers were not easy to maintain, but were required by the fact that the Bena had been divided politically as in pre-European days. The highland Bena in the extreme south came under the Songea District because Mbejela and other chiefs in that area had been in the former Ngoni sphere. In the Iringa portion of Ubena, Chiefs Lupembe and Kisuaga were directly responsible to the *Chef* while around Ilembula in the north, Bena *jumbes* and Sangu *wafumo* recognized Merere's paramountcy. When the Berliners decided to treat the Bena as a whole and turned their efforts to the Bena of the rivers in the Ulanga Valley, they had to deal also with officials of the Mahenge District.

Of the three German district offices with administrative authority in Ubena, the missionaries in the period before Maji-Maji conflicted most with Songea. Schumann had the temperament and missionary style of Merensky and wanted to spread his personal influence as far and wide as possible. Impatient for a response, he frankly expressed his gratitude when a tax post was established near the Lupembe Station in 1900 because the activities of the askaris caused the people to look to the Mission for protection.[1] To the south in Songea District, real friction developed from the time Schumann examined an *akida* about his tax receipts and claimed to be the *bwana mkubwa* or head European in Ubena. Lieutenant Albinus, true to the traditions of the military administration, interpreted this and the Mission's hostility to the Swahili language as signifying disloyalty to the Government. And true to missionary form, Groeschel at Jacobi and Klamroth at Milow in Upangwa helped to amass evidence of excessive force used by the officials. Tax collection on the frontiers of Songea in 1901, they asserted, had been accompanied by such rough tactics as hut burning, snatching of women, removal of cattle, and political disregard for local leaders.[2]

Carl Nauhaus attempted to smooth relations, advising the Committee not to publish comments on administrative practices. In an aside, he warned against treating people as parishioners before they

[1] Berlin *Jahresbericht 1900*, p. 61.
[2] Berlin Com. to von Götzen, 25 Sept. 1903 (T.N.A. IX A 3a).

were converted: 'If you do not regard the people as heathens, why go to them as missionaries?'[1] Notwithstanding this cool judgement, the parties involved proved to be difficult to reconcile. By 1902, Albinus was declaring that the main resistance to the Government came from mission areas and that Groeschel in particular harboured the cattle of delinquent tax-payers against confiscation.[2] The earlier feud in Langenburg might have been duplicated had the new Governor, Graf von Götzen, been less determined to court the co-operation of Christian missions in his attempt to recruit native agents locally and hasten the changeover to civil administration through traditional chiefs. The Governor therefore warned Albinus to be cautious in making charges. Turning to Schumann for help in his programme of regularized administration, Götzen met a stubborn refusal to compromise or to lift the matter above the level of personalities. He then appealed to the Berlin Committee, claiming that if chiefs were induced to collect taxes on behalf of the Government, the abuses perpetrated by unsupervised askaris and akidas could be avoided. The Committee refused to co-operate in this matter and declared that it was beyond the office of missionaries to introduce such political measures.[3]

The Berlin Mission suffered during the Maji-Maji Rebellion in part because it had not helped to rectify the political procedures of the Songea District. The rebellion broke out in August 1905 in the south-eastern portion of the colony, where it drew on discontents arising from European political control and economic innovation. Rebel cohesion was achieved by oathing in the name of a snake and by the distribution of medicine which, it was believed, would turn bullets to water.[4] At the beginning of September, the Ngoni chiefs, whose grievances were more purely political, joined the rebels and brought with them the peoples within their traditional sphere of influence.

The missionaries in Ubena clearly miscalculated the degree to which their record of support for local people would exempt them from anti-Europeanism. At the Jacobi Station, Groeschel was at first incredulous, for although he had for some time been aware of the coolness of Mpangire, the sub-chief in his neighbourhood, he could

[1] Nauhaus to Berlin Com., 5 Nov. 1901 (Berlin IX 1 8b).
[2] Albinus to Gov., 29 Apr. and 5 July 1902 (T.N.A. IX A 3a).
[3] Von Götzen to Berlin Com., 13 Nov. 1903. Berlin Com. to von Götzen, 11 Jan. 1904 (T.N.A. IX A 3a).
[4] See Iliffe, John, 'The Organization of the Maji-Maji Rebellion', *J.A.H.* viii, (1967).

not comprehend how Mbejela, always a warm host at his monthly visits, could join in a crusade pledged to eradicate all white men.[1] In September Mbejela refused to talk with missionaries and the sides became more sharply drawn when Groeschel offered the shelter of the station to the akida and askaris whose tax post near Mbejela's village was indefensible. It was soon learned that other askaris had been ambushed and a wealth in tax reclaimed. On 5 September a number of villagers departed from Jacobi and four days later Ngosingosi from the Iringa bank of the Ruhudji River came quietly to confer with his father Mbejela and then returned home to call out his people on the rebel side. After fending off a siege, Groeschel with another missionary and their families, the askaries, and over one hundred 'loyal' adherents were rescued by an expedition led by Schumann and withdrew to Lupembe. By the end of September the mission stations in the Songea District, Jacobi and Milow, lay abandoned and ruined.[2]

The Berlin Mission periodicals gave a full measure of credit to their men for containing the pagan onslaught:

> Our missionaries' brave and decided attitude has contributed greatly to the fact that the revolt has not been able to spread further in Heheland. It is especially pleasing that at the places threatened, the members of the congregations, the candidates for baptism and even a great number of pagans remained true to the missionaries and therefore remained out of the revolt.[3]

After the Mission absorbed the first shock, however, it was the *Schutztruppe* and auxiliaries supplied by pro-German chiefs that fought the war. Rebels penetrated to the neighbourhood of Kidugala where another large concentration of loyal people was to be found, and a few even reached as far as Ilembula in 1906, but Merere's warriors secured its defence. With the exception of Ngosingosi, no local leader in the Iringa District joined the rebellion. Chiefs and *jumbe*s rallied to the *Chef*, Captain Nigmann, so the Berliners reported, because they regarded him as the successor to Mkwawa: 'According to popular belief, the Hehe have no chief who can give them the medicine, the chief of the Hehe is the *Stationschef* of Iringa.'[4] Missionary reports suggest, therefore, that the method of

[1] Groeschel, *Christlicher Kulturarbeit*, p. 145.
[2] Groeschel, *Christlicher Kulturarbeit*, pp. 147, 152ff.
[3] Berlin *Jahresbericht 1905*, p. 124.
[4] *D.K.B.* (1906), 144.

administration and the perpetuation of pre-colonial spheres of influence contributed to tribal alignments during the Maji-Maji Rebellion. The timing of tax collection could not have been worse for the Songea authorities, for the appearance of Muslim functionaries crystallized popular grievances and alienation from the colonial regime.

When it came to reconstruction, the mission had a great advantage over the administration, which faced an enormous back-log of work and protracted judicial proceedings. The Berliners, in 1907, received permission to acquire extensive lands and began to develop their Bena stations as centres of separate, privileged Christian communities. Interdependence with the loyal people at Kidugala and Lupembe during the emergency, had hastened the social evolution of concentrated communities; Mission land had indeed become a refuge, and the boundary between pagan and Christian had been clarified and tested under fire. Karl Axenfeld, the Inspector in Berlin who began to take over from Merensky at the time of the Maji-Maji Rebellion, had suggested certain of its implications in an Annual Report, pointing out that the rebellion as a purely pagan movement was distinct both from the Ethiopianism present in the Natal Revolt of 1905, and from the earlier Bushiri Revolt. He argued that Islam, by being associated since 1891 with colonialism, had been part of the radical change provoking the war, and that evangelical respect for vernaculars and local customs, on the other hand, helped prevent racial friction. Axenfeld concluded in effect that white solidarity and the backing of loyal Christian Africans offered the only security in the future.[1]

The Iringa and Dar es Salaam officials did not, however, agree that colonial policy should be built upon white and Christian supremacy. The missionaries and administrators clashed and revealed their divergent policies over the issue of secular authority on Mission lands. The whole matter of land alienation had been difficult from the start, when Nauhaus had recommended the acquisition of the largest possible amount of land in Ubena. In May 1900, at the time Schumann began to apply for permission to buy land, the Berlin Mission was little more than a scattering of European households. Unfortunately, land regulations had just been promulgated the previous month, under which alienation in Iringa District was limited to

[1] 'Deutsch Ostafrika. Der Aufstand und seine Ursache', Berlin *Jahresbericht 1905*, pp. 96ff.

five hundred hectares per individual or firm. Schumann petitioned the Governor for grants of 2,500 to 3,500 hectares for each station, declaring that such estates would become places of refuge and centres where the baptized would wish to settle. In a tone redolent of Merensky at Botschebelo, he assured von Liebert that due to the sparse population of the region the land was not otherwise in demand and guaranteed that Mission lands would be administered exclusively by Europeans.[1] However effective these arguments were in South Africa, they did not move von Liebert. Five hundred hectares seemed to him enough land for a start, and he insisted that the consideration for further alienation to the Mission as to private individuals would be a record of improvement and cultivation of land already acquired.[2]

The limitation was even more severe than Schumann at first imagined, for until 1902 the Government maintained that a mission could purchase only a total of five hundred hectares throughout the the whole district. When von Götzen became Governor, he was bombarded by appeals from the Berlin Committee for relief and responded by conceding that each station could individually acquire the statutory limit while maintaining the development prerequisites for future increases. The Land Commission required for the survey of lands to be alienated assembled in 1904, but the final approval by the Governor had to await the cessation of the Maji-Maji Rebellion.[3]

After the final transfer of land to the ownership of the Berlin Mission in 1907, the next step in development of the station estate was to apply a general set of regulations for residence, the *Platzordnung*. The first version of a *Platzordnung* in German East Africa had been introduced in early 1897 by Carl Nauhaus because of the special circumstances at Ikombe, a station situated on a peninsula over which no chief claimed jurisdiction. Nauhaus requested leave of the *Bezirksamtmann* to impose communal obligations to plant trees, and to maintain roads, paths, and general cleanliness. The station head was to have the right to control access of new settlers and to prohibit any European influence harmful to the purpose of the Mission. Pagan dancing and ceremonies were forbidden, and special rules secured general moral standards. Nauhaus also requested the power

[1] Schumann to von Liebert, 23 May 1900 (T.N.A. IX 1 6).
[2] Von Liebert to Schumann, 27 June 1900, ibid.
[3] Von Gerlach to von Götzen, 30 Mar. 1903 (T.N.A. IX A 1). Land Commission Reports, 1904 (E.H. 21).

to evict persistent malefactors, although he did not think such drastic measures would be necessary. The *Platzordnung* in this instance was a measure to maintain order, not a proprietary dictate, and residents at Ikombe were encouraged to think of their plots as their own. Langenburg officials approved with the understanding that anyone dissatisfied with the regulations could withdraw, that the regulations applied only at Ikombe and that the missionaries must report any revisions or conflicts to the Government.[1] No such clearance with the district authorities preceded the inauguration of the *Platzordnung* in the Iringa District, however, and there it became a bone of contention.

If the missionary position improved in some respects after the Maji-Maji Rebellion, so did that of the administration in Iringa. German power had aquired a profound popular respect in Ubena due to the marching to and fro of troops among a people who were notoriously sensitive to the climate of authority. The message had been driven home by the trials and executions of leaders in the rising. Finally, the Ubena military post established during the emergency became a regularly staffed sub-station facilitating the closer administration of missionaries as well as Africans. Schumann clearly regarded the trial and conviction of a group of Bena for ritual murder in December 1908 to be a trespass on the part of the colonial government into a spiritual area.[2] On the other side, Captain Nigmann was not one to shrink from a challenge to his authority. During the ensuing quarrel between Schumann and Nigmann, people conspicuously avoided the mission, *jumbes* 'fished in troubled waters', and even Mission people took cases against their missionaries to the officials.[3]

The real principle at issue as the dispute developed was whether there would be a dual administration of the Christian community on the one side and tribal society on the other or a single administration through Africans responsible to the Iringa *Chef*. Nigmann's reaffirmation of the traditions of the District administration became explicit in mid 1908 when he noticed that the Berliners had staked out a claim for land in Usangu. The Mission had decided, in spite of retrenchments elsewhere, that it was imperative as a counter-move to Catholic advances to protect the evangelical sphere in Iringa by

[1] Nauhaus to Langenburg Station, 12 Jan. 1897. Von Elpons to Ikombe Mission, 23 Sept. 1897 (T.N.A. IX A 6).

[2] Berlin *Jahresbericht 1909*, p. 115. See *D.K.B.* (1909), 261.

[3] Berlin *Jahresbericht 1909*, pp. 114ff.

occupying part of Usangu. Merere Mugandilwa had died in 1906 and his successor did not have equal skills of postponement. Negotiations were complete and the land was already surveyed when Nigmann put up a strong protest on political grounds and threatened to block the alienation. Although the *Chef* was subsequently forced to accept the *fait accompli* in the case of the Usangu station 'Brandt', he by no means conceded the field.[1]

Schumann gave a new cause for official action when he contended that Mission tenants could cultivate freely on tribal lands because they were subjects not of tribal authorities but of the Kaiser directly. Indeed the land policy in Iringa encouraged the missionaries to disregard tribal authorities. Whereas in Rungwe alienations occurred by direct purchase from chiefs, sanctioned by the *Bezirksamt*, in Iringa they were arranged through the official land agency or 'Fiscus'. The local *jumbe* participated only as a member of the Land Commission, to assure that adequate compensation was paid for rights of cultivation or occupied *tembe* homesteads. But Nigmann would not tolerate the bypassing of headmen in matters of African rights. An official circular asserted that local chiefs continued to have the role of landlords to whom all strangers must apply for the right to hoe. Next, after it became evident from complaints at the Ubena substation that missionaries at Ilembula used forceful sanctions to hold children at school, it was announced that school attendance was not compulsory. Schumann protested that the whole mission system would collapse unless tenants were bound by the *Platzordnung*, which stipulated that all children must attend school and warned that to undermine missionary authority was to reduce European prestige and invite rebellion. Nigmann argued to the contrary that disregard for traditional authorities and an overbearing manner raised the same danger.[2]

The more Nigmann learned of Schumann's methods, the less he liked them. In his judgement, the tactic of urging people to settle on Mission lands where they became fee-paying tenants turned free peasants into unfree mission people, subjected and held through 'a highly temporal and thoroughly illegal apparatus . . . in dependency of the harshest form conceivable.' This interpretation was surely an overstatement. On their side the missionaries had justification in

[1] Schumann to Nigmann, 16 Sept. 1908. Nigmann to Schumann, 24 Aug. 1908 (T.N.A. IX A 3a). *B.M.B.* (1907), 413ff.

[2] Nigmann to Schumann, 3 Jan. 1909 (T.N.A. IX A 3a).

protesting that heretofore there had been little evidence of a consistent administrative policy:

> We are in the founding period of a young colony. Laws and established regulations are still being created and they frequently fluctuate. What is valid in one district is not in another; even in one and the same district different Chefs are not of the same opinion. Earlier regulations are cancelled and new ones put in their place. Uncertainty, incompleteness and confusion therefore prevail.[1]

The days of local initiative were rapidly passing. Under the administration of Governor von Rechenberg, the colony was hastened along the course of centralization plotted by von Götzen. The Colonial Secretary, Bernhard Dernburg, subscribed to von Rechenberg's conviction that German East Africa was not 'white man's country' and after his visit to the colony in 1907 returned home to make a policy statement guaranteeing non-whites equal rights before the law, protection for the labourer, and action to counter those attitudes of German civilians symbolized by the *kiboko* or whip which they almost all carried as a symbol of mastery.[2] The new legislation limiting the rights of private individuals to inflict punishments served Nigmann in pressing his case against the Berliners. Furthermore, the *Chef* gained the direct support of the bureaucrats in Dar es Salaam because they disliked the Mission's persistent reference to South African experiences and the importance of White Supremacy. The Governor dispelled the missionaries' notion that settlers would soon enter the Southern Highlands, and in the light of the mood in Dar es Salaam, the wrong approach was used when the Mission applied for alienation of part of the Mufindi Forest Reserve on the grounds that a carpentry training school would prepare artisans to be employed by settlers.[3] The invocation of a South African precedent also misfired, official rejection being summed up in a curt marginal note: 'This d...ned South African baas management won't go here.'[4]

The Berlin Committee, unappreciative of the temper in Dar es Salaam, kept up the South African line, for example, by declaring that the administration was destroying a decade of Mission work in 'training of people and accustoming them to discipline and willing

[1] Schumann to Iringa Station, 16 Dec. 1908 (T.N.A. IX A 3a).

[2] *D.K.B.* (1908), 216ff.

[3] Berlin Com. to Dernburg, 22 Jan. 1909. Rechenberg to R.K.A., 2 May 1909 (T.N.A. IX A 3a).

[4] On Berlin Com. to Gov., 19 May 1909, ibid.

obedience to Europeans'.[1] In an equally inept attempt to exploit differences among officials, Schumann tried to use the pro-settler and pro-missionary attitudes of the touring Under-secretary von Lindequist to strengthen his position.[2]

Negotiations over an acceptable form of *Platzordnung* brought the Berlin Mission into line. Nigmann demanded drastic revisions effectively depriving missionaries of secular authority, and Schumann again could not rise above the subjective level in order to gain a compromise. The matter had to be turned over to Martin Klamroth, the Berlin Mission's chief missionary in the Dar es Salaam area, to be worked out with the Central Government. In effect, the new *Platzordnung* ended the possibility of a privileged Christian status and assured that Mission lands would be treated politically in the same way as other areas. Mission *jumbes*, to be appointed by the administration and responsible directly to it, were charged with tax collection, execution of official instructions, settlement of minor cases, and submission of major ones to the *Chef*.[3] By this official control of civil affairs on Mission lands, temporal sources of missionary power were much curtailed. But the day of the military administrator as an independent agent was also over. Nigmann received a rebuke for being so aggressive in reclaiming jurisdiction and was warned that the missions had a right to administer the revised *Platzordnung* as a contractual agreement. Von Rechenberg's intention to avoid undue intervention in missionary affairs was displayed when officials in Langenburg complained of Berliner autocracy. In response, the Governor merely pointed out the appropriate spheres of official concern: the encouragement of Mission education to Government standards, assurance of the freedom of labour, and ample provision of land even in the form of reserves for the future if development requirements had not been met.[4] In 1911 and 1912, in spite of its defeat on general native policy, the Berlin Mission received generous increases in alienated land.

The position of the Lutheran and Moravian missionaries in the Southern Highlands cannot be described in terms of a simple impact. Political relations in Rungwe created a pattern of give and take with

[1] Spiecker to Gov., 22 May 1909, ibid.

[2] Schumann to Nigmann, 2 Jan. 1909, ibid.

[3] Berlin Com. to von Rechenberg, 24 June 1911 (T.N.A. IX A 3a). For the *Platzordnung* and its revisions, see Appendix A.

[4] [Von Rechenberg] to Iringa Station, 15 Nov. 1909. Von Rechenberg to Lohr (Langenburg) 7 and 30 Jan. 1911 (T.N.A. IX A 3a).

Africans, while in Ubena a traditionally subject people exposed to German military operations and thinly spread in homesteads could easily be treated as a peasantry to be mobilized under new leadership. The Merere dynasty represented a different style of African politics and society, whose leaders resented the levelling tendencies of the evangelicals and sought political advantage by collaboration with officials, not missionaries. But many missionary efforts in Africa contended with a similar diversity. The special ingredient in the Southern Highlands must be sought in the opposition of missionaries and local administrators. In particular, the Berliners with their partisan involvements helped to create a situation demanding closer examination of political conditions by officials. The manner in which von Prince had to modify the area of Merere's paramountcy is a good example. The missionaries for their part served as critics able to expose incidents of excessive punitive action, although it must be remarked that all too often criticism came from the Berliners not for the sake of better government, but rather to serve as a stick to beat out apologies for petty personal insults or to increase missionary prestige. Only in the proposals for a court circuit in Rungwe does it seem clear that a larger good came first. Nevertheless, better administration no doubt followed from the increased European staff assigned to Langenburg and Songea as a consequence of missionary publicity.

CHAPTER V

Early Christian Communities

THE political events of the early colonial period profoundly affected the preconditions for Christianization in the Southern Highlands. In turning to the narrower history of Christian communities and missionary strategy relating to social issues and church foundations, the rapidity of development during the German regime must be kept in mind. The transition did not, of course, take place simultaneously everywhere; the popular rush to missionary schools which typified the awakening to new values came in Rungwe about 1900 and in Ubena not till a decade later. In terms of missionary policy, an early stage of physical establishment and local missionary initiatives, was followed by a period when the metropolitan authorities began to appreciate the special characteristics of German East Africa and exerted pressure for reform and elaboration of missionary practice.

The Germans excelled in the pioneer stage. Their stations won the applause of Governor von Schele when he toured Langenburg in 1894. Dr. Kerr-Cross, miffed at the primitive housing allowed Livingstonia missionaries outside the headquarters station and generally dissatisfied with the ascendancy of Laws' centralizing policy, lavished praise on the four 'beautifully built' and fairly autonomous Berlin stations at the north end.[1] Although Rungwe and other Moravian stations were less than monumental, they rapidly became regulated centres of industry. Within a year, Rungwe reported a fixed salary scale with overseers and brickmakers at the top, menial tasks performed by women and children at the bottom. In contrast to the Berliners who unashamedly imported their labourers from Bandawe and Karonga, the Moravians tried to develop a local supply. This, however, was frustrated by the economic complacency of the Nyakyusa-Kukwe and their refusal to act as porters beyond their own country.[2] Even at Rungwe, therefore, the numbers of strangers inevitably increased. They were drawn not so much from

[1] Kerr-Cross to Livingstonia Com., 23 Aug. 1894 (N.L.S. 7877).
[2] *H.M.B.* (1893), 7, 13.

Nyasaland as from the refugees who had infiltrated from the raid-torn rift corridor and formed a reservoir of relatively ready workers to compensate for the refusals of self-sufficient Kukwe villagers. These immigrants had frequently known forms of dependency before, but in Rungwe, where bondage did not exist, they had remained unassimilated to the exclusive communal life and economy of the villagers. The mission stations provided a substitute corporate life for them.[1]

Nyiha and Safwa made up the majority of the immigrant station settlers in Rungwe, the Ndali and Nyiha the majority at Rutenganio in the area between Rungwe and Karonga. Safwa prophecies of relief from the yoke of Merere had led to a widespread prediction that heroes would come from the south to end the misery and introduce a new way of life. A prophetess had once declared: 'The spear that will come to do away with these stones the Sangu fortress, Utengule, will come from the distance! And it will come with many things. No one of us will recognize all the things that the spear will bring from the distance. And the stones near Medjere will have no power against the spear.' Christians later interpreted the prophecy so that it fitted their world: 'And we say now: the spear is the white men, who have come from the distance. And the many things that the spear was to bring are, table and chair, pen and paper, clocks and tools, and so on.'[2] The role of prophets in mobilizing resistance on a supra-tribal scale to meet the challenge of colonial power has received considerable attention. In many less dramatic and more parochial ways, as in this adjustment by some Safwa, prophetic traditions eased transition for a people under stress.[3] On the Moravian side, the idea of building communities from uprooted peoples corresponded with a highly symbolic tradition, the gathering of souls at Herrnhut.

The Berliners had longer to wait before finding a situation suited to their South African Botschebelo model. Neither the personality of their first resident Superintendent nor conditions among the Nyakyusa conformed to the prototype. Carl Nauhaus, the chief linguist as well as executive officer, led his colleagues in notable

[1] Meyer to von Soden, 12 Feb. 1892 (T.N.A. IX A 1). Fülleborn, *Deutsche Njassa*, p. 493. *H.M.B.* (1898), 9f.

[2] Kootz-Kretschmer, *Die Safwa*, ii, 192f.

[3] Ranger, T. O., 'Primary Resistance and Modern Mass Nationalism', *J.A.H.* ix, 3 (1968), 447f. The Congo would appear to offer closer parallels to the Safwa–Nyiha style of prophetism.

research on language and ethnography in the early years. With the aid of Kumoga, some other Africans, and Kerr-Cross, he progressed rapidly in learning, analysing, and writing down Kinyakyusa. At a conference at the Scottish station Ngerenge in December 1892, it was agreed to adopt a standard orthography for the closely related Ngonde, Kukwe, and Nyakyusa dialects. Nauhaus, who by that time had outstripped Kerr-Cross and Meyer in language studies, was commissioned to translate an African fable to be printed at Bandawe for use as a primer for the whole language area. This project, and the contemplated annual meetings to discuss language problems, failed to mature because Kerr-Cross resigned in 1894 and the development of the Overtoun Institute at the new Livingstonia headquarters caused the Scots to cease publishing literature in vernaculars which were of secondary importance in their strategy of church growth. Nauhaus, however, continued to be in contact with the Livingstonia staff and found them deeply sympathetic, so that in time he as well as the Moravians looked to Livingstonia for indications of future stages of development in the Southern Highlands.

Soon after the 1892 Ngerenge conference, the Berliners held their first service in Kinyakyusa and thereafter Nauhaus kept up pressure to translate new portions of the Bible for each succeeding Sunday. In hopes of increasing missionary influence and as an adjunct to language study, he started a school at Wangemannshöh in June 1892, to which Mwakatungile brought fifteen alert boys. By the end of the first week, however, these students demanded calico for their labours and when refused abandoned the class to kitchen boys and other employees of the mission. Until the value of education became appreciated or a more powerful authority came into being, village boys did not attend. Nauhaus commented philosophically that 'from a state of nature to compulsory education is a long, trying path' and consoled himself that by the end of 1893 at least a few men had become literate enough to help with translations.[1] The Moravians also encountered and refused demands of village students to be paid for the work of learning when the Rungwe school began in 1893.

Almost immediately after the Rungwe school failure, von Eltz liberated a large group of women and children from one of Mlozi's slave caravans and distributed them among the missionaries at Rungwe, Wangemannshöh, and Manow. The reactions to this sudden acquisition of involuntary dependents dramatized the differing

[1] *B.M.B.* (1893), 155f., 525. *B.M.B.* (1894), 327.

attitudes of Moravians and Berliners. The Moravians debated the principle in a negative spirit, influenced by the terms of the Cracow legacy which supported their work and the prospect of the freed slaves falling under the 'bad influence' of the askaris.[1] For publication, Meyer called the colony a 'useful nucleus', but he also deplored the distraction from evangelization among Rungwe peoples and never shared the joy of the Berliners who concluded that freed slave children repaid teaching because they were under direct paternalistic control and could be required to attend.[2]

By 1895, even without any enthusiasm from people native to Rungwe, a normal missionary pattern had emerged on all the older stations. The little elementary schools met anywhere from four to to ten hours per week, following a curriculum balancing religion and literacy. Of the two societies, the Berliners pronounced themselves most satisfied. Their four stations, eight missionaries preaching in Kinyakyusa, vernacular translations of Bible excerpts in the Press, the routine of morning prayers, elementary schools, instruction of catechumens, and Sunday worship including hymns set to African melodies, all conveyed the impression of achievement and stability.[3]

On the Moravian side, discontent with the lack of progress in spiritual matters persisted. To lay greater stress upon the community, Meyer set about regulating life at the Rungwe Mission. Recognizing that intensive contact could only occur where a degree of control existed, 2,500 acres of land around the Rungwe Station had been purchased in 1894. The absence of some headmen from the ceremony of transfer indicated that this extensive alienation was unpopular, but Meyer felt the need to encourage labourers to become self-reliant farmers, and to provide land in lieu of bridewealth for the freed women who married local men. Under stipulations laid down at this time, settlers were free to remain or leave, but those who chose to stay were to regard themselves as subjects of Jesus, obliged to hear and respect his word, abstain from work on Sunday and forego theft, lying, and whoring. Under these new rules, obedience to the rules rather than labour constituted the basis of the community.[4] A background for this reform lay in the Moravian values of individualism and voluntary communal association, but an added inducement for reconsidering social policy in 1895 came from the exodus from

[1] Conference Minutes, 24 Nov. 1893 (Herrnhut R15 MIb).
[2] *B.M.B.* (1894), 327. [3] *B.M.B.* (1894), 459. *B.M.B.* (1895), 469.
[4] *H.M.B.* (1894), 340f. Rungwe deed, 25 May 1894 (T.N.A. IX A 6).

Rungwe of freedwomen, followed by most of the other settlers. The missionaries accepted this demonstration with self-criticism and resolved to be more tolerant of African ways. Later they came to appreciate the opportunity to restart with a clean slate as a blessing which permitted the construction of a Christian community on a sounder basis.[1]

At this time, however, the Kukwe still did not provide many adherents of the Mission. To the Moravians, both they and the Nyakyusa seemed to be lacking the prerequisites for conversion; they had no sense of sin and unscrupulously stole from the Mission. In one notorious case, a headman robbed cloth from the missionary's house after attending a service. Those belonging to the little station community, on the other hand, boasted two promising catechumens and labourers who behaved well enough to be favourably compared with 'very many white men and very many Christians'.[2] Meyer kept down the number of settlers in order to avoid tying the Church to Mission land and to ensure that the core would be solidly Christianized when expansion into the villages became possible. Balancing values in the community presented a dilemma, however, for the only source of converts was those settling as employees and tenants; yet to introduce too many strangers or to increase the proportion of pagans might in the Superintendent's view harm the nascent Christian morality.[3]

Christian teachings and tribal customs came into conflict in February 1897, well before the outward movement took place. As it happened, the first convert, or 'first fruit' in the idiom of the Moravians, was a Kukwe woman, Fiambarema, who had come to the mission in 1894 for medical care. As she recovered, she resolved to remain near the Mission, joined religious instruction for catechumens and outstripped the others. When Fiambarema made her first declaration of faith, the missionaries responded sceptically, believing that no local person possessed a sense of sin profound enough to make the wish for a saviour genuine. Fiambarema persisted and her open confession during a service released the cautious missionaries from their doubts. The baptism, in recognition of the work of the Holy Spirit, was soon arranged and the event precipitated a notable increase in the number of Kukwe catechumens.[4]

[1] *H.M.B.* (1896), 177ff. *P.A.* (1897), 280.
[2] *H.M.B.* (1896), 21. [3] *P.A.* (1897), 378.
[4] *P.A.* (1897), 284. *H.M.B.* (1897), 210. Bachmann, T., *Ich Gab Manchen Anstoss*, ed. H. W. Jannasch (Hamburg, 1964), pp. 71f.

The conversion of a person with vested interests in the traditional social and economic system focused sudden attention upon the teachings of the white men. It did not take long before the Kukwe grasped that the undertakings of Fiambarema as a Christian threatened a revolution in the rituals of kinship and traditional distribution of wealth. The social reaction did not touch the convert herself but concentrated on the catechumens, especially women who did not live on the station. These came to Traugott Bachmann, a young missionary left in charge of Rungwe Mission at this time, asking: 'What can we do? All the villages are in a state of excitement about this baptism. We want to be children of God but the people find fault with us and curse us.'[1] One husband demanded the return of his bridewealth cattle because his wife was going to serve God. The son of another adherent pleaded with his mother to be a child of God merely by listening, pointing out that the local chief was the arbitrator of her problems and she could follow but one code.[2] Rumours that Mwakapilile wished to drive away the usurping missionaries caused Bachmann to call upon the deputy who generally conducted relations with the Europeans. It surprised him and indicated the gravity of the situation when Mwakapilile received him personally. When assured of unswerving respect in temporal matters, the prince promised to punish the perpetrator of the unfounded rumour of his anger. Although headmen necessarily sympathized with the popular reaction the spiritual contest remained on the level of common people employing witchcraft and did not in this case involve the sacred aspects of chiefship. A boycott of paths leading to Rungwe and the planting of 'deadly' potions coincided with an illness of Bachmann. His recovery was celebrated by the small congregation as proof of their new immunity to the 'breath of men' or spiritually powerful public opinion.[3]

Up to this point, Bachmann had been a narrow pietist. His work at Rungwe since his arrival in 1893 had been with freedmen, supervising in the garden and then teaching school. In dealing with these factious dependents, he showed himself to be a strict disciplinarian and a pessimist about the unconverted African. Conversion in his mind implied total rejection of the normal world. In instructing catechumens before baptism, he described the 'new life' in Christ in rigidly anti-tribal terms. Jesus would be their chief, no more bridewealth would be paid or received, and all rights in cattle would be

[1] *P.A.* (1897), 385. [2] *H.M.B.* (1897), 220, 358.
[3] ibid., 221. *H.M.B.* (1898), 6f., 9f.

resigned in order to gain release from the shackles of materialism and the source of ill feeling.[1] After he fell ill and interpreted it as a struggle with the Devil in the form of African magic, Bachmann's own conversion to an extremely pro-African position began to take place. He ultimately became the champion of adaptive Christianization, but at first had no quarrel with the clear distinctions that had been drawn by Meyer: Christians must disapprove of abdominal autopsies to determine whether death had been caused by witchcraft, repudiate funeral sacrifices, and forego ownership of cattle distributed through the kinship structure. Rejection of bridewealth was part of this rigorous separation of Christian from non-Christian, although bridewealth in the end became a matter for compromise and acted as the weathercock of shifts in policy. In the early days, however, betrothals took place mainly between adherents living on the station who consented to the new procedures. It was indeed a positive attraction for young men that as Christians they could wait for God to provide, rather than having to assemble the required cattle and work for the parents of an intended bride.[2]

The trial of strength with Kukwe communal rituals increased the self-assurance of the little Christian community at Rungwe, which thereafter developed rapidly. Africanisms where they supported the Church were encouraged, for example, in the names the converts adopted at baptism to symbolize rebirth. Fiambarema became Numagile, 'I have found Him.' Rambasika, one of the original labourers and catechumens, took a name meaning 'I am saved.' The Moravians also recognized that their form of confession had an analogy in customary practice. In Moravian practice, the individual conference before communion was a standard form of religious counselling. The need for an intimate discussion of feelings and trespasses also existed in Africa, and even more in a society where conflicts between traditional and Christian values tended to produce anxieties. Among Rungwe peoples, the custom of 'speaking out' constituted a very important form of confession of ill will preliminary to reconciliation, and when the missionaries adopted this healthy psychological device, they enabled Christians to expose their inner suspicions of witchcraft or animosity towards the missionaries or their fellows.[3]

[1] *H.M.B.* (1897), 358. See also Bachmann, *Manchen Anstoss*, pp. 74ff.

[2] *H.M.B.* (1897), 213, 263.

[3] *P.A.* (1898), 630ff. See also Wilson, M., *Rituals of Kinship Among the Nyakyusa* (London, 1957), p. 8.

Another stage saw the leadership formation in local age villages paralleled in the appointment of deacons to assist with services, to advise about the readiness of candidates for baptism, and to help judge in cases of discipline. A very Moravian practice, one highly unconventional in local African society, was the designation of two women as well as two men.

As a consequence of this development in the later 1890s at Rungwe Station, the Mission became a desirable place to settle. It provided security from askaris, a plot of land, opportunities to earn some cash, and a community spirit. In the screening of the many would-be residents, it became conventional for applicants first of all to approach Numangile-Fiambarema as the senior Christian who would intercede on their behalf.[1] The recognition of her status was a further stage in the emergence of the role of women in the leadership of the African Moravian community.

This story of intense internal development must be seen in part as a reaction to the increased exclusivism of the Kukwe villagers which closed them to Christian preaching. Bachmann's reputation for hostility to cattle-owning and bridewealth, two principal components of the kinship structure, continued to have repercussions. He had only to appear in a non-Christian area to excite fears that the askaris would not be far behind to confiscate cattle.[2] At Rutenganio, the missionaries reacted to Kukwe indifference with the most extreme kind of station exclusivism. Kretschmer called the Kukwe 'selfish, self-righteous, and self-complacent' in contrast to immigrant station residents, mainly Nyiha, who were appreciative and amenable to discipline.[3] The proposal of the missionaries at Rutenganio to acquire more land near them in order to remove a village which they alleged contaminated the morality of their Christian settlement, raised an important matter of policy which was warmly debated at the General Missionary Conference of October 1898, when the future course of development in the Nyasa Province was being charted.

The main business of the Conference was to draw up a Provincial constitution. In the original instructions of 1891, the Livingstonia rules for pioneer missionaries had been followed; seven years later, however, the Brethren naturally looked to their own precedents for a prototype and used the constitution of the Province of South Africa-

[1] *P.A.* (1898), 634. [2] *P.A.* (1898), 634.

[3] The Ndali were also regarded as evil influences. *H.M.B.* (1897), 263. *P.A.* (1898), 626f.

West as the draft for discussion. Two major areas of concern, station rules and church development, received warm debate as the differing experiences and temperaments of the missionaries themselves became evident. In regard to station life, Bachmann revealed his new direction by passionately opposing the motives of the Rutenganio missionaries for forcing the removal of a non-Christian village, and he succeeded in so far as the purchase of land for this was agreed to only as an exceptional measure. In fixing rules for church discipline and admission to various degrees or classes of religious instruction, the desire to draw a clear line between pagan and Christian continued to be strong, but in comparison with the South African model, it accommodated more of the local conventions. The softening of attitudes towards custom appeared particularly with respect to bridewealth, which the Nyasa Brethren resolved to tolerate, even while reiterating that the exchanged cattle presented difficulties. Some of the missionaries were inclined to be even more flexible, but Superintendent Meyer came down on the side of precise and explicit rules to avoid confusion among Christians. Later, Africans would share in the Christianizing process more formally through the appointment and installation of congregational spokesmen and the rearing of a cadre of evangelists to be apprenticed to missionaries until ready for independent work.[1] The schoolmaster in Meyer seems to have been present in his desire for clarity as Christians assumed these new responsibilities. And given the unsettled political situation and the unreceptive attitude of the people beyond the station, the Conference went about as far as it realistically could.

The world missionary activity of the Moravian Church required careful economic planning and early movement towards financial autonomy in new provinces. Spartan missionary habits had to be matched in East Africa by a conscious effort to make residents on station lands self-employed rather than dependent upon wages paid out of funds from abroad. How to achieve financial autonomy was one of the subjects of discussion at the 1898 Conference and it remained a perennial item on agendas thereafter. Even before Director Baudert declared in 1900 that all Moravian missions must exercise rigid restraint and never again expand impulsively on the assumption that Providence would provide, steps had been taken to set up a trading company to encourage economic development in

[1] Minutes of the General Missionary Conference, 17–20 Oct. 1898 (Herrnhut, R15 MIb 4).

the Nyasa Province.[1] This initiative could not have been more timely, for at the turn of the century the economic impact consequent upon effective colonial control was causing a serious inflation in the indigenous economy. Bad harvests added to the pinch, which caused even the Brethren to invest in cattle as a means of riding out the changes in value.[2]

A lay trader, Adolf Stolz, and then Ferdinand Jansa, a merchant missionary who had served a commercial apprenticeship in Liverpool, came to supervise the new enterprises. Under their management, a trading network was extended from a special headquarters, at first located at Ipiana near the lake and later at Kyimbila, an entirely new place situated in the foothills near the new road running from Mwaya on the lake to New Langenburg. This road extended gradually through the Moravian field, going through the Igali Pass and on towards Lake Tanganyika, its construction executed by men labouring in lieu of cash payment of tax, and by those hired and paid through a direct subsidy from the colonial government. As the *Bezirksamtmann* intended, the making of the road was the making of a labour force.[3] The Moravians' contribution to economic development did not aim, as did Zache, at the eventual settlement of European farmers in Rungwe. Rather, they sought to encourage a cash economy and claimed in 1900 to have been responsible for introducing whatever coin circulated in the highland area. Shops sprang up next to churches and Kyimbila became a focal point of a variety of activities. Although it had not at first been thought of as a mission station, the once unpopulated neighbourhood rapidly became settled and warranted a full religious schedule.

Zache saw that the Moravians profited greatly from their ability to distribute through their mission stations at a very low overhead cost, and he objected to the Janus-faced operations which permitted the trading organization to qualify for a 25 per cent reduction of freight charges on the steamer *Wissmann* while the Mission as a charitable organization claimed a 3,000-mark freight and customs rebate.[4] As he predicted, the Moravians were able to kill competition from Hansing & Co. and other German firms, but the field was not empty. Muslim traders soon became established as very effective

[1] *P.A.* (1901), 462. [2] *P.A.* (1900), 257.

[3] Zache, Hans, 'Die wirtschaftlichen Verhältnisse des Nyassagebiets', in *Verhandlungen des Deutschen Kolonial-Kongresses 1902* (Berlin, 1903), pp. 555f. See also, *P.A.* 1900–2 for notes on economic affairs.

[4] Zache to Gov., 17 Feb. 1902 (T.N.A. IX A 6).

rivals and the Berlin Mission also influenced conditions of trade. The Berliners never separated their supply and trading activities organizationally, yet their turnover of yard goods was great enough to cause Meyer to suggest that their practices amounted to covert trading, because of the large difference between the cost of the cloth and its assigned value when distributed as wages.[1] Employees of the Berlin Mission, it would appear, were not at this time paid in cash, which would have permitted them to buy anywhere, but were tied to a kind of 'company store'. Besides keeping people in a dependent condition, this merged operation required the Superintendent to devote to business affairs the time that might have been well spent in religious and educational work.

In many other respects as well, the Berlin Mission could not match the orderly progress of the Brethren after 1895. Superintendent Carl Nauhaus struggled against the Mission's entrenched paternalism during a difficult period when it was understaffed, and had too wide an area to administer. As leader of the East African Mission, Nauhaus displayed more the instincts of a teacher than a ruler. He reflected the spirit of Wangemann's 1882 *Missionsordnung*, still nominally the standing instructions for missionaries, which anticipated an early progress towards self-supporting indigenous churches led by Africans. Unfortunately, the disillusionment over the Bapedi National Church had sapped the vigour of the Director's initiative in this direction so that seminary graduates after 1890 did not come to the field with these values to the fore. As apprentices to Nauhaus in the Konde Synod, however, the probationers saw in practice a very modified paternalism deeply imbued with respect for African potentialities.

Nauhaus possessed a definite charisma. From the time he settled at Ikombe in 1894, he developed a large following, established fraternal relations with the priest of the Pali-Kyala cult, and generated an atmosphere of good will never achieved in the early years in the troubled Manow–Wangemannshöh areas. It was under the influence of Nauhaus that the first catechumen reached the point of baptism.[2] As Superintendent, he attempted to correct some practices which led to untoward complications. By July 1896 at the conference approving the first baptisms, he advised against public confrontation with pagan religion and medicine, recommended a quieter wrestling

[1] Hennig to Axenfeld, 28 Feb. 1912 (Berlin I 5 64).

[2] *B.M.B.* (1894), 15. *B.M.B.* (1899), 761 f.

for the souls of sinners, and criticized as erroneous the missionary involvement in judicial processes, owing to the fact that it robbed valuable time and fostered a false image of missionaries. To illustrate the last point, he asserted that those who wanted to bring a case were too evident among those who turned up in church.[1] Not all his colleagues agreed and, as we have seen, Bunk executed a contrary policy by being actively partisan both during Nauhaus's absence from Langenburg in 1897 and afterwards in relations with the Bena.

A meeting of the Konde Synod in October 1899 helped to put the affairs of the Berlin Mission into better order. Nauhaus had protested to home authorities against the continuation of Bunk as head of the Bena-Hehe contingent because he had no practical knowledge of 'real' missionary work, did not maintain proper relations with Africans or in the missionary brotherhood, was tactless with the administration and lacked the wider perspective essential to leadership.[2] The Synod decided that Schumann should become Vice-Superintendent for Ubena, a choice heartily approved by Nauhaus as the saving of the new area where in his opinion such a false start had been made. But given the limits of personnel available, the cost had to be covered by sacrifice elsewhere and because Schumann had been expected to start a training school for helpers at Wangemannshöh, Nauhaus had to step into the breach. 'With very divided feelings I accept my removal from Ikombe to Wangemannshöh. The work at the seminar of training evangelists who shall take the Word to the people, I greet enthusiastically, just as, despite all my love for Ikombe, . . . I must at last regard the voice of the Synod to be the voice of God.'[3]

The responsibilities of seminary leadership and administration did not complement one another in a time of active expansion and difficulties with officials. Nauhaus attempted for the first time to resign the Superintendency in September 1900, declaring that he could not convince himself that his calling was to be Superintendent rather than a missionary, and that one excluded the other.[4] It should be understood that when Nauhaus referred to the missionary vocation, he had in mind particularly the example presented by the Nyasaland missionaries. Enthusiasm for church and school develop-

[1] Nauhaus to Berlin Com., 23 July 1896 (Berlin IV 1 8b).
[2] Nauhaus to Berlin Com., 7 Apr. 1899 (Berlin IV 18b).
[3] Nauhaus to Berlin Com., 13 Oct. 1899 (Berlin IV 1 8b).
[4] Nauhaus to Berlin Com., 13 Sept. 1900 (Berlin IV 1 8b).

ment under the Scots had been fired by the 1900 Conference celebrating the twenty-fifth anniversary of the Livingstonia Mission. The educational hierarchy held the central position in the Livingstonia church strategy. Closer to home, improved education was also made necessary through the insistence of the administration of German East Africa upon a standard Swahili curriculum, a pressure felt in Langenburg through the *Bezirksamtmann's* threat to introduce Government schools if the missions could not offer equivalent facilities.[1] When Director Gensichen visited East Africa in 1901, he refused to appoint a new Superintendent and Nauhaus seems to have been satisfied that the Director accepted the priority of instituting a sound educational system. Gensichen watched with apparent approval as a curriculum was drafted and revised by the missionary conference, and his published report of the inspection reflected the urgings of Nauhaus and others. The programme never materialized, however, for Gensichen failed to make available the staff for double missionary occupancy or assignment of specialist teachers at each station. Instead, he fell back into the pattern of favouring industrial over literary education, and in effect vetoed co-operation with the Government by refusing to recognize Swahili.[2] With great disappointment, Nauhaus in October 1901 closed the seminary because of the pressure of administrative desk-work as Superintendent, and for lack of any substitute schoolmaster. He did not hide the fact that the suspension of helper training was a last resort and a regression in missionary development.

The relations of Nauhaus with his superiors in Berlin exploded in 1903 over the issue of who should decide the posting of personnel. The man in question was Martin Klamroth, a university graduate and later a distinguished missionary. Merensky in Berlin had decided that Klamroth should have all the usual station experiences of a Seminary man before being permitted to specialize. Nauhaus believed that Klamroth should at once begin teaching in the Wangemannshöh school, where the future of the Church was much more at stake than on stations paternally presided over by isolated missionaries.[3] As his differences with the Berlin Committee extended to many other questions as well, Nauhaus came to regard Merensky as his particular

[1] Zache to Gov., 14 Sept. 1901 (T.N.A. IX B 1).

[2] Nauhaus to Berlin Com., Sept. 1903 (Berlin IV 1 8b). See also Genischen, Martin, *Bilder von unseren Missionsfelder in Süd und Deutsch-Ostafrika* (Berlin, 1902).

[3] Merensky Memorandum, Mar. 1903 (Berlin IV 1 8b).

antagonist. Under attack by the Committee for his pride and independence, Nauhaus delivered a rejoinder calculated to rock the Berlin Missionshaus on its paternalistic foundations. Many passages of this revealing document deserve quotation, for Berlin missionaries did not often defy authority in such a way or so incisively.[1]

In my capacity as leader of this mission, I believed that after the first baptisms in Kondeland, a helpers' seminary should be opened in which the necessary assistants to missionaries would be educated. In my view, the right moment for opening helpers schools was allowed to pass in all our regions in South Africa and throughout our whole mission. This error I wished to avoid here, which is why I considered the creation of a seminary so early. In Berlin I presented this idea to our Inspector, Herrn D. Merensky, in the presence of Brother Schumann and had, so it seemed, a sympathetic hearing.

Nauhaus went on to regret the lack of support for the seminary and the consequent lag of missionary work. In a peroration, he returned to the theme that the directives from the Committee had harmed rather than aided the development of the field:

The one thing the fathers lack is practical knowledge. Men who are born in Germany, live there and never do continuous practical work as real missionaries, can have no clear insight into the requirements of this work. Men who only devote their leisure time to the mission cannot comprehend the details of this work. *Experts* must be elected to the Committee. That is the only way I see to save our mission in all its regions. It is noteworthy that one expert, Herrn D. Merensky, already sits on the Committee and I am convinced that the remaining members of our committee are ever grateful to have one expert in their midst. One is not enough. Every being has a certain point of view by which he judges and acts. No one comprehends everything and the experiences gathered at Botsabelo 20 to 30 years ago are not valid for all areas and times.

In my conception, we missionaries stand to the Committee neither as mercenaries to their employers nor as German soldiers to their commander in chief, that is in a relationship of absolute obedience. Rather, we stand to the committee and to missions generally as individual shareholders in a corporation to one another.

A return of real brotherhood between the Committee and its missionaries will awaken a new life on the entire mission field.

Change came too slowly in the Berlin Mission to keep this gifted missionary in a position of administrative responsibility. By 1904

[1] Nauhaus Memorandum 'Pro Conscientia', Sept. 1903 (Berlin IV 1 8b).

Schumann had already become an autonomous Superintendent of the Bena-Hehe Synod and the principal consequence of the change came in the Konde Synod, where Schüler, a young man with the inclinations of a parochial station patriarch, was placed in charge.

While he had remained leader of the Mission, Nauhaus was refused permission to make study tours to learn from the experience of others. Once relieved, however, he was allowed at the end of 1904 to make an extended trip of nearly three months to Nyasaland, the highlight of which was a conference to discuss the possibility of a united Christian Church in the environs of Lake Nyasa. *En route*, he called at the U.M.C.A. stations, where a lively discussion of Christianization of African customs took place because the U.M.C.A. already contemplated baptizing the wives of polygamists and tolerated circumcision as a social practice. The U.M.C.A., he reported, 'just preaches . . . no cultural improvement is intended.' On the other shore of Lake Nyasa at Livingstonia, now in the full bloom of the development of the Overtoun Institute, another style prevailed, one as congenial as ever to the visiting Berliner owing to its emphasis upon the education of Africans. To Nauhaus, the reliance upon native agents and Laws' concentration on an institutionalized centre offered much better prospects than the Berliners' sprawling decentralization. The idea that a revival could take place with obvious grass-roots congregational feeling also impressed the visitor. Livingstonia Mission, he reported, had achieved the greatest results of any mission on the Nyasa.[1] Some differences in social attitudes did exist. The Presbyterians equated beer drinking with orgies and made temperance a primary objective, while drinking was treated tolerantly by the Lutherans. Because converts tended to identify ethical prescripts as articles of faith, the question of beer was already in 1904 the subject of dispute between Christians from the Berlin sphere and those from Livingstonia churches, wherever they met.

At the inter-mission conference, Nauhaus participated fully in discussion, having given much thought himself to the desirability of a common church development not confined by denominationalism. This idea received a sympathetic hearing, but its corollary of a common language proved to be a stumbling-block. In the supra-national

[1] Nauhaus Tour Report, 24 Sept.–15 Dec. 1904 (Berlin IV 1 15). By being exposed mainly to the institutionalized centre of Livingstonia, Nauhaus did not grasp the conflicts between the revivalists and educators at this stage in its development. See McCracken, John, 'Livingstonia Mission and the Evolution of Malawi, 1875–1939' (unpublished Ph.D. diss., Cambridge, 1967), pp. 273, 285f.

institutions, Nauhaus proposed that Swahili should be the church language, and upon encountering the determination of the Scots that English should serve this purpose, he concluded that a united church must be limited to German territory where Swahili would be the lingua franca.[1]

Yet admiration for the style and accomplishments of the Livingstonia Mission went on unabated. Nauhaus found a kindred spirit in James Henderson, headmaster of the Overtoun Institute, to whom he must have confided his disappointment with the development in his own Synod. Henderson seems to have suggested that the disconsolate Berliner join the Livingstonia Mission, and received a generally positive response from Nauhaus during his leave in Berlin:

> It is not so very easy to leave one's old sphere of work even in one's thoughts. But as matters are just now in our Mission I decided to wire 'Yes' as an answer to your question: 'Might I mention your name either for work at the Institution or at one of our stations?' I would consider it an honour to be privileged to work in the Livingstonia Mission. Perhaps at some later date our Berlin Mission may see its way to work on different lines and then perhaps I may be of some use with what I would in the meantime learn in the Livingstonia Mission.[2]

At this time the Livingstonia Committee was bent upon reasserting greater control over the direction of the Mission's growth, which had been dominated too much, in their view, from Nyasaland by Laws. J. Fairley Daly's veto against the nomination of Nauhaus, on the grounds that a Lutheran might find it difficult to adjust to Presbyterian rules and that a Scot would be preferable,[3] may have been part of this reaction.

The policies of the retired Superintendent did not survive long in the Konde Synod. Under his inspiration in 1903 the Ikombe congregation had mounted a substantial missionary effort of their own, sending relays of evangelists to Muhanga near Iringa to keep alive the activities of the easternmost station of the Berlin Mission in the Southern Highlands, a feat especially remarkable in view of the pronounced provincialism of the Nyakyusa. The subsequent period saw the ascendancy of parochialism and ethnic particularism. The Konde Synod developed no common language, but recognized three church vernaculars, to serve Buwanji, Ukinga, and Unyakyusa. On

[1] Nauhaus Tour Report, 27 Sept.–15 Dec. 1904 (Berlin IV 1 15).
[2] Nauhaus to Henderson, 3 Feb. 1906 (N.L.S. 7865).
[3] Daly to Laws, 16 Feb. 1906 (N.L.S. 7865).

at least one issue, that of bridewealth, helpers who had been trained in the Nauhaus era protested against a missionary attitude which placed control, discipline, and uniformity of European practice before sympathy with African conditions. It had been officially recognized as early as 1901 that the practice might justify itself in the Christian community as a kind of dowry. The East African missionaries in conference agreed not to regard the custom as sinful, as it was treated in South Africa, but the majority thought it ought nevertheless to be abolished as dangerous.[1] This attitude prevailed in the Bena Synod, but the Konde Synod voted in 1904 to allow bridewealth as the legitimization of marriage. The missionaries grew more indecisive as the variance in principle became clear. African suspicions may have been heightened by the harsher discipline imposed in 1908, the year Nauhaus was shifted to the Bena-Hehe Synod to run the Kidugala School. Until that year, the 'greater *Bann*' of excommunication had not been employed. Feeling that their progress and interests were being threatened, some Nyakyusa helpers exchanged letters among themselves alleging that the white men wanted to hold down Africans. To free the hesitant missionaries of their scruples about uniformity, Schumann from Ubena specifically stated that he had no objection to Christian bridewealth, the principle was incorporated in the Konde Synod, and the agitation quietened.[2]

The differing conditions in the Konde and Bena Synods contributed to their divergence. Whereas the Nyakyusa and others demanded constant alertness, Bena compliance opened the way to ripe paternalism. Schumann personified South African proprietary attitudes and allowed the paternalism of missionaries serving under him to go uncurbed. The Ilembula Station, built up and presided over by Martin Priebusch, exemplified not only the operation of a semi-autonomous missionary unit in the Bena pattern, but also the tendency of the Berliners to champion the Bena people. It was not long after the station was founded that Priebusch began to undermine the influence of the Sangu authorities and to encourage a sense of identity in the subject Bena. Attendance at station services rapidly reached the hundreds and preaching places in the countryside were sought. Priebusch exploited a rivalry between *jumbe*s in 1903 to gain permission to establish a regular outpost at Muhandazvanu's settlement. In the same year he promoted his first baptized, Mataji

[1] Report of Joint Synod Meeting, Kidugala, 20–29 July 1901 (Berlin IV 1 8b).
[2] Steinborn, *Kirchenzucht*, pp. 136, 157. Richter, *Berliner Mission*, p. 689.

Muselema, to the position of evangelist at four preaching places and reported that the restraining power of chiefs seemed to be diminishing.[1]

Ilembula became itself a small chiefdom. A preliminary land survey in August 1904 created such a firm popular impression of control of the land by the missionary that people living in the neighbourhood began to show special respect to Priebusch and 'offered' to give two days a week as voluntary labourers in the mission fields, very much in the tradition of communal labour for chiefs. Because in the same year work on mission station roads was credited towards taxes, a further blurring of functions became possible. Priebusch did not bother to make distinctions between political and other sources of his authority and cheerfully reported great religious progress. Steady attendance at Sunday services stood at four hundred, two men were baptized, and the class of catechumens numbered twenty. Mataja Muselema helped with the instruction of eighteen children at the station elementary school, but the other bush schools sprouting up throughout the parish created a need for many more evangelist teachers. The rapidity of the entire development is revealed by the fact that of the three men sent to the new Kidugala Seminary in 1904, two were yet unbaptized.[2]

To cap his chief-like position, Priebusch came into his own as a medical man by vaccinating over twelve hundred people against smallpox. After this initial popular contact, he continued to be active in preventive medicine and hygiene, innoculating in the face of another plague and organizing a huge round-up and incineration of rats. Tribal religious practices, weakened in the Sangu sphere by lack of Bena leaders, wilted even further in the face of the protective function assumed by the Mission. The former *mganga* in the congregation symptomized a general transfer of faith, though the other adherents, still fearing his charms, insisted that he sit apart.[3]

Ilembula boomed even during the Maji-Maji hostilities. The highly personal standard by which its success had been judged, however, became clear in mid 1906, when Priebusch went on leave and his deputy, unable to manage all the activities of station and parish, suspended itineration and some school activities, resolving to concentrate upon improving quality. By normal standards, Christianization had not progressed very far in the parish: one-third

[1] *B.M.B.* (1904), 70ff. Berlin *Jahresbericht 1903*, 123.
[2] Berlin *Jahresbericht 1904*, 138. [3] *B.M.B.* (1905), 533.

of the catechumens examined just after the departure of Priebusch were judged to be unready for baptism. Yet pressure for instruction and baptism did not subside. Thirty children under fourteen, too young for adult baptism under Mission rules, clamoured for it and the deputy missionary felt obliged to submit their case to the Synod for decision. Mature candidates also presented themselves in great numbers, causing the missionary to avoid visiting preaching places where he might be asked to supply a resident helper.[1] The undifferentiated power and authority of the Berlin Mission at Ilembula, together with its pro-Bena posture, had generated this response. Tightening its grip after the Rebellion, the Iringa administration necessarily burst the bubble of popularity, by regularizing the indirect methods of rule in the district. Chiefs and *jumbe*s became better instructed about rights and duties, and being more certain of their authority within the colonial structure they began to lodge complaints against the activities of Mission helpers. At the outstation of Ihanga, the helper Jesikaka was charged with alienating the people from their chief. When a German official ordered Jesikaka to teach children only, he refused to obey without instructions from Ilembula. Relations worsened when Jesikaka refused to drink *pombe* after a sacrifice and was accused of proven disloyalty to the chief.[2] Upon his return from leave, Priebusch would not accept the new official support for tribal authorities and complained bitterly that Nigmann allowed them to make trouble with impunity. But the balance of power had shifted and many of the helpers had indeed little sense of purely religious evangelization. All except Mataji Muselema were suspended and withdrawn from outstations in 1908–9, causing a drastic curtailment in parish work. Priebusch himself received a setback by being forced to return a fine levied for adultery under customary law, which the officials judged him unauthorized to administer.[3] The difference between chiefdom and Christian parish thus became clarified in political terms between 1908 and 1911, although the influence of Priebusch as patriarch of Ilembula and its environs survived the First World War and down to 1940.

In one area, Unyiha, the Moravians made contact with the people on a broad tribal basis comparable in some ways to the relationship between Mission and tribes at Ilembula. This development was

[1] Berlin *Jahresbericht 1906*, 114. Ibid., *1907*, 116. [2] *B.M.B.* (1907), 538.

[3] Nigmann to Schumann, 4 Jan. 1909. Schumann to Gov., 24 Mar. 1909. Von Rechenberg to Iringa Station, 14 July 1909 (T.N.A. IX A 3a).

significant for the Nyasa Province not merely in theory, but also as an example of a practice different from that prevailing in Rungwe station communities. The Mbozi Station in Unyiha was founded by Traugott Bachmann in 1899 under auspicious circumstances. Five years had elapsed since the last Sangu raid and memory of the Ngoni had long since faded, so that after a half century in palisaded villages, the Nyiha could allow their fortifications to deteriorate. The cohesion bred of this defensive way of life remained, however, and when chiefs agreed that missionaries should come to their villages, substantial audiences were already on hand. The Nyiha had earned reputations as migrants ready to work for the Scottish missionaries, as well as at Rutenganio and Utengule. Some in returning home had brought with them the influence of, and receptivity to, missionary ways. This vanguard of Christianization spread word of the benefits associated with the white men, praised the virtues of literacy and introduced the observance of Sunday as a day of rest.[1] When Bachmann first met his new parishioners, however, these advantages were not apparent. He could not deny their enthusiasm: numerous Nyiha came singing and dancing to fetch him and Meyer when they set out from Utengule to search for a station site; but his impressions on this journey were coloured by his Nyakyusa experiences. The Nyiha seemed dishevelled and dirty in comparison with the tidy Nyakyusa, and their language rang dissonantly in his ear.[2] Bachmann later adored the Nyiha and became too certain that he had found the key to *Volkskirche* success to dwell upon drawbacks.

For all that he had experienced in Rungwe, Bachmann remained at first only half converted to African values, and the emergence of Mbozi as the scene of an important experiment occurred as much by accident as design. The area's water shortage was one advantage: although Mbozi was situated near a series of springs assuring a regular supply, its quantity was limited and would not permit a large number of people to be settled permanently at the station. The ceaseless demand for work encouraged the erection of an impressive complex of buildings. Sometimes Bachmann employed as many as three hundred men without exhausting the available labour and when the period of construction ended, the success of coffee-growing experiments offered another source of employment and resulted in extensive planting. At the end of the first year, Bachmann, still a

[1] *P.A.* (1901), 465, 468. Kootz-Kretschmer, *Die Safwa*, i, 2f.
[2] Bachmann, *Manchen Anstoss*, pp. 81f., 90ff.

stern pietist trying to impose his ideas of appropriate self-restraint, abruptly released a whole aggregation of labourers because their nightly festivities seemed too riotous. After razing all huts, he decided to institute a new system of station life excluding all but the few who showed genuine religious interest and respect for order. Simultaneously, Bachmann devised an ingenious scheme for giving equal opportunities for work and reaching large numbers of the people. As there were twelve chiefs in Unyiha, he instituted a schedule of taking workers from each chiefdom in turn for a month, thus exposing many to the station routine of labour and prayer while exciting the jealousy of no chief.[1]

In Unyiha also, traditional religion and superstition offered little overt resistance to Christianity. Chiefs lacked a strong mythical charter and had limited ritual functions, while the people's sense of tradition had suffered through over fifty years of disruption. A prophetess flourished briefly during the transitional period of dispersal from defensive concentrations and growing awareness of colonial demands. Her message merely stated that the oppressors would pass and referred to no retributive power.[2] Officials discouraged this political messenger, while Bachmann tackled another religious phenomenon, the cult of the iron-worker. The smelting of iron had declined because of the disturbed conditions of the nineteenth century and most furnaces were in disuse, but beliefs in the sacredness of the smelters' office retained more religious content than any other and by popular conviction furnaces could not be successfully operated without the proper preliminary rituals. He therefore constructed a furnace in the traditional style and managed before a large audience to render iron. Before long, Mbozi reports claimed as a further religious victory the presence of a former *mganga* in his congregation.[3]

Bachmann and his principal helper, Nkasima, developed vernacular religious and elementary school materials. By 1905, a hundred and seventy pupils attended station and off-station schools and pairs of Christians covered the countryside as evangelists, able to visit some eighty villages regularly.[4] The success might have been limited to Unyiha, had its implications not been so ardently advertised or so readily appreciated by the Board in Herrnhut. All Bachmann's great zeal became attached to the proposition that the Church must

[1] *H.M.B.* (1916), 11ff. *P.A.* (1903), 234.
[2] *P.A.* (1902), 16. Wilson, *Peoples*, pp. 29f.
[3] *Moravian Missions* (1906), 218. [4] *Moravian Missions* (1906), 217ff.

grow from the Christianization of tribal customs and he was able to look back upon his early rigidity in imposing European standards of morality and discipline as something present in most missionaries which needed a process of softening, or 'unlearning'. He lectured his colleagues on the dangers of superimposing alien values and favoured some form of Christian teaching so adapted to African idiom as to be equally intelligible to the pagan and the adherent.[1] When Director Hennig toured East Africa in 1905–6, Bachmann had a full philosophy to present and won assurances that the Mission Board approved of such an adaptive approach.

Hennig even supported Bachmann's proposal to tolerate polygamy during the transitional stage in Christianization. Although this degree of accommodation did not become a general policy because other missionary agencies would not go so far, Bachmann moved towards it in Unyiha, believing that 'God does not make the ugly distinction between monogamy and polygamy.'[2] He did not discipline a certain Christian who kept a senior wife in his household as 'his mother'; nor, after a conference with the congregational council, did he rigidly exclude from fellowship another earnest Christian who reverted to polygamy from a sense of responsibility for his discarded second wife. These compromises assume importance when it is remembered that those under Church discipline were generally ostracized socially; both Moravians and Berliners wished to keep the way open for reconciliation, but they instructed their congregations to treat a person under discipline 'not as a friend'.[3] Bachmann's conservative attitude towards African society led him to apply discipline leniently and reluctantly and to become ever more opposed to certain tendencies in the Christian communities elsewhere in the Nyasa Province. Whereas he had attacked bridewealth in his early days at Mbozi as representing a form of 'slavery' of women because they seemed to do all the work, he afterwards accepted that this payment and the traditional distribution of labour were part of a woman's duty and self-respect. Finally, noticing the new equality of women in Christian communities, he grew concerned that their status might damage family solidarity.[4]

Ilembula and Mbozi represented the contrasting styles of the Berliners and the Moravians as they first developed a mass base.

[1] Bachmann, *Manchen Anstoss*, pp. 101 ff., 110 f.
[2] ibid., p. 113. [3] Steinborn, *Kirchenzucht*, p. 36.
[4] *Moravian Missions* (1906), 218. *H.M.B.* (1910), 108.

Although Bachmann may have been eccentric among the Brethren in his highly adaptive outlook, he nevertheless conformed to the Moravian practice of steering clear of secular political involvements, kept the religious aspects of his work in the foreground, and fully utilized confession, counselling, and continuing instruction for the baptized. His off-station agents radiated from a strong religious base. Priebusch at Ilembula, on the other hand, did not probe deeply into motives or individual affairs and depended upon his personal reputation and broad contact to establish an extensive influence. Nigmann correctly noticed that after the Maji-Maji Rebellion the Berliners tried to collect their adherents on their own property, in contrast to the Moravians who went to the people at their homes.[1] The proprietary model, so basic to the difficulties of Nauhaus with the Berlin Committee, continued to prevail in the Iringa District because it was suitable in times of war, and to rally the subordinated Bena. Changes occurred when East African officials repudiated South African premises and forced the missionary authorities to do likewise. The agent of reform was not a local missionary, but an Inspector, Merensky's successor, who had fresh ideas and for whom East Africa was the prime concern.

[1] Nigmann to Gov., 3 Jan. 1909 (T.N.A. IX A 3a).

CHAPTER VI

Church Foundations

FROM the time of the Moravian Director's tour in 1905, the Evangelical missionary efforts responded more and more to internal and external pressures which impelled them fairly swiftly towards advanced church constitutions and the provision of superior educational facilities. In the Southern Highlands their own burgeoning congregations, official pressure, and competition with the Roman Catholics were the most prominent factors. The same considerations existed elsewhere in the territory, along with a far greater concern about the spread of Islam, and these issues provided the basis upon which Protestants could build inter-church co-operation.

The most constant pressure, and one unique to German East Africa, came from a central administrative policy of educating Africans in the Swahili language for employment in official service. State-run education originated in 1892, and evolved without the deference to missionary institutions that was typical in British colonies. In German East Africa, the State schools not only underwent constant upgrading themselves, but also produced curriculum outlines and literature to be used by private educational institutions. Some of the means by which the Government induced various missionary agencies to conform remained indirect, for example by threatening to start one of their own schools, to be staffed by teachers trained at the Tanga School, who usually came from the coast and appeared to the Christian missionaries a vanguard of Islam in the interior. In terms of direct subventions to mission schools, a certain amount of material support came from the 'Fund for the Spread of the German Language', which in East Africa went to encourage not the European imperial tongue but standard Swahili.[1] Certain funds also permitted the Government to give books and other school materials to missions which used the Swahili Curriculum. The local district administrators who served as school inspectors frequently displayed an enthusiasm for education which led them beyond

[1] See Wright, M., 'Local Roots of Policy in German East Africa', *J.A.H.* ix, 4 (1968).

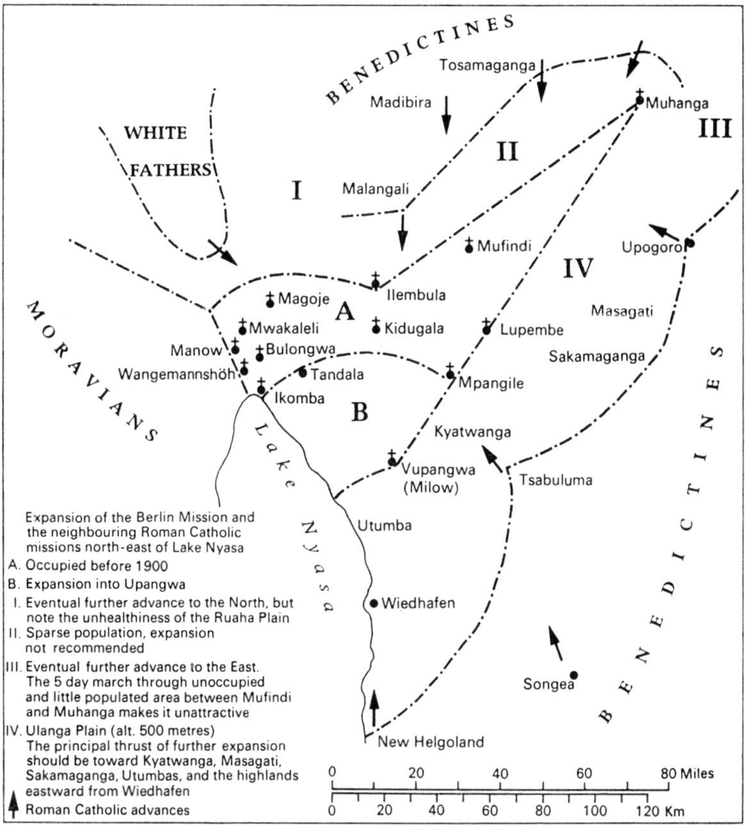

Map IV Strategy Map by Martin Klamroth [1902]

mere observation; African authorities were impressed with the necessity of providing education for their young people.[1]

The question of vernaculars and the presumed connection between Swahili and Islam inevitably exercised those in Germany concerned about general missionary principles, and metropolitan preconceptions impeded the adjustment of policy on the field. From the time support for the Tanga School had first been included in the Imperial Budget, the Evangelical Mission Committee had attacked any item implying an

[1] On the whole, the Roman Catholics identified themselves with officials far more than did the Protestants, by situating their stations near district offices and exploiting the stress upon education. The Benedictines were known to construe official support for education as an order for compulsory attendance in their schools. See Mueller, F. F., *Kolonien unter der Peitsche* (Berlin, 1962), document 78.

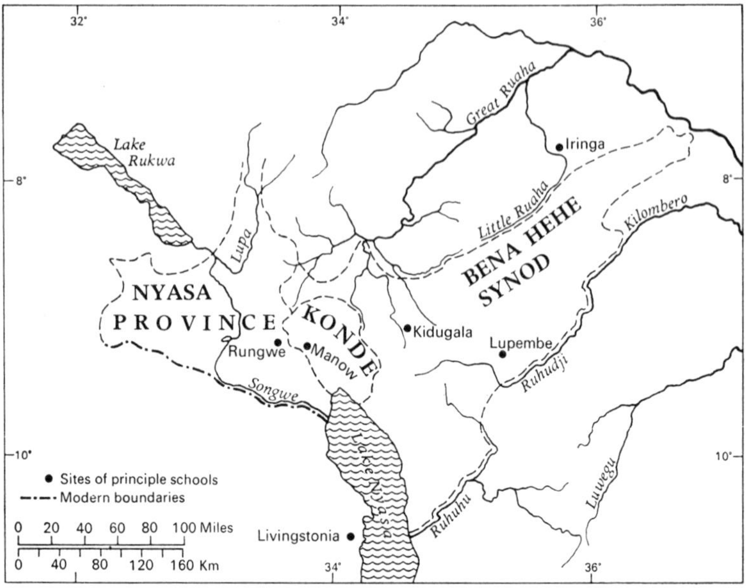

Map V German Mission Spheres [1914]

official sponsorship of Islam. Although colonial officials protested that coastal Islam was politically innocuous and the mass of the people were lost to the Christian religion, the Protestant lobby succeeded in eliminating the salary for a Koranic teacher.[1] The next educational issue to become a bone of contention sprang from the effort by German nationalists to compel the teaching of German in order to block the spread of English in West African colonies. In defence of their vernacular policy, the Evangelicals reacted against this, and secured a provision that German would be compulsory only if another foreign language were taught, and that missions would not be placed under any pressure to introduce a language other than the vernacular.[2]

In December 1897, Gustav Warneck urged those attending the Continental Conference to take a more active part in colonial education in order to exert influence to preserve the vernaculars. He assured them that they need not scruple to accept financial aid from 'Caesar', as they had already earned it by creating vernacular literatures and

[1] A.A.K.A. to Gov. (received) 28 June 1895 enclosing Memorandum by Evangelical Committee, composed by Warneck and signed, among others, by Buchner of Herrnhut and Schwartz of Leipzig, 28 Dec. 1894 (T.N.A. IX B 1).

[2] Kolonialrat Proceedings, 23 Oct. 1896 (D.Z.A.P. R.K.A. 6969).

linguistic aids. The memorandum elaborating this new direction and demanding imperial support for Evangelical educational institutions presented the religious and pedagogical reasons for education in the vernacular, and the social and cultural reasons against Europeanization.[1] It remained a subject of hot metropolitan dispute, however, as to whether Swahili ought to be considered a vernacular in interior regions of East Africa.

The Benedictines had led the way in making arrangements to protect missionary priorities in the interior.[2] The Roman Catholics, the Anglicans, and the Bethel missionaries, having all spread out from coastal bases, always employed the Swahili lingua franca and did not become involved in discussion of its religious content. At Kisserawe near Dar es Salaam, the Bethel missionaries quickly agreed to co-operate in a system of Government subsidies and the Roman Catholics made sweeping promises to develop standard schools. Had fulfilment of the requirements been immediate, the expense would have far exceeded the funds available to the administration. Götzen, counting the expenses of a territorial education system as part of the cost of elaborating the civil administration, requested 20,000 marks in 1901 for the education of Christians.[3] The failure to secure this sum temporarily limited the ability of the administration to buy conformity, and allowed a transitional period in which the Protestants adjusted their policies.

Of the Protestant leaders in the Southern Highlands, Nauhaus most favoured a Swahili curriculum and Schumann opposed it most. Schumann's attitude, reflecting the tension between missionaries and officials, prevailed in 1901, when the Berliners were requested by the Langenburg *Bezirksamtmann* to establish a standard school. They declared that they did not feel it their duty, so early in their development, to create schools to facilitate the work of the local officials. They also objected to what they saw as a rule that Christians in official service must give up the practice of their religion, a misinterpretation which provided an opportunity for them to declare that though training to respect authority was essential, education must

[1] Memorandum composed at Continental Conference, Bremen, May 1897, enclosed in A.A.K.A. to von Liebert, 9 Dec. 1897 (T.N.A. IX B 1).

[2] For full details, see Wright, M., 'German Evangelical Missions in Tanganyika 1891–1939, with Special Reference to the Southern Highlands' (unpublished Ph.D. diss., London, 1966), pp. 212ff.

[3] Von Götzen to A.A.K.A., 15 May 1901. A.A.K.A. to von Götzen, 18 Jan. 1902 (T.N.A. IX B 1).

glorify the *Divine* Authority, not that of the State.[1] Neither the Berliners nor the Moravians entered into the plan for co-operation when it first appeared. Zache, as the *Bezirksamtmann* in Langenburg, became frustrated at the entirely negative response to his more modest request for interpreters with literacy in the local language who could also make themselves understood in Swahili. He complained bitterly at the educational backwardness of evangelical agencies with fourteen stations in his district, some ten years old: 'I request, therefore, that education of the natives of Langenburg District should not be left exclusively in the hands of the missions.'[2]

Near the Iringa District headquarters another kind of dispute took place. A Koranic school had long existed at the *boma* and the discontent of African functionaries with the Catholic teaching which began in 1901, caused the German officials to find reasons to suspend co-operation. The *Chef* reported that his people considered attendance at the 'mission' school to be a form of enslavement and recommended establishment of a purely secular school, to safeguard 'the unlimited confidence of the Africans enjoyed [by officials] until now'. A German lieutenant offered to serve as teacher.[3] But the central government refused to condone such a school. An appeal for funds to maintain the secular school at Songea, and the desire of the *Chef* of Mahenge District to start a *boma* school without reference to the newly arrived Roman Catholics, were similarly turned down. The lack of sufficient funds to set up an entirely State system played as much part as the desire to avoid antagonism in the missionary lobbies in Berlin. Financial restrictions also applied at Langenburg, where Zache, unable to make good his threat of a State school, explored ways of persuading the missions to co-operate. Among other things, he proposed that the central government place more emphasis upon the rewards for good examinations, and suspend customs relief, the added revenue to be expended in educational grants to conforming schools.[4]

The Directors at Herrnhut and Berlin, Buchner and Gensichen,

[1] Schumann for Joint Konde and Bena-Hehe Synod, 30 July 1901 (T.N.A. IX B 1).

[2] Zache to Gov., 14 Sept. 1901 (T.N.A. IX B 1).

[3] Iringa Station to Gov., 18 Mar. 1902 (T.N.A. IX B 13). Iringa Station to Gov., 21 Nov. 1901 and von Götzen to Iringa Station, 24 Dec. 1901 (T.N.A. IX B 1).

[4] Zache to Gov., 24 Feb. 1902 (T.N.A. IX B 13). Zache to Gov., 12 Sept. 1902 (T.N.A. IX A 3).

responded jointly, firmly, and negatively to official insistence upon the use of Swahili as a language of instruction. As a minor concession, they offered to assist in educating any boys sent to their schools with a prior knowledge of Swahili. Although Nauhaus privately urged accommodation, this dictum from headquarters remained in force and the missionaries in Langenburg maintained a 'cautious reserve' towards manoeuvring officials.[1] In Germany, Director Buchner proved to be an unrelenting foe of Swahili, going so far in a speech before the Kolonialrat in 1905 as to declare that it was so irredeemably mixed with Islam that every expedient ought to be employed to obstruct their joint penetration. On this initiative, the Kolonialrat passed a resolution that schools should promote German instead of Swahili as the lingua franca. Later, after the reversal of this policy by the missions, realists such as the Berlin Inspector Axenfeld noted that this resolution was carried only with the help of supporters of German as a nationalistic symbol, who had little feeling for the religious motive of deterring Islam.[2] Immediately, however, Buchner's opposition to Swahili was adopted and expanded by Julius Richter, a member of the Berlin Committee. Richter delivered a diatribe during the Kolonial Kongress in 1905 against the pernicious influence of Islam everywhere in Africa as anti-European and a hindrance to true civilization. Isolating East Africa as the scene of the worst danger, he envisaged a mosque alongside every coastman's hut, and took the official support for Swahili to be blatantly pro-Islamic.[3] Various experienced missionaries differed. Fr. Acker of the Benedictines pointed out that Swahili as a lingua franca was an accomplished fact, and suggested that Richter study the difference between the Waswahili proper and the Wangwana who may have had a veneer of coastal culture but were not truly Islamized. Carl Meinhof, the respected linguist, proposed that missions take the offensive in adopting and Christianizing Swahili, a suggestion that won the support of the Leipzig Director, von Schwartz. The Leipzigers had already recognized the practical situation and although they still taught in the vernacular, anticipated the early incorporation of Swahili.[4]

[1] Buchner and Gensichen to A.A.K.A., 10 Feb. 1902, enclosed in A.A.K.A. to Gov., 20 Feb. 1902. Zache to Gov., 24 Feb. 1902 (T.N.A. IX A 3).

[2] Axenfeld, Karl, 'Die Sprachenfrage in Ostafrika vom Standpunkt der Mission aus betrachtet', *A.M.Z.* xxxv (1908), 556ff., 570.

[3] *Verhandlungen des Deutschen Kolonial-Kongresses, 1905* (Berlin, 1907), pp. 510ff.

[4] ibid., 531ff.

The Buchner–Richter position received a *coup de grâce* from the new Director of the Herrnhut Moravians, Paul Hennig, when he came to East Africa. Hennig had to consider the situation not just in the Nyasa Province, but also in the Tabora area, where the Moravians had taken over the work of the London Missionary Society. Von Götzen's impatience to fill the need for literate civil functionaries had led him to instruct all district officials to urge native authorities and all the people to attend instruction. At Tabora, where Superintendent Stern pleaded that his headquarters would not permit instruction in Swahili, the Governor responded with an ultimatum: 'The main benefit to the administration in its agreement with the missions would be destroyed by the non-adoption of Swahili in the curriculum. The Government would be obliged to re-introduce its own schools in the interior in competition with the mission schools in order to gain subordinate officials competent in Kiswahili.'[1] At Tabora and Ujiji, State schools were indeed authorized in 1905 for lack of a mission alternative and this proof of von Götzen's earnestness affected Hennig's assessments.

By 1905, the Berlin Mission also began to respond to the demand for secular education in Swahili. As a consequence of the transfer of the Usaramo field from Bethel to Berlin, the former headmaster of the Kiserawe School, Pastor Cleve, moved to the Bena Synod to take charge of the Kidugala Seminary, which had been endowed in 1904, along with Manow, as a centre for training evangelists. During his short stay of something over a year, Cleve developed the school at Kidugala in two branches, one for secular education including Swahili and German to prepare boys for public life, and the other for the primary religious task of training evangelists.[2] The eagerness of the administration to encourage this development was proven by the grant of school materials even though the intention to alter the standard curriculum had been announced.[3] Zache's comment that an important reason for local opposition to Swahili was that the missionaries did not speak it themselves, appears correct. Cleve had solved this problem in Bena country, and Hennig, expressing his disagreement with Buchner's policy and determined to recommend the Swahili curriculum, stated that a similar school would be established

[1] Gov. to Stern, 15 Nov. 1901 (T.N.A. IX A 3).

[2] For the fluctuating career of central schools in the Bena-Hehe Synod, see *A.M.Z.* xliv (1917), 20ff.

[3] Deputy Gov. to Cleve, 24 Feb. 1905 (T.N.A. IX B 13).

in the Nyasa Province as soon as an education specialist could be trained in Swahili at the Oriental Seminar at Berlin. The Langenburg *Bezirksamtmann* reflected the subsequent change in climate on this issue. In May 1906 he reported that the Moravians 'now, *finally*, intend to introduce Kiswahili instruction' and recommended the delivery of a hundred and twenty Swahili primers 'in the interest of the good cause and the importance of introducing this language.'[1]

After his inspection in 1905–6, Bishop Hennig recommended that the future African Church develop along three lines: centralized middle-school education, congregational and provincial self-government, and the social integration of Christian and tribal communities. The usual considerations partly governed this new statement of aims: the impoverishment of the home treasury, the rigours of the tropical climate and inadequate prospects of recruiting white missionaries, presented serious problems, especially in a region of rapidly expanding Church membership. On the social side, developments at Mbozi and Utengule demonstrated that off-station evangelization could be successful, even if it continued to be popularly held in Rungwe that people could be Christians away from the station only after a period of training in residence. Further encouragement for Hennig's conclusions came from the performance of the helpers who had been schooled at Rungwe in 1902–4. Finally, after close, enthusiastic observation of the methods of the Livingstonia Mission, Hennig declared that 'it seems plainly to be God's method that Africa shall be won for the Gospel by means of Africans'.[2]

Hennig had power to adopt the Livingstonia model and he took it over quite literally. Rungwe School should become a central institution for the advanced education of the brightest and best students from all tribes, through a common language and common standards. These men would become the core of the future united Church, for Hennig accepted that the hierarchy of education established the hierarchy of the Church and assistant teachers would progress to the rank of certified teachers and thence to special theological training to become pastors. The Rungwe complex was also to contain industrial, religious, and secular education side by side. The one difference was

[1] Zache to Gov., 30 May 1906 (T.N.A. IX B 13). See also Hennig to von Götzen, 29 Jan. [1906] (T.N.A. IX A 6).

[2] *Moravian Missions* (1907), 51, 18. *A.M.Z.* xxxiv (1907), 72ff.

that Swahili instead of English was to be the common language of the central school and the United Church.[1]

These educational goals required time and new personnel to be realized and the Nyasa Province moved more easily in another of the directions mapped out by Hennig, the reduction of distinctions between Church and tribe, in which Bachmann had pioneered. Superintendent Meyer had always hoped that a whole tribe could be Christianized by capturing an aristocracy, as the C.M.S. had done in Buganda. The character of politics in Rungwe did not lend itself to this approach and Merere had been a continuing source of disappointment. The opportunity seemed to come as an outgrowth of Bachmann's work at Mbozi, for although the Nyiha themselves did not have a strongly centralized kingship, the neighbouring Nyamwanga did. Bachmann became very excited by the prospect of converting the ruler Mkoma and Christianizing the people from top to bottom. There were good prospects of success because the principal agent, Ambilishiye, was himself related to the ruling family through his mother, his father having been a Nyiha *mganga*. Ambilishiye had been introduced to the Moravians through his brother, a trusted helper at Rutenganio and a member of the first Rungwe training course. He settled at Mbozi and had risen to be one of Bachmann's principal helpers when his brother came to prepare for his assignment to found a substation at Mkoma's capital. After his brother fell from grace for divorcing his wife and marrying a pagan, Ambilishiye became the appointee for this delicate task of approaching a tribal head.[2]

Ambilishiye's qualifications as an evangelist included his apprenticeship with Bachmann and command of the Nyamwanga tongue. Although lacking a central school training, he possessed what the Moravians considered a sufficient background for helpers in early stages of Church development, that is, acquaintance with a good number of Bible stories, ability to witness to a living God as Creator and Saviour, literacy, and a variety of miscellaneous information picked up on the mission station together with a sense of discipline, cleanliness, and order.[3]

The situation at Mkoma's court in 1907 was critical. The paramountcy survived in colonial times by collaboration, mainly by providing an ample supply of labourers and porters to the Langenburg authorities. Yet because the international boundary cut through the

[1] *A.M.Z.* xxxiv (1907), 259–74 *passim*. [2] *H.M.B.* (1917), 6, 26ff., 47.
[3] *H.M.B.* (1915), 80.

Nyamwanga country, the female governor in the South, the Waituika, had been recognized by the British as an autonomous paramount. In addition to this territorial loss, Mkoma was subject also to German regulations depriving him of his former plenty of domestic slaves and of the right to kill human beings as ritual sacrifices. Mkoma fell ill in 1907 and, since he was an old man, a great debate developed because the council of *wasongo* deemed it imperative in case of his death to sacrifice a wife, if not slaves as in the traditional practice. The tension at this time owed much to the influence of the recently established Mwenzo station of the Livingstonia Mission. Although there had been constant contact between the Nyamwanga and the Scots ever since the Stevenson Road had been cut through their country, it was December 1900 before a missionary, Dr. James Chisholm settled regularly at Mwenzo. In 1905 came the first baptisms and by mid 1907, the time of the chief's illness, there were three hundred catechumens and over 3,500 children enrolled in sixty-three schools.[1] Christian impulses from the south had preceded the arrival of Ambilishiye from Mbozi.

Ambilishiye followed upon a letter from the leading helper at Utengule and later the first ordained pastor in the Nyasa Province, Msatulwa Mwashitete, who had been a trusted slave assigned as major-domo to the Waituika Mwenisungu from 1897 until 1900, when he escaped. Msatulwa had advised Mkoma to end the practices of sacrifice and adopt Christianity. This message caused a stir and Mkoma expressed a willingness to 'talk things over'.[2] This task Ambilishiye assumed, after diplomatically making his first act a pledge of loyalty to the chief.

Besides cultivating the royal family generally, Ambilishiye soon found a close ally in a son of Mkoma's first wife. Tjesumbi, later baptized Alinane, had protested even before the arrival of the Moravian evangelist against the prospective burial sacrifice of his mother. Beyond the personal concern, this protest reflected a widespread anxiety about the human sacrifice. Children evaporated from Ambilishiye's school at the rumour that the perturbed spirits responsible for the bad harvest would be appeased by the offering of children attending Christian instruction. Rather than fleeing, Alinane adhered

[1] *Missionary Record* (1901), 268 ff. Ibid. (1908), 24. See also Fülleborn, *Deutsche Njassa*, p. 493. Coxhead, *North-Eastern Rhodesia*, pp. 44 f.

[2] Mwashitete, M., *Ways I Have Trodden*, trans. M. Bryan (London, 1932), pp. 16f., 32.

even more firmly. During the absence of his teacher he preached in 1908 and on his own initiative went to the Livingstonia Station at Mwenzo to acquire the literature he heard had been printed in Chinyamwanga.[1] By the time Bachmann made his first visit to Mkoma's in early 1909, many people attended school and services and two were ready for baptism. He had to deal too with the impact of Christianization, which concerned the Langenburg authorities who feared that the one really viable paramountcy in the district was being subverted.[2] Bachmann, of all missionaries, did not wish to menace customary social and political arrangements and resolved to retain the confidence of Mkoma.

In the event, a crisis was inescapable, for the two candidates for baptism represented special points of friction between Christian and tribal ideas. The woman, Kapuleya-Ndondolilwe, met opposition from her husband who protested that her duties would be neglected. Bachmann replied that her Christian obligations would reinforce her sense of responsibilities in the family. Alinane presented a more complex and political difficulty, having been accused of a crime against the tribe for burying a child in foreign cloth rather than following customary law by using either locally woven fabric or none. The normal punishment for such an offence was death, which Mkoma felt obliged to impose precisely because the case involved his son and an especially acute challenge to his role as defender of tribal values. A rational defence of Alinane's action, on the basis of the scarcity of local cloth failed, but after a protracted negotiation, an alternative compensation was agreed. As a final preliminary to the ceremony of Baptism, Bachmann assured the chief that Christians would be obliged to participate in the rituals of the State and generally respect civil order as understood by the tribe.[3]

When the baptisms took place, Mkoma attended, Bachmann preached in Chinyiha and Ambilishiye put the questions to the candidates. This apparent reconciliation only glossed over the underlying problem of the Church in this area, and the Chief in a final interview promised not to obstruct the Christian effort so long as it did not interfere with his ritual functions. Precisely what line he would draw remained in doubt and in 1910 Ambilishiye had a pos-

[1] *H.M.B.* (1917), 60.

[2] *H.M.B.* (1917), 61ff. See also Iliffe, J., 'The German Administration of Tanganyika, 1906–1911: the Governorship of Freiherr von Rechenberg' (unpublished Ph.D. diss., Cambridge, 1965), p. 401.

[3] *H.M.B.* (1910), 107f., 111f. Ibid. (1917), 67ff.

ition strong enough to allow him to suggest with impunity that the practice of praying to the ancestors in the event of misfortune should be suspended. On the Moravian side there was also some restraint, for Bachmann decided to hold back from further baptisms in hope of converting the Chief. Progress in this direction was hampered by the death of Ambilishiye in 1911, but evangelization continued and Bachmann concluded that Mkoma seemed to be Christian 'in spirit' even if his office precluded his baptism.[1] When the aged chief finally lay on his death-bed in 1914, the *wasongo* again expressed the determination to carry out traditional funerary sacrifices, but the Christian party had gained considerable strength and could appeal to Mkoma's express wish that no human life should be taken. At the moment of his death, a sharp clash of wills occurred before the Christians won the compromise of slaying a hen instead of a woman.[2] The Nyamwanga episode closed at this point because the strategy of capturing a tribe at its head depended upon the quality of authority exercised by the chief. A paramount like Mkoma, the master of life and death, tested by pre-colonial stress and colonial collaboration, was not likely to develop in a purely colonial environment. The importance of the episode rests mainly in the fact that it sustained the fires of Moravian missionary imagination in a formative period for Church policy.

One reason for Bachmann's visit to Mkoma in 1909 had been the expansion of the White Fathers into the western part of Nyamwanga country. This competition was only a minor manifestation of the conflicts between Evangelicals and Catholics which became increasingly frequent and severe in the Southern Highlands as networks of schools and outstations intermeshed. Nyamwanga proved to be a fairly straightforward case to resolve because of the authority of the chief and the Moravian advantage in having a poised and well-connected African agent. Worse clashes occurred with the White Fathers in Usafwa and western Usangu, and with the Benedictines in Ulanga and on the Songea frontiers.[3]

The Roman Catholics had claimed since 1892 that the Congo Act and derivative legislation prohibited official delimitation of mission spheres, but conceded that short-term agreements might be made

[1] *H.M.B.* (1917), 66, 71f., 120. Bachmann, *Manchen Anstoss*, p. 115.

[2] *H.M.B.* (1916), 258f.

[3] Files full of details about 'confessional rivalry' are available. For the Moravian sphere, see Meyer to Iringa Station, 30 [Sept.] 1904 (T.N.A. IX A 2). For the Berlin sphere, see T.N.A. IX A 3a.

between contending societies. Such voluntary treaties did not in fact resolve the problem. By 1908 disorder arising from confessional rivalries reached such a peak that von Rechenberg proposed a general separation. Because the impartiality of local officials was not accepted by the disputants, the delimitation was to be arranged either by a special commission from Germany or in a conference chaired by the Governor. Von Rechenberg's personal drafting and correction of this dispatch, in his barely decipherable handwriting, shows how serious he took the situation to be. Religious conflict existed throughout the territory, and the description, even where not directly applied to the Southern Highlands, was extremely apt:

> The White Fathers and the Herrnhuters in their struggle over the triangle formed by Bismarchburg–Langenburg–Kilmatinde . . . no longer fight with fictional occupation of giant stretches of county by means of outposts consisting mostly of a single coloured 'helper' or 'catechist', but through an encroachment upon the established mission sphere of the opposing confession. This process would have led in the Langenburg District, as already on Kilimanjaro, to a chessboard arrangement of the two confessions, were it not for the *Bezirksamtmann's* timely success in blocking some especially forward posts.
>
> The appeal to Africans in the struggle should be considered as a separate issue. The heightening of African self-confidence in matters relating to European missionaries may be a touchy problem. This aspect may become especially important if the confrontation goes so far that appeal to the state power appears to be the last resort. The officials in that case will judge almost always on the evidence of Africans, probably pagan and Mohammedan, who alone in these cases can be interviewed as impartial witnesses.
>
> It is regrettable that many missions, despite all their declarations against Islam, combat the other Christian confessions much more than Islam.[1]

Colonial Secretary Dernburg agreed that maintenance of order took precedence over freedom of conscience, and authorized von Rechenberg to call a general conference if agreements could not be reached voluntarily. Meanwhile the Colonial Office consulted the metropolitan spokesmen of the feuding denominations and received characteristic replies: the Berlin Mission favoured a general separation along tribal lines, claiming Kiwanga's district as part of greater Ubena; the Moravians offered restraint in Unyamwesi for equivalent restraint in Usafwa by the White Fathers; and Hespers, the venerable Catholic statesman, again put forward the arguments for

[1] Von Rechenberg to R.K.A., 4 Nov. 1908 (T.N.A. IX A 1).

freedom of religious movement and commented that religions must coexist in Africa as in Germany. He then announced that the Benedictines, White Fathers, and Holy Ghost Fathers would negotiate with non-Roman missions over particular points of friction.[1] Many agreements were in fact made, and reduced the level of conflict enough to obviate the threat of overall official regulation. Von Rechenberg's successor, Heinrich Schnee, maintained the principle of religious freedom while acting energetically against disturbances caused by disputes. Schnee confined himself to warnings that the unseemly antagonism gave an advantage to Islam and misrepresented Christian ideals.[2]

The Berlin Mission, by assuming responsibility for the Usaramo Synod, began to work in a Swahilized setting as well as to enjoy enhanced prestige by representing Protestant interests before the Government. It therefore moved into a key position as co-ordinator of territorial missionary co-operation. When Karl Axenfeld, after succeeding to the leadership of the Executive Office and Seminary in Berlin, also became the Inspector for German East Africa, the tone and direction of the Berlin work was transformed. Axenfeld took up the problems of Islam, Catholic competition, education, and Church development, with the efficiency he had previously displayed in reorganizing the finances of the Society as Metropolitan Inspector.[3] Furthermore, through his contact with Berlin officialdom and informed public opinion, he became committed to the reform programme associated with Dernburg. Once again, concern to transfer the government of the Church to Africans formed a *leitmotive*. Financial retrenchment on all mission fields had been ordered in 1905 and the following year Axenfeld had announced that self-restraint must continue. The long pause in ordaining African pastors had ended a few years earlier in South Africa and the Berliners returned to the 1882 *Missionsordnung* with its principles of self-government and, most emphatically, self-support.[4]

Axenfeld criticized the old authoritarianism of the Berlin Mission,

[1] Berner to Dernburg, 31 Dec. 1908. Hennig to Dernburg, 12 Jan. 1909. Hespers to Dernburg, 2 Jan. 1909 enclosed in Dernburg dispatch 12 Jan. 1909 (T.N.A. IX A 1).

[2] Schnee to Axenfeld, 11 Jan. 1913 (Kidugala 2). Schnee to Mahenge Station, 14 Jan. 1914 (T.N.A. IX A 3a).

[3] See Axenfeld, Karl, *Eben-Ezer: bis hieher hat der Herr geholfen* (Berlin, 1907). Richter, *Berliner Mission*, pp. 334ff.

[4] Richter, *Berliner Mission*, pp. 381f.

and, after the reorganization of the constitution in 1906, actively used the advice of committee members with high reputations as students of mission work and Africanists, including Julius Richter, Carl Meinhof, and Diedrich Westermann. The Vice-President, and subsequent President, of the Society from 1909 to 1914, Max Berner, was also the official mediator between Protestant Missions and the Imperial Government. With this fresh and influential circle in control, the Berlin Mission entered a sunny period.

Surveying the condition of German East Africa, with its extending railways and increasingly effective administration, Axenfeld became convinced that a social revolution was afoot, in the course of which the younger generation of progressive Africans would adopt a world religion, either Islam or Christianity. Rather than react to Islam as a menace to be countered by official repression or tribalized Christianity, he thought that the new classes could be captured positively by full missionary participation in the Swahili medium educational system. The new policy for the Berliners in German East Africa therefore became twofold: to develop a self-supporting native church, and to associate the church or churches with other evangelical Christians and with the élites by creating educational institutions rising to official standards.[1] Policy statements, in contrast to those of the time of Nauhaus's troubles, all recognized the factors of economic and social mobility, standard education and the territorial language, and the rapid expansion of the Church. Axenfeld had not fixed the idea of the size and scope of a national church in East Africa, much as that was his goal, for he realized that its evolution would depend on the effectiveness of Swahili education and the permanence of the social revolution.[2]

As a sane organizer, Axenfeld analysed the mission situation with methodical thoroughness. The multiplicity of dialects, he saw, offered a temptation to missionaries to become preoccupied with petty differences that inhibited the building of a viable, vigorous church. Too well schooled in standard theory to discard the mother-tongue for basic evangelization, he pointed out nevertheless that central institutions for training evangelists inevitably led to a single 'synodical language', and appealed to linguists to distinguish languages in groups. This would simplify the creation of Christian literature in sub-synodical vernaculars; he proposed that such a literature should

[1] Berlin *Jahresbericht 1908*, pp. 76ff., 89f.
[2] *B.M.B.* (1909), 125, 132.

be developed wherever the population exceeded 50,000. If local vernaculars could be printed in hand presses at mission stations, most resources could then be devoted to Swahili. As part of this emphasis, all new missionaries were to receive a Swahili language course at the Oriental Seminar.[1]

In a speech before the Annual General Meeting in December 1907, the new Inspector laid down the priorities for missionary work. With candid self-criticism, he stated that missionaries must learn how to vacate the pastorate in favour of the native clergy: 'In East Africa especially, we must sustain the conviction that the defective performance of natives is often more valuable than the good [performance] of the foreign missionary, and the more so because it lies so deep in the blood of us Germans, and even more us north Germans, that we must do everything ourselves, at least regulate everything. . . .'[2] On the principle that not every missionary could become a bishop but that all could be teachers, a special course on educational methods was held at Kidugala in 1909 to give the missionaries some idea of how to go about upgrading station elementary schools and village bush schools. In the seminaries, too, increased time went into giving African personnel more training in educational methods.

The most consistent ally of Axenfeld in his territorial programme was the C.M.S. From the start, the Anglicans of the C.M.S. had co-operated with the Government fully and to a greater extent than any German society. The C.M.S. in 1906 had been able to present twenty-four scholars at the Mpwapwa District Office for examination in the standard subjects, including German. The fruit of their efforts was not only the warm commendation of the examining official and the grant of a premium, but also the appointment of three Christians as *akidas* in the district in 1907.[3] Then, just as the Government succeeded noticeably in 'stirring the heathen chiefs to seek education', the C.M.S. committee in London, in view of the shortage of missionary recruits and funds, decided to concentrate in British territory, expecting that the Germans, too, would wish national consolidation. But the Germans were unenthusiastic and Bishop Weston of the U.M.C.A. declared emphatically that English

[1] *A.M.Z.* (1908), 561ff., 572f.
[2] *B.M.B.* (1909), 125.
[3] Rees's memorandum of interview with Lt. Lademann, Mpwapwa, 26 Jan. 1906. Peel to Baylis, 1 Feb. 1908 (C.M.S. A 8/01).

missions must not be weakened in such a way as to encourage the administration to 'sit on' foreigners. The Committee therefore decided in January 1909 to rescind its decision and remain in German East Africa.[1]

The climate for co-operation was excellent as Axenfeld looked for ecumenical friends. After its period of restraint, the C.M.S. in Ugogo urgently required facilities for training at all levels, and did not wish to send men to Freretown for fear of their alienation. Yet coastal influences approached their own doorstep with the railhead. The Anglicans felt the pinch: funds from London were very scarce and the administration threatened to set up a State school if the C.M.S. did not undertake to educate sons and nephews of chiefs and *jumbe*s. The Muslim overtones of State education frightened the C.M.S. as much as any other society. When, as a consequence of mutual interests in China, leaders of the Berlin Mission and the C.M.S. came together, they recognized that German East Africa, too, presented problems of mutual concern. Axenfeld offered either the hospitality of Berlin, or to come to London himself, 'to discuss with you common work against Islam, common representation before the Government and [*sic*] others.'[2] Islam was the keynote of ensuing conversations held at the Edinburgh Conference between Axenfeld and the Revd. Rees of the Gogo Mission.

The Berlin Inspector's conception of the menace of Islam was eclectic and abstract rather than practical. It had sources in missionary literature, the atmosphere of propaganda in Germany and his own sense of an urgency to animate Christianization. Axenfeld believed that the very process of colonization favoured Islam and stated repeatedly that the time of decision between the two religions was near, as for example: 'In all probability the religious future of West and East Africa must be decided in a generation. Whatever has not been taken under Christian care in this time-span will surely fall to Islam.'[3] In German colonial circles the political line of suspecting the loyalty of Muslims could be used to argue for a Christian priority in official policy. A different tone was appropriate in dealings with the C.M.S., and Axenfeld placed stress there upon the winning of élites. A Swahili language policy served as the strongest medium for

[1] Rees to Baylis, 15 Aug. 1907. Memoranda, 20 Oct. 1908 and 30 June 1909 (C.M.S. A 8/01). Weston to Travers, 23 Oct. [1908] (U.M.C.A. A 1 17).

[2] Axenfeld to Rees, 15 Oct. 1909 (C.M.S. A8/01).

[3] *Verhandlungen des Deutschen Kolonial-Kongresses, 1910* (Berlin, 1910), pp. 633, 635.

accomplishing this end and he sought co-operation in sponsorship of the periodical *Pwani na Bara* and the new simplified Swahili version of the Epistles, both edited by Martin Klamroth. In return for C.M.S. help, the Berliners could offer the services of Klamroth as a mediator with the Government in Dar es Salaam, and in Berlin those of Berner who 'has always the right, and when *he* likes, to approach the Chancellor and the Colonial Minister alike. . . . The Government never acts without Mr. Berner's advice, and never deals with any missionary matters apart from him.'[1]

The conditions favouring a C.M.S.–Berlin alliance caused the German societies of the northern part of German East Africa also to think in territorial terms. Educational pressure at Moshi prompted the Leipzig Mission to assign a teacher to the *boma* to prevent the importation of a Government schoolmaster to look after the instruction of askaris and official dependents of various classes. Yet the Leipzigers resented the whole thrust of official policy and complained at the 1910 Kolonial Kongress that the administration, for all its pressure, produced only rootless collaborators and had no real aims in education.[2] The Leipzig Mission on Kilimanjaro had by this time achieved an enviable position in popular-tribal education, built up from the time they had closed their initial boarding schools in favour of day attendance. The three-year teacher-training course begun in 1902 by Johannes Raum contributed greatly to the capacities of the Mission.[3]

The Bethel Mission did not evolve with the clear sense of priorities that distinguished the Leipzig Mission. Its nationalist origins, the inexperience of its staff, and the belated assertion of single-minded executive direction, had hampered the whole effort. The Shambala in the twentieth century proved to be willing adherents and apt scholars, albeit complex and allegedly non-religious in their motives. After 1907, however, affairs in the Bethel Mission became better organized and Ernst Johanssen, one of its original missionaries, took the task of establishing a field in Ruanda as an opportunity to

[1] Memorandum, 26 June 1910 (C.M.S. A8/01).

[2] Leipzig *Jahresbericht 1910*, p. 85. *Verhandlungen des Deutschen Kolonial-Kongresses, 1910*, pp. 706f.

[3] If education of girls can be taken to be an index of broad social influence, the fact that girls exceeded boys in elementary schools by 1913 is significant and unparalleled by other missions. See Weishaupt, M., 'Unsere Mission in Deutsch-Ostafrika', in Paul, D. ed., *Die Leipziger Mission, daheim und draussen* (Leipzig, 1914).

apply his hard-won experience in an attempt to Christianize a whole people.[1]

Evangelical co-operation, it may be concluded, was based on experiences following official initiatives in the realm of education. Against the progressive assumptions of rapid modernization and social movement, most Evangelicals upheld a more conservative social philosophy. The full official curriculum, all agreed, did not allow enough time for religious instruction; Christian values were at least as important as academic and practical instruction, to use the terms of Axenfeld.[2] This consensus was retrospectively summarized by Oscar Gemuseus, the Rungwe Moravian educator.

> We were all fully convinced that it was our duty to keep the natives in their own nationality as much as possible; to deliver to them a genuine and adequate knowledge of Christian life, and to prevent with all means to breed a kind of black European. Therefore we preferred Swahili, as an African language, to German, and had good experiences with it. After a few months my pupils were all able to give contributions to our Christian monthly paper, 'Pwani na Bara', edited in Dar es Salaam, which was a chain linking together all Christians of the whole colony. They would never have been able to have a paper for themselves in a European language. Besides, through our teaching Swahili, we made the Government schools, with their non-Christian influence, dispensable.[3]

The Evangelical Mission Conference held at Dar es Salaam in 1911 must be regarded as the antecedent of the Tanganyika Missionary Council established in the 1930s. It represented the kind of ecumenical co-operation which did not rush, enflamed by the spirit of the moment, into pledges of church union, and seemed a very cool affair in comparison to the Kikuyu Conference of 1913. In the tradition of the Continental Conference, rather, the proceedings dealt with practical common concerns, of education, Islam, language and culture, and migrant Christians, none of which impinged upon the respective theological positions of the participants.

Two important addresses, delivered by Martin Klamroth and Bruno Gutmann, focused upon different means of combating Islam. Each dealt with the detribalized and the tribe, but Klamroth emphasized the *wangwana* as the strategic element to be captured while Gutmann

[1] *A.M.Z.* xxxv (1908), 63ff. Johanssen, E., *Führung und Erfahrung*, 3 vols. (Bethel, 1934–8), i, 83ff.; ii, 85f.

[2] Berlin *Jahresbericht 1909*, p. 86. See also Leipzig *Jahresbericht 1911*.

[3] Gemuseus to Mackenzie (in English) 29 Apr. 1924 (N.L.S. 7818).

argued that the most important work lay in stabilizing the tribe so that it could resist the infiltration of demoralizing coastal influences. Klamroth's posture naturally reflected his situation in Dar es Salaam, the urban magnet for many Africans, where his congregation was made up of clerks, cooks, servants, and askaris from many areas.[1] He had also undertaken research which indicated that the estimates of the spread of Islam had been exaggerated. In conclusion, Klamroth suggested that when African agents became more evident in Christian efforts, the appeal of Islam as the more 'African' religion would diminish. Gutmann did not deny the importance of first-class schools for the Christian élite or the need for improved education at every level, but with his priorities set on the tribal fortress, communal morality, kinship and Christianized rituals, he was bound to be suspicious of any education causing alienation from the community.[2] The dialogue between the tribalists and the progressives, which persisted down to 1941, was thus brought into the territorial missionary forum.

Practical progress at the 1911 Conference included agreement to continue with a Bantuized Swahili version of the New Testament, and to produce a Christian pamphlet series on geography and other works in Swahili to serve as supplements and alternatives to official materials. Agreement was also sought on the standardization of local missionary practice. Here the main concern was to minimize local differences so that Christians who had left their native areas could easily join other congregations. Church union was not being anticipated. All delegates agreed to admit to instruction, but not to baptize polygamists, to respect certain age limitations on infant and adult baptism, to expect literacy of candidates but not to make it absolutely requisite, and to issue identity cards as recommended by the C.M.S., to smooth the reception of travellers.[3] On the other hand, variations in practice existed and were revealed especially by the C.M.S. representative who, as the lone Anglican, noted certain ethical and national inclinations. On the discipline of teachers in cases of adultery, for example, all societies meted out some penalty, but the C.M.S. alone judged the sin as grounds for lifetime exclusion from teaching. The Revd.

[1] Dar es Salaam Mission Report, 1910 (Berlin III 10).

[2] *A.M.Z.* xxxviii (1911), 523f. See also Klamroth, M., *Der Islam in Deutschostafrika* (Berlin, 1912), and Gutmann, B., 'Christianisierungsprobleme eines Bantustammes im Spiegel der Heidenpredigt', *A.M.Z.* xxxviii (1911), 69ff. (Beiblatt.)

[3] *A.M.Z.* xxxviii (1911), 526ff.

Rees also had puritanical reservations about allowing Anglican converts to come under the influence of German missionaries who so manifestly enjoyed drinking and smoking. These details did not, however, mar his appreciation of the areas of co-operation, the proposed collection of tribal law and traditions, collective sponsorship of Swahili publications, and the continuation committee to prepare for the next meeting.[1]

Soon after the August Conference, Karl Axenfeld landed at Dar es Salaam intent upon following up his preliminary discussions with the C.M.S. and Moravians about active co-operation along the central railway line. At Dar es Salaam, he found the new Governor, Heinrich Schnee, bent upon a programme of religious neutralization in the civil service which not only entailed discouragement of Muslim functionaries holding religious office at the same time, but also a strong desire for Christian recruits. The Governor's hopes were high for substantial increases in subsidies to missions for educational and other welfare services. Greatly optimistic, Axenfeld proceeded to Ugogo to discuss his proposal for a joint Swahili Central School in Morogoro, with Stern of the Tabora Moravians and Rees of the C.M.S. This school was to be all things to all people, training teachers to the Government standard while laying stress on Scripture and tribal self-respect, giving the students entirely free choice of official or mission service while assuming that most graduates would go into Christian standard schools, and providing that future mission teachers could practise as evangelists in the Morogoro area, where the symptoms of the age of improvement, plantations, railway, and growing commercial activity, abounded.[2]

The discussions in Ugogo ended positively, with a resolution to let the Berlin Mission make arrangements for buildings, and accepting the designation of Carl Nauhaus as Director of the joint normal school. Nauhaus was certainly the best appointee available to the Berliners, but once again, it meant that the Southern Highlands lost talented personnel to regions of colonial concentration. A few Bena attended the Morogoro School in 1914, but were soon repatriated on account of the war.[3]

The Southern Highlands remained to be visited at the end of

[1] Rees to Baylis, 12 Sept. 1911 (C.M.S. AB/01).

[2] Axenfeld Memorandum, 9 July 1912 (C.M.S. A8/01).

[3] For further discussion of issues surrounding the Joint School, see Wright, 'German Evangelical Missions', pp. 242ff.

Axenfeld's tour. The social revolution there was not caused by Islamization or economic development to the same degree as in the Centre and North. A sense of the larger scene came through the migrants who went increasingly to the developing regions after 1909 and returned with coastal names and manners and brought back charms thought to be the more potent the more distant their origin.[1] But it was much more Government insistence on education and religious rivalry among Christians that accounted for the sense of a new era, and a landslide of attendance in bush schools. By 1913, the Nyasa Province claimed 7,931 pupils, the Konde Synod 6,586, and the Bena-Hehe Synod 5,515.[2] Education, therefore, remained in the forefront. Axenfeld presented a plan for the systematic improvement of elementary schools at the joint meeting of the Berlin Southern Highlands Synods in November 1912. Henceforth, each synod was expected to maintain standing school committees chaired by the leader of its seminary, to provide all teachers with printed curricula and course plans monthly and to assure inspection of records. It was hoped that improved teacher training and Swahili instruction in the upper grades of all full station schools would make for a smooth path up the newly elaborated educational hierarchy, even if there were many obstacles, such as the mature age of many chosen to be evangelists, the diversity of languages, and the tendency of missionaries to hold the best students on their own stations.[3]

The constitution of an indigenous church formed a principal matter for consideration at the Kidugala General Synod. Although Axenfeld recognized after his arrival that the pace of change imposed no internal necessity for progressive church legislation, he appreciated that the Livingstonia and Moravian Missions had gone far ahead of the Berliners in setting up the framework for self-government. Furthermore, the need to encourage financial autonomy had no end, and the Bena Synod required droves of African evangelists if it was to make good the aspiration of bringing the whole Bena people under the Lutheran Church. The Bena Christians responded well to the declaration that support of evangelization in contended areas was a form of self-defence. Efforts at intensive Christianization fell by the wayside for both Berliners and Benedictines. New graduates of the

[1] Ubena Post Report, 1 Jan. 1913 (T.N.A. IX A 16).

[2] P.A. (1914), 153. Berlin *Jahresbericht 1913*, p. 221.

[3] Weichert, L., *Das Schulwesen deutscher evangelischen Missionsgesellschaften in den deutschen Kolonien* (Berlin, 1914), p. 15.

Kidugala Seminary moved into fresh areas in Ulanga rather than into established parishes. But the sense of emergency provided an interesting diversion from normal peasant life and stimulated congregations performed remarkable feats; many volunteers went off to the religious campaign, supported materially by the major stations such as Lupembe and Ilembula. The Catholics claimed that Chief Kiwanga had called for their teachers rather than the Protestants and that the evangelists and missionaries from Lupembe, who finally won the battle for the Masagati area of Ubena, had employed terroristic tactics.[1] Aggression certainly occurred on both sides and more than once officials had to come in to ascertain the true wishes of a *jumbe* or to impose a neutralized zone. The Berliners showed their primary commitment by assigning one of their few university graduates at Pommern, south of Iringa, to direct strategy in the easterly Hehe-Bena area.[2]

The Constitution adopted in 1912 represented more a promise for the future than an immediate evidence of shared responsibility in the Berlin Synods. The seminaries continued to train evangelists and teachers who were *not* expected to work autonomously and Axenfeld did not look forward to early ordinations, much to the relief of the Leipzig Missionaries who apparently regarded him as impetuous in matters of church development.[3] For all that he had seen in East Africa, Axenfeld did continue to believe that change was rapidly making traditional values archaic. His attitude towards custom never approached the Gutmann or Bachmann view that it was a source of morality. For the Berlin leader, it was simply an enriching quality not to be trampled by modernity. Hennig's commendation of the Mbozi model of tribal church never made a deep impression upon Axenfeld.[4] And because Axenfeld became Director of the Berlin Mission in 1913, his opinions were likely to deter any local missionary from excessive romanticism about a Volk being a religious end in itself. Without being burdened with theoretical systems, Schumann could still be conservative and until the war regarded the Africans of his Synod as too 'unripe' to carry through the financial and legislative responsibilities outlined in the Constitution.[5]

[1] Schäppi, F. S., *Die Katholische Missionschule im ehemaligen Deutsch-Ostafrika* (Paderborn, 1937), pp. 195ff.

[2] Richter, *Berliner Mission*, p. 690.

[3] Paul, *Die Leipziger Mission*, p. 195. *A.M.Z.* xliv (1917), 26.

[4] Hennig to Axenfeld, 28 Feb. 1912 (Berlin I 5 64).

[5] Berlin *Jahresbericht 1913*, p. 102.

The Moravians had progressed much further than their Berlin neighbours in church development. Superintendent Meyer had from the start made periodic reviews and moved ahead with steady deliberateness. Yet just as missionaries had disputed alternatives in the 1890s, so the counciliar democracy of the Provincial Commissions and growing African self-expression led to controversy. Hennig had postulated a three-pronged effort including central school development, increased self-government, and social integration, as if these all complemented one another. In fact, the potential contradiction between tribal Christianity and élite formation always existed, and became increasingly explicit in the Nyasa Province from 1908 to 1915, when the war caused the cessation of regular missionary activities.

Oscar Gemuseus, very shortly after his arrival in East Africa, championed the progressive position which recognized modern conditions as fundamentally different from traditional life. Gemuseus was the educator Henning had promised to train at the Oriental Seminar for leadership of the central school. He could not have arrived at a more suitable moment, for African helpers attending the Provincial Conference in September 1908 quite candidly spoke of their problems and aspirations. With a certain diplomacy, they opened by speaking of the difficulties for themselves and all their people in adjusting to the mass of strange and contradictory things in the colonial era. At the heart of the matter lay the question of pay. Why, they asked, did they receive less than carpenters, masons, and cooks, and substantially less than Government employees? Certainly their education was equal or superior. The answer was predictable: In the special service of the Kingdom of God, all must learn to make do with little. This grievance of church workers in time became lessened as the special status became one of social significance and by accepted custom remained poorly paid. There were adjustments, however, which had to be made both within the Church and by those who could not accept the conditions. Gemuseus continually struggled to secure the rights of the new élite, while some missionaries, foremost among them Bachmann, contended that distinctions should not be made by material means.

Another discussion in which Africans participated in an especially significant way concerned the line to be drawn between tribal customs and Christian ethics. The experimentation at Mbozi in 1908 began to affect the policy considerations of the whole Province, and

Bachmann encouraged every sign that missionaries would preserve tribal customs. Gemuseus came into his first recorded confrontation with Bachmann by stating that polygamy was in origin unnatural, and where men and women were equal in number, it created a shortage of women, and led to child marriage. Bachmann adhered to his position that family structure must be preserved at all cost, and went on to point out that although in Rungwe polygamy was equated with heathenness, it was not so among the Nyiha. Gwalusako, a Nyakyusa and a former polygamist, spoke for the progressive African position by stating that polygamy was whoring and if it seemed different to the Nyiha, it was simply that they had not yet recognized it as such. When the question of compromise of the more rigid Christian position came to a vote, Gemuseus alone opposed it, because it led to uncertainty and in effect might slow progress towards full Christianization and modernity. Others either agreed for the sake of agreement or positively favoured the less stringent rules in order to increase access to the Gospel. As a result, the Provincial Order was revised to allow all wives of polygamists to be baptized, and in the related matter of inheritance, the general custom was to be followed except that widows were not to be passed on as wives to polygamous households. Finally, polygamists were allowed to live on mission land.[1]

Polygamy could be treated either way, as Superintendent Meyer noted in his comments on the 1908 Conference. Other matters, such as rituals relating to twin births, rites of passage, death and burial, and traditional medicine, remained beyond the pale. Meyer suggested that Gemuseus had been given a vote too early in his career in East Africa to use it with a proper understanding of the country. The position of the new school Director obviously jarred the progress of development as projected by the Superintendent, and in an effort to regain his former control, he proposed that the education system be put under a committee rather than a single director, perceiving quite clearly that given the progressive stand of Gemuseus, and his powers as Director, the impossible situation of two provincial heads might result.[2] In time the personal threat posed by the new man receded,

[1] Minutes, Allgemeine Missionskonferenz, Sept. 1908 (Herrnhut, R15 MIb). In a refinement carried in 1910, only first wives who were in a monogamous relationship at the time of their baptism were allowed to become office-holders in the church. Minutes, 1910 Conference (Herrnhut, Qb Protokolle).

[2] Remarks on 1908 Conference (Herrnhut R15 MIb).

but Meyer had to live with the reality of a clear conservative–progressive split in his province.

Gemuseus quickly summed up the educational needs and conditions in the Nyasa Province, conveying his own and Hennig's determination to raise the Rungwe School to Government standards in order to forestall a State school. Not only ought the middle school to be expanded, but the shortcomings of station schools had to be overcome through the distribution of teaching and learning materials, and by inspection. The educational pyramid solidified in the years before the war. The students of the Rungwe School achieved impressive results and the efforts of both the Berliners and the Moravians at the lower levels in the Langenburg District made it possible for the *Bezirksamtmann*, Dr. Stier, to discount Islam as an expansive force and to recruit most of his agents from among Christians or those under Christian influence. Schnee's instructions to give preference to Christians posed no difficulty in Langenburg where they had better general education than Muslims. Stier also gave the missions every support, from the grant of a church plot near the *boma* to supplying free school materials. In 1913, the advanced section of the teacher-training course at Rungwe caught his eye and he forwarded Meyer's request for books in expectation that some of the graduates would become civil servants.[1] The next year, after the Central Government had given the Moravians an additional cash subvention of 400 rupies, he found to his chagrin that all graduates went directly into mission service. Gemuseus declared outright that he not only needed the twenty-five teachers in mission schools, but also refused on principle to place them in the moral peril of official service.[2]

This husbanding of resources for the work of the Church and the continued suspicion of officialdom caused enmity on the part of Stier during the last months of the German administration. Mission records show, however, that this overt obstruction of the will of the administrator was only one of many negative acts. The Moravians generally underestimated the effectiveness of officials as judges of local cases, especially because the two assessors in the court at New Langenburg were coastmen. Only years later did a revaluation take

[1] New Langenburg to Gov., 20 Jan. 1913 (T.N.A. IX A 16). Ibid., 19 Mar. 1913 (T.N.A. IX B 19).

[2] Gemuseus, O., 'Die Tätigkeit in der "Mittelschule" in Rungwe, 1914–1916' (MS., Rungwe School, 1940).

place. For example, the missionaries did not fully understand the symbolism and recurrent practice of 'sprinkling the homesteads' with a compound made of parts of the human body to assure prosperity. Contemporary missionaries accused the courts of witch-hunting when a case of murder for this ritual purpose was prosecuted.[1] At other times, they tended to believe that charges against a Christian were valid only if other Christians affirmed them.[2] Such loyalty must have reinforced the impression made in earlier years that Christianity and colonial rule did not go unquestionably hand in hand, a consideration worth taking into account when churches as proto-political institutions come under discussion.

The graduates of the Rungwe School, and men from shorter training courses before Gemuseus's time, became an élite of the Church which rarely surrendered to the temptations of higher pay in the civil service. After Ambilishiye's brother became morally disqualified for the position of evangelist, he easily obtained a lucrative clerkship at New Langenburg. Ambilishiye himself exemplified the normal desire of church workers to have a reasonable if not competitive wage. He went on a kind of strike demanding that helpers should receive a month's freedom to cultivate their fields without loss of pay.[3] The issue ultimately at stake in the pay question was more than its cash value; it also concerned the kind and degree of subordination of the agent. So long as salaries were subject to the dictate of individual station heads, the teachers or evangelists remained in a relationship of personal dependence.

Africans educated in this period at the Rungwe School had high aspirations. Gemuseus was obliged to introduce a course in German when it became evident that the students would cross to Nyasaland to acquire English primers and literature to gain command of a European language. Preferring to spend his energies otherwise, Gemuseus tutored Ruben, his leading African teacher, in German and then entrusted the course to him.[4] The degree to which the congregations identified themselves with the achievements and status of these educated men became even more evident at the General Church Conference of 1913. As a result of the Provincial Constitution of 1910, the representative bodies providing for increased lay

[1] Gemuseus, O., 'Über Zaubermedizin' (Herrnhut, Nachlass Gemuseus, 1932).

[2] Gemuseus and Busse, *Ein Gebundener*, p. 74.

[3] *H.M.B.* (1917), 47. *H.M.B.* (1910), 20.

[4] Gemuseus, 'Mittelschule, 1914–1916'. '50 Jahre' (Herrnhut, Nachlass Gemuseus).

participation in Church affairs had been established. The General Church Conference, the Elders' Conference, and Congregational Assemblies, had slightly different regulations. At a Congregational Assembly all adult members had a voice in the public deliberations, but votes were given only to each adult male aged twenty or over. The Elders' Conference comprised the elected elders, men and women, as well as helpers and community overseers who owed their positions to appointment by the missionaries. At the General Church Conference, held every two or three years, the missionaries met representatives from each parish, whose number varied in proportion to the parish membership.[1]

As its first duty, the General Church Conference was to produce a code of regulations for the indigenous church. In the discussion, African delegates tended to line up on progressive and conservative sides, following the noticeable parties among the missionaries. One matter only was initiated by a delegate. In the context of congregational income, a spokesman from Ipyana reminded the missionaries of the request by teachers for higher pay. Meyer quickly discouraged any idea that such a matter would be regulated by a representative gathering and informed all present that the missionaries would determine a policy and each individual missionary would communicate the result to his congregations.[2]

Gemuseus encouraged his advanced students to think of themselves as the future leaders of the Church: to back up this promise with concrete evidence, he insisted that graduates of the school in 1914 and after should receive a uniform salary, making them more a Provincial staff than employees of single missionaries. The graduates discovered, however, that most of the missionaries refused to pay them on the promised scale, leading them to suspect that the whole publicity for the future of the African Church was a hoax. Their disillusionment affected the tendency of the most progressive Christians after the war to seek professions outside the Church. In 1914 and 1915, the matter of status for Africans deepened the gulf between progressive and conservative missionaries. Bachmann, the chief of the tribalists, found cause to criticize every special consideration given to Rungwe students. Gemuseus defended the theory and

[1] Provincial Constitution, attached to Minutes, Allgemeine Missionskonferenz, 1910 (Herrnhut, Qb Protokolle).

[2] Minutes, Allgemeine Kirchenkonferenz, 1913 (Herrnhut Qb Protokolle). The agenda will be found in Appendix C.

practice of leadership training and refused to expect his protégés to work as hard as ordinary labourers during their midday stint in the garden.[1] By the time of the British invasion, Meyer had not succeeded in reconciling the two positions and so important questions about the future of the Church remained open.

[1] Gemuseus, 'Mittelschule, 1914–1916'.

CHAPTER VII

War and the Scottish Interlude

BY the beginning of the First World War, missionary activity in the Southern Highlands had reached a stable level of organization with nominal African participation. The Berliners had been forced to surrender the premise of white supremacy and to regard their stations as centres of education and bases for frontier evangelization rather than as Christian preserves under missionary rule. The Moravians had made notable advances in activating constitutional provisions for consultation with their parishioners. In both missions, the groundwork for African self-reliance had been laid, though had peaceful conditions continued, the missionaries would probably have been satisfied only with a long period of tutelage before the recognition of autonomy. When active warfare took place in the south-western zone of Tanzania between 1916 and 1918, bringing conditions of turmoil and trial for the churches, which were stripped of missionaries, African leadership quite naturally became more conspicuous.

Two years of siege economies and cautious administration preceded the invasion of 1916. This period of phony war, during which the human and material resources of the territory were carefully quarried, led to a political climate of positive interdependence between black and white which conditioned the reception of, and attitudes towards, the British as occupiers. Initial skirmishes had taken place in the first days of the European war because Colonel von Lettow-Vorbeck ordered his companies to attack points beyond the frontiers in order to place the enemy on the defensive. In the south-west, this order became implemented in actions leading to the Battle of Karonga. After this German initiative, inaction prevailed as each side merely defended the frontier. A troop build-up occurred on the German side in 1915, bringing with it the inevitable demands upon the countryside for commissary supplies. At this point, the missionaries who had been rejected as recruits in the medical corps of the forces because of the policy of preserving administrative normalcy, found themselves welcomed as contractors to supply provisions for the newly stationed troops.[1]

[1] Gemuseus, 'Mittelschule, 1914–1916'.

The Brethren drew a line between such legitimate services and others opposed to their religion, and balked at smuggling propaganda across the border into Nyasaland to foment African unrest. The German administration sought in East Africa as elsewhere to use its alliance with the Turks for the purpose of activating supposed pan-Muslim allegiance to Istanbul. Proclamations of a Turkish–German

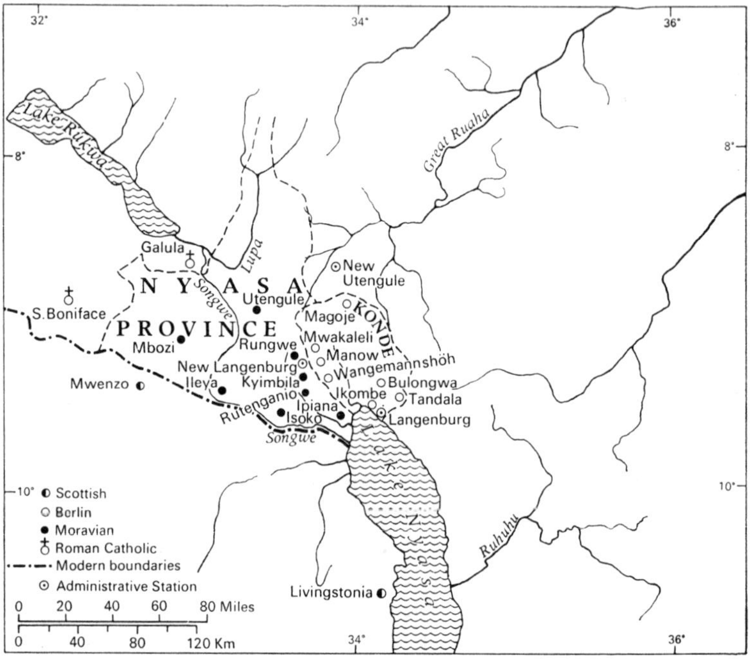

Map VI Nyasa Province and Konde Synods [1914]

jihad had a bizarre, far-fetched quality, and achieved little more than an initial advantage by exploiting anti-colonialism. *Jihad* itself had a minimal place in the Muslim traditions in East Africa, but the idea of a German–Muslim alliance was plausible owing to the careful German religious policy, with its demonstrated sympathy for Islamized societies. Zanzibaris balked at co-operating with the war efforts of their English colonial overlords because of enduring goodwill towards the mainland.[1] John Chilembwe, in preparation for his rising against the regime in Nyasaland, addressed a letter requesting German aid to the district officials at Tunduru in southern Tanzania. The

[1] Smith, H. M., *Frank, Bishop of Zanzibar* (London, 1926), p. 191.

message was relayed to Schnee, who endeavoured to infiltrate *jihad* propaganda hoping to encourage dissidents.[1] As the leading resisters were Christian and the Chilembwe Rising quickly died under vigorous colonial reprisals, the German effort was bound to be fruitless. Yet officials persisted, singling out the Moravian missionary Uhlmann in Bundali as the agent to arrange for the literature to be disseminated southward into Nyasaland. The project misfired. Uhlmann

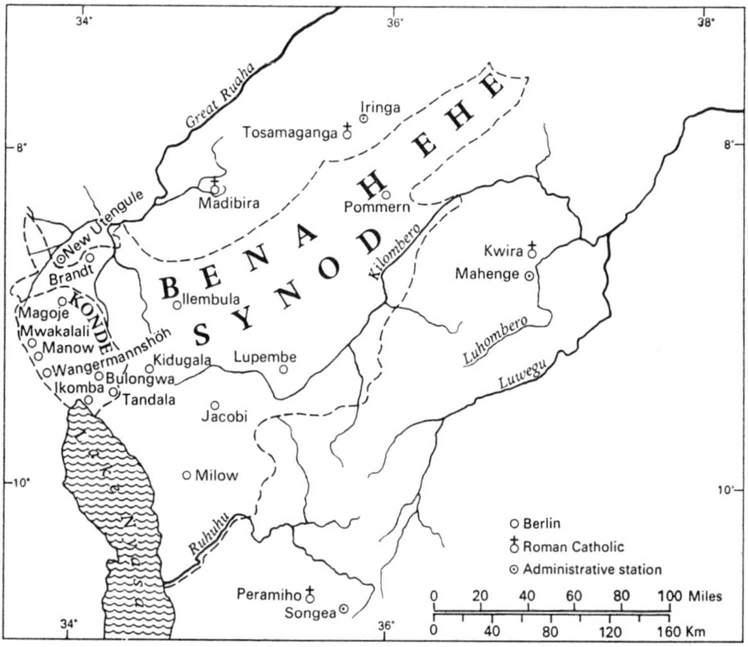

Map VII Bena-Hehe and Konde Synods [1914]

was a pacifist and in refusing on grounds on conscience to collaborate in any call for *jihad*, he received firm support from his colleagues.[2]

The cloud of official disfavour at missionary defiance dissipated somewhat when Gemuseus, having closed the Rungwe School in 1915 for lack of funds, became a contractor to supply grain for the local garrison. By a shrewd choice of barter goods and areas not already exposed to such demands, he soon became the most successful of the commissary agents in the district, at least until enough money had

[1] Mwase, Simon, *Strike a Blow and Die*, ed. R. Rotberg (Cambridge, 1967). Schnee Circular, 14 Mar. 1915 (T.N.A. IX A 16).

[2] Gemuseus, 'Mittelschule, 1914–1916'.

been earned to enable the reopening of his school at the beginning of 1916. The new school session continued but a short while, however, for beginning in March 1916, German East Africa received a co-ordinated invasion from three sides, Smuts attacking from the north, the Belgians from the west, and Northey from the south-west. As Northey advanced, the defending forces withdrew, employing guerrilla tactics which kept the British from being able to claim a total victory. The British occupied New Langenburg and the mission stations of the Nyasa Province and Konde Synod without opposition.[1]

The missionaries had clustered together with their families, the Berliners at Magoje in Buwanji, the Moravians at Rungwe, to await events. From there, they were called in, briefly paroled, and then detained for deportation. The determination to purge enemy missionaries, as opposed to allowing them to remain at their posts on parole as Smuts did in the northern parts of the territory, came about because of the conditions in the Southern Highlands, where missionaries were the most widely influential of European agencies.[2] Northey looked upon missionaries as a 'danger and a weakness', believing that their stations were centres of enemy supply and intelligence and necessary to his own forces as military camps and hospitals.[3] Altogether, the Commander opted for a thorough campaign in the south-western sector, the keynote of which could be taken from his early criticism that the British in the preceding years on the Rhodesian front had been excessively inactive. Northey, like von Lettow-Vorbeck, believed that offensive action alone secured defences.[4] This aggressive attitude continued to prevail well after the decision to remove German nationals. As the Moravians awaited their transportation down the lake from Mwaya, they had opportunities to communicate with Nyakyusa Christians, one of whom, with prescience, declared: 'If the enemy treats you in this way, how will they treat us?'[5]

To understand the relationship between the British and the Christians of the Langenburg District, a grasp of both political and military backgrounds is called for. The political officers assigned to the South-

[1] The literature about military aspects of the war is enormous, but a return to the original documents is well rewarded.

[2] See Wright, 'German Evangelical Missions', p. 253.

[3] Northey to C.O., 7 July 1916 (C.O. 691/1). Northey War Diary, 1 Oct. 1916 (W.O. 95/5329).

[4] Northey War Diary, 21 Apr. 1916 (W.O. 95/5329).

[5] Gemuseus, O., 'Erinnerungen von Bruder Oskar Gemuseus vom Sommer 1916 im damals deutschen Nyassa-Gebiet' (Herrnhut Nachlass Gemuseus).

ern Occupied Territory were headed by Hector Duff, Chief Secretary of the Nyasaland Government. Given the manner in which official attitudes towards religious organizations in Nyasaland had hardened in the aftermath of the Chilembwe Rising, Duff's support of the Northey policy towards missionaries and the subsequent suspicion of African teachers and leaders of both the Moravian and Lutheran communities, was almost inevitable.[1]

From the military point of view, the entire region continued to be insecure so long as the German force remained at large and highly mobile. The men of Rungwe were obliged to turn out for labour as porters, as the British extended their activities through the Livingstone Mountains and into Iringa District supply lines. Hector Duff had the task of deploying his subordinate political officers in such a way as to assure this flow of manpower, while at the same time attempting to impress the Nyakyusa with the impartiality of British justice.[2] Standard attitudes generated by war propaganda had led him to think of himself as the bearer of a superior administrative tradition, but the cruelty of at least one of his subordinates seemed more evident to Christians than benevolence. Nor could the back-log of disputes left undischarged by a preoccupied German administrator be attended to at once, owing to the war situation. Altogether, the years 1916 and 1917 saw little stabilization of colonial conditions in Rungwe.

Left to their own devices, the Christians responded in a variety of ways. Notwithstanding the tensions of the whole situation and the absence of missionaries, a remarkable stability prevailed in the Church. The one outbreak of real syncretism was transient. This crisis occurred at Kyimbila at a time not precisely dated, but probably about the end of 1916. Testimony gathered afterwards by Gemuseus enabled him to reconstruct the affair in the following way:

> Not long after we were deported, the call went out through all Kondeland: Come to Kyimbila, where the Holy Ghost has appeared! From great distances the Christians came to observe the wonder. What had happened? A youth of perhaps thirteen [or] fourteen years had fallen into a trance and spoke in other tongues, especially German, which he had never learned. The students from the Rungwe Middle School could understand him. Now an evil confusion arose in the Kyimbila congregation. To be specific, an elder and a teacher, formerly a student in my school in Rungwe,

[1] See Shepperson, G., and Price, T., *Independent African* (Edinburgh, 1958), ch. 8.

[2] Duff Report, 15 Sept. 1916 (C.O. 525/69).

> encouraged this 'medium', as the youth may well be designated, to appear in a communion service. Others, especially some women and girls, joined in, became caught up in ecstasy, and ran about without any sort of clothing. Thus the movement went rapidly downhill to the demoniac, even to a shocking travesty of communion. . . . [1]

A cool analysis of the forces at work in this scene could be rendered in part because the phenomenon did not spread or have any apparent permanent effect upon the larger body of Christians. That the movement disappeared as rapidly as it came, Gemuseus credited to the firm, quiet actions of elders from the neighbouring Rutenganio congregation, who came to restore order. The backers of the medium yielded to the majority preferring orthodoxy, the teacher later migrating to South Africa, and the medium himself withdrew to a remote mountain village, never again to have anything to do with Christianity or trances.[2]

Quite clearly, the months after the British occupation did not create the kind of pressures productive of schism. Members either lapsed, or coalesced more firmly in a defensive posture, with their leadership intact and ethical norms sufficiently internalized to lend stability. Whether the British political officers knew of the Kyimbila incident is doubtful for at that time the Christian communities do not seem to have been so closely observed as they were in 1917.

On New Year's Day 1917, the spare military prose of Northey's dispatches reported one aspect of the suffering endured by the men who carried munitions and supplies over the mountains into Ubena and Songea: 'All this time the supply difficulties have been getting greater; many carriers desert on the road over the Livingstone Range and many die of the cold.'[3] Christians began to make lists of their kin who never returned from this labour, and their numbers were disproportionately great because as a semi-autonomous community with dubious loyalty, they had been most heavily drafted. By bearing down on Christians, Duff and his assistant for Nyakyusa country, Major Wells, were enabled to placate non-Christian princes. Typically, some of the princes attempted to ingratiate themselves at the expense of others, by reporting on Christians. Polokoto, near the Rungwe Station, had a special reputation for this. Sakalija Mwakasungula retired to the protection of his old prince, Mwankanje, who granted permission and gave materials for the construction of a chapel.

[1] Gemuseus, '50 Jahre' (Herrnhut, Nachlass Gemuseus).
[2] ibid. [3] Northey War Diary, 1 Jan. 1917 (W.O. 95/5329).

From his independent centre at Kikota, Sakalija could in time move throughout the countryside to encourage Christians.[1] The initiative displayed in this move was duplicated many times and a number of individuals in Ubena, too, operated as autonomous yet orthodox evangelist-teachers. Those who remained at mission stations in Langenburg District fared much worse. In the early months of 1917, relations between the British and the Nyakyusa deteriorated owing to the hard times and continued calls for labour. When a detachment of German forces retreated from the direction of Tabora and passed through the Safwa corridor, the charge was made that Christian teachers had given information to the enemy. No evidence was ever produced to prove this allegation and Christians believed that Wells had maliciously invented the story. Under martial law, however, it sufficed to assert that the teachers were a continuing source of treachery. Responding to the abuse of their fellow captives, the first group to be deported declared their innocence and stated aptly: 'We are sacrifices in a European war.' Two leaders from each of eleven Moravian and Lutheran stations, the cream of the educated Christians, were eventually arrested and transported to Zomba, where they remained from March 1917 to the middle of 1919.[2]

Meanwhile the Christians in Langenburg continued to be regarded with anxiety. Assemblies were prohibited, and Sakalija remembered an order given out to all authorities to the effect that 'if you find them at prayer, we will punish them, because they are praying for their Europeans.'[3] British actions heightened the sense of identity as Christians for some, but not all members. Given the dangers of being a Christian, many men particularly in Mbozi and at Ipyana, on the western Nyakyusa lake shore, took a second wife and opted out of the system of restraints associated with the Christian ethic. One Nyiha chief sponsored a tribal dance and punished Christians who disobeyed his order to attend. Among the Safwa, certain Christians left the Utengule station and later became actively anti-Christian.[4] In general, the period before the coming of African and Scottish missionary support may be considered one of sorting out, when the more Christianized areas such as Rungwe demonstrated the extent to which the new values had been assimilated, while the tenuous Christian

[1] Gemuseus, *Sakalija Mwakasungula*, p. 13. [2] Gemuseus, 'Erinnerungen'.
[3] Gemuseus, *Sakalija Mwakasungula*, p. 13.
[4] Z.f.E.S. xxiv (1933/4), 191f. Gemuseus, '50 Jahre' (Herrnhut, Nachlass Gemuseus).

impact in such areas as Usafwa and Unyiha made it difficult for the Christian communities to sustain themselves.

Naturally the Scottish missionaries in Nyasaland concerned themselves with the fate of the mission fields in the occupied territory. James Hetherwick, head of the Church of Scotland Mission (Blantyre), became alarmed immediately by reports that the German missionaries would not be allowed to return to the field. Dissatisfied with the 'vacillation' displayed by the Governor of Nyasaland about the future disposition of the stations, Hetherwick appealed to Laws at Livingstonia for co-operation in caring for the vacancies, and applied pressure through metropolitan channels for a recognized extension of the Presbyterian sphere.[1] Dr. Arthur of the Church of Scotland, Kikuyu, telegraphed in support: 'suggest co-operation Nyasaland Livingstonia utmost importance Central African Presbyterianism recommend Hetherwick tackle situation.'[2] To J. H. Oldham, Secretary to the Continuation Committee of the Edinburgh Conference and Convener of the newly organized Conference of British Missionary Societies, this claim looked like an incipient ecclesiastical scramble. His alternative plan, calling for an overall, preliminary allocation, received approval from the Colonial Office and from Horace Byatt, the Administrator of the Occupied Territory in East Africa, who wished to see responsibility lodged clearly, albeit temporarily and provisionally, with loyal agencies.[3]

The Nyasaland Administration, after the Chilembwe affair, had its own standards of security by which all religious organizations were suspect. Whatever plan might be drawn up and applied elsewhere, Nyasaland missionaries were kept at arms length until after the arrest and deportation of the 'unreliable' Christian leaders. For purely medical purposes, a physician from Livingstonia, Dr. Prentice, had been called into Langenburg to help cope with an outbreak of bubonic plague. Other problems—the unabated commandeering of food and porterage, a *rinderpest* epidemic, and disillusionment with the effectiveness of British power to conclude the war—also contributed to Duff's considerations, as he came around to the view that official personnel could not manage alone. He resolved to ask for a few British or Allied missionaries 'of the right type' to counteract the

[1] Hetherwick to McLachlan, 7 Aug. 1916 (EH 8).

[2] Arthur to Ogilvy, quoted in Oldham to Steel-Maitland, 24 Jan. 1917 (C.O. 691/13).

[3] Byatt to C.O., 3 May 1917 (C.O. 691/10). See also Oldham's Memorandum on Spheres, 23 Mar. 1917 (T.N.A. S.M.P. 04).

influence exercised over Africans accustomed to mission tutelage, by 'the half educated native teachers, *capitaos* and other ex-mission subordinates and hangers-on who have been left behind.'[1] With this, in mind and expecting the hostilities to be over in a few months, Prentice extolled the magnificence of the field awaiting the Livingstonia Mission.

Representatives from Blantyre, Livingstonia, and the U.M.C.A. sat down to work out details of occupation following the outline proposed by Oldham, whereby the U.M.C.A. would occupy the Songea District, the Blantyre Mission—Iringa, and Livingstonia—Langenburg. The fixing of concurrent religious and political boundaries entailed the partition of the Berlin fields among all three British societies, which Laws denounced, but the others preferred.[2] This partition did not come at once, for continuing hostilities revived Duff's reservations about allowing white missionaries into the occupied war zone. In November 1917, following a conference with Laws, he agreed to admit African agents into the Langenburg District west of the Livingstone Mountains.[3] Because Songea and Iringa remained entirely out-of-bounds for Africans as well as Europeans, the teachers from Livingstonia entered Rungwe a year earlier than the agents of the U.M.C.A. or Blantyre Mission moved towards their new regions.

Laws appealed to the Nyasaland congregations to support the Langenburg effort as their own foreign mission and they did so, yet material support for the large undertaking remained inadequate during the African missionary period. Nevertheless, three evangelists, two carpenters, and three other helpers were sent north in mid December 1917 to make headquarters at Rutenganio and to concern themselves with Rungwe and Usafwa.[4] Mbozi and Unyiha, meanwhile, were reached by men from Mwenzo. At the time of their arrival, the mission stations had been unoccupied for a year and a half, furniture and materials of military utility had been stripped, and the plantations were left to rot, as they seemed to have no commercial value. Politically, the Christian community had been accused of pro-German sympathies and deprived of many natural leaders. Duff's

[1] Duff to Gov. Zomba, 25 June 1917 (C.O. 525/73). Ibid., 15 Nov. 1917 in dispatch 21 Jan. 1918 (C.O. 525/78).

[2] Bp. Fisher to James Reid, 6 Oct. 1917 (N.L.S. 7816).

[3] Laws to Fisher, 20 Nov. 1917 (N.L.S. 7816).

[4] Laws Report, 19 Dec. 1917, quoted in Com. Minute, 16 Apr. 1918 (N.L.S. 7816). For a general physical description see *P.A.* (1917), 28f.

motive in allowing the Nyasa to come was manifestly political, in that he wished to spike the potential for 'false prophets' and to introduce benevolent agencies to disprove the German propaganda that the British were only malicious militarists. Confidence in the British was not a Christian virtue when Yoram Mphande, leader of the Livingstonia party, took up residence. He, his family, and colleagues, were subjected to hostility and boycotts of food until he gradually established his bona fides.[1] This he did in a variety of ways, by sharing the economic depression of the Rungwe peoples, by interceding on behalf of the Christians with officials, and by establishing excellent relations with the teachers still at liberty. The task of approaching local church leaders was a delicate one. A breakthrough in this respect occurred in April 1918, when Mphande called Sakalija Mwakasungula, Fiwombe Kilindu, and Lazarus Mwanjisi as well as three others, for a conference at Rutenganio. Not only did he earn the respect of these leaders, he also recognized them as missionary agents, thus paving the way for their full integration into the Livingstonia establishment.[2] The tack and comity of the Nyasa Presbyterians, as well as the large-mindedness of local leadership in the tempestuous Rungwe area, did much to preserve the cohesion of the Christian community at this critical juncture.

After the Armistice came in November 1918, five teachers from the Blantyre Mission, one from each of its major stations, came into the Iringa District under the guidance of Yoram Mphande. A different kind of problem existed in this relief effort, for the sphere of the Church of Scotland lay a great distance from its headquarters at the south of the lake, and the scattered stations of the Bena-Hehe Synod were situated days away from one another. To officials, the Nyasas seemed little more than caretakers, but to the Bena they were welcome helpers. When A. M. Anderson, the missionary from Zomba came in 1919 to inspect the Presbyterian spheres, he met extremely demonstrative crowds of Bena. In the course of visiting twenty stations in Langenburg and Iringa, he baptized two hundred and fifty people and administered communion to seven hundred. Anderson returned home captivated: 'The native Christians so appealed to me on the spot to do my utmost for them that I had to promise, and eventually I had no choice but to offer for the work myself in the conviction that the door has been opened to us and we cannot but enter and do our

[1] Mackenzie Report, 5 June 1920 (E.H. 23).
[2] Gemuseus, *Sakalija Mwakasungula*, p. 14.

best.'[1] Before his new assignment, Anderson used his leave in Scotland in 1920 to carry on a personal crusade on behalf of Iringa, presenting the area as one officially delivered to the Church of Scotland and part of the imperial 'Legacy of Duty'.[2] His personal enthusiasm always exceeded the capacity of his society to respond, and throughout his career in the Southern Highlands, he seems to have consistently received a half of what he requested, as for example when only two rather than four European missionaries were assigned to Iringa.[3]

The man picked to head the Livingstonia Mission in 1920 was D. R. Mackenzie. As a former missionary at Karonga he had a thorough grasp of the language and customs of the Ngonde–Nyakyusa peoples. The new white personnel chose not to encroach upon the parish work of Nyasa and local evangelists, who continued to have primary contact in Ukinga and Usafwa while the Scots concentrated on clinics and schools in the larger centres. The physical condition of mission buildings in 1920 left much to be desired, for the decay caused by neglect, official occupation, and vandalism had been capped in May 1919 by a series of earth tremors. According to official reports, the tremors made wrecks of the mission stations of Madahani, Bulongwa, Tandala, Mwaya, Mwakaleli, and Kyimbila.[4] According to Mackenzie, however, Rungwe Station had suffered most: 'Rungwe is the tragedy of the Moravian Mission. There is not a trace of either church or school, as these buildings were built of sun-dried bricks, and when the roofs fell in, the bricks quickly returned to their original mud.'[5]

Both Mackenzie and Anderson in 1920 assumed that the Presbyterian Church would become permanently established in Tanganyika. The Free Church had strong evidence to support this expectation, for both Gemuseus and Nauhaus had written to Laws specifically entrusting the Berlin and Moravian congregations to the care of Livingstonia. Subsequent moves had been cleared with the British Moravians, who requested a continuation of the arrangements and promised to support the work by supplying or subsidizing two missionaries.[6]

[1] Anderson to Oldham, 18 Sept. 1920 (E.H. 23). See also Iringa District Report, 31 Mar. 1921 (T.N.A. S.M.P. 1733).

[2] Anderson, A. M., *New Mission in Africa*, pamphlet, Nov. 1920 (E.H. 13).

[3] Church of Scotland, *Report of the Foreign Mission Committee, 1919*, pp. 9f., 44f.

[4] Hollis to C.O., 13 June 1919 (C.O. 691/22).

[5] Mackenzie Report, 5 June 1920 (E.H. 23).

[6] United Free Church of Scotland, *Report on Foreign Missions, 1919*, p. 32.

For the Church of Scotland, however, there had been neither invitation nor confirmation from the Berliners. Complications in its position arose as a consequence of the Treaty of Versailles, whereby, under Article 438, property of enemy missions was reserved from the operation of general economic clauses calling for the liquidation of German property. Instead, trustees of the same denomination as the former mission were to hold the property. Interpreted legalistically, Lutherans could claim a prior right to Lutheran fields. To add to the criteria for legitimate succession, it was decided at the Crans Meeting in 1920 that the preferences of German societies should be considered. The American Lutherans, although they were the obvious co-religionists who might claim denominational rights, had their hands full in northern Tanganyika, and specifically renounced any intention of entering Iringa. Other societies, however, came forward with claims; the C.M.S. because of the ethnographic and geographic contiguity of Ugogo, and the Dutch Reformed Church because the Berliners had made them their preferred deputies.[1]

Axenfeld plainly did not care for the Church of Scotland, whose leaders had in the heat of war made extremely hostile statements about German missions. At a widely publicized meeting in Glasgow, the Chairman of the Church of Scotland Foreign Mission Committee had stated that German missionaries shared 'the fatal spirit of megalomania' that ruined their nation, and from being a glory had become 'a hissing and a shame'. Ironically, this statement came just after the German missionaries had delivered an eminently international memorandum to their Colonial Secretary.[2] In discussion with Oldham in 1920, the Berliners made it clear that they regarded the Iringa arrangements to be illegitimate. Oldham, who appreciated every nuance of the situation, advised the Scots to 'go right ahead', while also warning that the 'Lutheran character' of the Church must be upheld. To this, Anderson responded that no African would be able to define the difference between Lutheran and Presbyterian forms except in petty details.[3]

Ecclesiastical disparities had a more sensitive reading in Rungwe, where the Lutheran practices seemed more ceremonial than the

[1] C.B.M.S. Memorandum, 9 Mar. 1921 (C.O. 691/54).

[2] See Confidential Memorandum for Dr. Solf, 18 May 1917 (D.E.M.R. R.K.A.) and 'Declaration' by German Members of the Edinburgh Conference Continuation Committee [1917] (Gibson Papers).

[3] Oldham to McLachlan, 13 and 14 Sept. 1920 (E.H. 8). Anderson to Oldham, 18 Sept. 1920 (E.H. 20).

Moravian ones. While respecting the Lutheran character, Mackenzie hoped to level differences and unify the church in the district, by making the different congregations more aware of one another and by developing a single centre for advanced education. In order to preserve the opportunity for convergence, he postponed action on petitions from people of the Moravian sphere for full church sessions and a Presbyterian constitution, until the stationing of a European missionary in the Berlin side should produce similar wishes.[1]

Reconstruction of the missionary effort, having been put off by war conditions, uncertainty of tenure, and the confusion in the new British mandate administration, finally began when the Livingstonia, Blantyre, and U.M.C.A. custodianship of Berlin Mission property was recognized by the Tanganyika Trust, a special adjunct of the Conference of British Missionary Societies created to hold the assets of German missions until a final disposition could be made. Reconstruction took place in much the same way in Iringa and in the Rungwe–Mbeya Districts, being characterized by the revival of education and helper training, an extension of activities into frontier areas particularly as a defence against the Roman Catholics, and perhaps most significantly, by formal measures of increased congregational self-government. The primary means of re-establishing contact with teachers and catechists was the refresher course, for in both areas, an initial rustiness and reserve had to be overcome. At the end of 1921, Anderson organized a six-week course for forty-four Bena teachers and from that time more and more of the prominent teachers made known their willingness to work under him. The revival of the mission staff could not, however, keep pace with the vast demand for village schools. Each month brought added requests. Between March and August 1921, Mackenzie reported an increase of from 38 to 57 schools in his area, and from Iringa came a statement that every petty chief had petitioned for 'Mr. Anderson's schools'.[2]

Both supervisors conducted boarding-schools at their homes, in which English became the featured language. The whole-hearted teaching of a European language belonged to the Scottish missionary practice. The British administration in Tanganyika also favoured its national language far more than the Germans had theirs, so that the education policies of the two agencies coincided without friction.

[1] U.F.C., Committee Minute, 16 Nov. 1920 (E.H. 23).

[2] Mackenzie to Daly, 26 Aug. 1921 (N.L.S. 7816). C.S., *Foreign Mission Report 1922*, pp. 58, 63.

Mackenzie foresaw a future time when his students would need English for their participation in the Presbyterian Synod of Central Africa. As for Swahili, he recognized its value as a territorial language but criticized its culture outlook as meagre: 'For such purposes English is an open door; Swahili is a partially open peephole. . . . Swahili will keep the people in mental and spiritual bondage.'[1] Anderson took a more political line in his boarding-school attended by the well-born, including relatives of Merere and Kiwanga. His ardent advocacy of English on nationalistic grounds was expressed in the school's curriculum and in an extra course held at midday for Nyasa and Bena staff members at Kidugala.[2]

Once the congregations began to show renewed life, questions about the direction of church development became more urgent. Mackenzie had come to Langenburg intending to discourage exclusive Christian villages. When he broached this idea to the Moravians, they raised no objection, for they were more aware than Mackenzie of the efforts of their brethren to achieve a parish base beyond the mission compounds. Meyer, too, would have taken the opportunity for a new effort to relocate the balance of religious efforts away from mission land. But Berlin stations also entered the picture and Mackenzie prided himself on striking at the roots of the old excessive paternalism. In an allied reform, he advocated freedom of marriage, ending the stricture against marriage between Christians and non-Christians. These measures represented no real discontinuity with the theory of the German missions. It was rather the enthusiasm of the new missionaries from Livingstonia and their fresh approach, with its practical evidence of liberal attitudes towards African leadership, that contributed to their popularity. Burgeoning congregations included prominent chiefs. Numbers of people returned to communion.[3]

In Iringa, Anderson did not call for reform of the station pattern. Although it was impossible to compel all the residents who had dispersed to return, he attempted to follow them up. The three great stations, Lupembe, Kidugala, and Ilembula came through the war in good communal condition, thanks to the *jumbe*s Nigmann had forced upon the Mission. The efficiency of the system displayed itself

[1] Mackenzie to Ashcroft, 29 Apr. 1924 (N.L.S. 7818).

[2] C.S., *Foreign Mission Report 1923*, pp. 60f.

[3] Mackenzie to Ashcroft, 23 Feb. and 28 Mar. 1921 (N.L.S. 7816). Ibid., 17 Apr. 1924 (N.L.S. 7818).

best at Kidugala, where the house and garden of the *jumbe* Lupituko were maintained by the people among whom he enforced spiritual and civil obedience.[1]

Revival began once more to take place through evangelistic campaigns. The standard pattern of the Nyasaland Church was carried into Rungwe by teams of evangelists radiating from Karonga. The local Christians responded quickly and carried the practice into their own hinterlands. Voluntary participation in such efforts had also been known in German times, particularly when wide areas might otherwise be occupied by the Catholics. The Roman Catholic challenge in the early 1920s was strong everywhere. To meet it, volunteers from Utengule worked in High Safwa, deaconnesses from Ilembula occupied Brandt, and Lutherans in southern Ubena rallied to meet the usual emergency in Ulanga.[2] Whereas officials in the Rungwe District looked on benignly as the Church became invigorated, those in Mahenge and Iringa took umbrage at Protestant expansion, which they saw as a challenge to administrative and tribal authorities. Anderson started an English school in Iringa town in 1922 despite the objections of the District Officer, and in the next year concluded that his sphere called for an extensive rather than intensive coverage if it were to be preserved from Catholic advances facilitated by official preference.[3]

The frontier struggle in the Mkasu sub-district of Mahenge offered a particularly severe example of the conflicts which arose. The Capuchins had received administrative blessing to establish schools in Mkasu, but successive deputations of Bena petitioned Anderson at Kidugala to send teachers. Lupembe, as ever, was a strategic base for operations in Ulanga, so Anderson assigned his European colleague, Watson, to that station in order to release Ellerton, the Nyasa teacher formerly in charge, and as many Bena catechists as possible to occupy Mkasu.[4] The District Officer was outraged by the insolence of the teachers, the aggressive behaviour of Anderson and his Nyasa agents, and the generally autocratic way in which the Protestant contingent claimed the area. For the sake of order, administrators deposed one offending teacher and appealed in vain to Anderson to postpone reopening Protestant schools. His

[1] C.S., *Foreign Mission Report 1922*, pp. 57, 59. Ibid., *1923*, p. 62.

[2] C.S., *Foreign Mission Report 1924*, p. 61. U.F.C., *Foreign Mission Report 1924*, p. 95.

[3] D.O. Iringa to Acting C.S., 18 Sept. 1922 (T.N.A. S.M.P. 1228).

[4] Anderson to McLachlan, 23 Nov. 1923 (N.L.S. 7607).

reply demanded not only that the old Lutheran bush schools but also their surroundings must be recognized as belonging to the Protestant sphere. The Mkasu incident closed in 1924 when formal religious partition was declared to be illegal and the Protestant advantage in popularity could serve as a reliable indicator of whose schools would be established.[1]

The question of how far the Presbyterians should introduce their form of church government came under full debate in 1923, on the occasion of a visit by Frank Ashcroft, the Secretary of the United Free Church Mission. The moment for constituting the Presbyterian Church of Central Africa was approaching, and it was possible that the Southern Highlands congregations would make up a Presbytery within the Synod of Central Africa. As a preliminary to organizing a regular Presbytery, Ashcroft encouraged the formation of a joint missionary conference in Tanganyika and the election of sessions or councils of elders in the various congregations.[2]

Ashcroft also had other perspectives to keep in focus. He represented the Tanganyika Trust and had made trips to Germany to confer with his society's predecessors, the Basel Mission, over the Gold Coast, as well as with the Berliners over East Africa. The task of the conciliator came naturally to Ashcroft, but it had practical justifications too, arising from the inability of the Scottish missions to fully supply the required staff and funds to maintain their activities in Tanganyika. Employing the precedent of co-operation in the Gold Coast where individual Germans were employed by the Presbyterians, he sounded the Berliners about sending out some of their former missionaries. Once in East Africa, he found his own missionaries reluctant to go along with this admixture of nationalities, and Anderson adamantly opposed any work with Germans. The Iringa supervisor asserted resentfully that the Livingstonia Mission proposed to bring in the Berliners 'behind his back' in Ukinga. Because he imagined that a joint missionary council might one day be dominated by Germans, Anderson refused to establish this link between Iringa and the Livingstonia sphere.[3]

Anderson also acted cautiously in the matter of ordaining elders. The form of sessions and ordination was introduced, but only Nyasa men were in fact installed. In the Bena-Hehe area, congrega-

[1] (T.N.A. S.M.P. 1733, S.M.P. 15330).
[2] U.F.C., *Foreign Mission Report 1923*, pp. 121 f.
[3] Mackenzie to Ashcroft, 17 Apr. 1924 (N.L.S. 7818).

tional councils of 'deacons' retained much the same character and status as elders had under the Berlin Mission. That is, the enhanced authority explicitly granted to elders ordained under the Presbyterian constitution did not come to Bena churchmen. The *status quo* did not remain entirely inviolate, however. An important departure from former practices supporting paternalism took place when at Anderson's instigation councils reluctantly voted to require that contributions to the church should be in cash rather than the conventional service of labour to the Mission.[1]

In the western sphere, Mackenzie went through with the election of elders, stopping short of formal ordination. This decision implied no lack of confidence in the capacities of the local people, especially the Nyakyusa, but reflected the indecision of certain leading Christians as to whether to commit themselves to the Central African Church or to await the possible return of their former missionaries. By one account, leaders from the main Moravian congregations attended the meeting of the Presbytery in Livingstonia in 1923 and in the presence of Ashcroft were questioned about their preferences. Sakalija Mwakasungula, the respected older man among them, led the group to a unanimous decision to await further developments.[2] Sakalija's role at that point and later is of great interest because he was to a degree politically neutral, as the men who had been exiled were not. Ambokile, to take the example of a prominent church leader who had endured detention and enforced personal service for South African officers in Zomba, had returned to his home in 1919 to encounter the same hostile official and the sad tactic of intimidation. Wells at this time said that German missionaries were being punished and ransomed, and that any statement of continued loyalty to them would be punishable by a year of imprisonment. Before releasing Ambokile and the others, he made them hand over the clothing in which they had come from Zomba and told the sick men to dress themselves in banana leaves. At the end of this passage in his autobiography, Ambokile concluded 'and so he punished us. We however thought we would have a reckoning with him if the Germans returned to the country.'[3] In 1923, when the Christians received the first intimation that some German missionaries might indeed return, the Rungwe District Officer protested to Dar es Salaam and cited

[1] C.S., *Foreign Mission Report 1923*, p. 62. Ibid., *1924*, pp. 61 f.
[2] Gemuseus, *Sakalija Mwakasungula*, p. 15.
[3] Gemuseus, 'Erinnerungen'.

the current prophecy that 'the British Government is shortly to be supplanted by another Government' as evidence of the political significance that would be attributed to any breach in the exclusion of the ex-enemies.[1]

The confusion of the German administration and missionaries resulted as much as anything from their association in the thought and actions of British officials. Some men who had suffered also, may have identified Church and State, but Sakalija represented those who had stayed behind and worked happily with the Presbyterians.

Again, on 6 August 1924, Mackenzie put the question of joining the Central African Church to an assembly of congregational representatives in the Moravian area. A minority were at that time opposed, and as ordination to elder status was tied to the proposition and was much desired, he decided to hold them back until the next meeting, in hopes that unanimity would then be achieved. When the representatives reconvened three weeks later, the mood was unchanged.[2] At the same time, the Livingstonia Mission made an impressive demonstration of its willingness to promote Africans to the ministry by arranging a large festival at Kyimbila for the laying on of hands, ordaining Yoram Mphande who thereafter assumed full responsibility for Utengule and its surroundings.[3] This gesture had its effect when the Moravians resumed full charge of the province, but pending the return of Gemuseus many preferred to watch and wait.

Just as Yoram Mphande distinguished himself in the Utengule area, so George Nyasuru ably supervised the parishes of the Livingstone Range. Political experience in the mountains did not entail persecution of Christians as in Rungwe. Yet special social and economic factors arose out of the war. In the early stages, due to the blockage of imports, the wheat cultivated in the neighbourhood of missions as a peasant crop suddenly commanded a large internal market. A period of prosperity as the granary of the besieged inhabitants of German East Africa was followed by the era of the campaigns of Northey, whose supply routes criss-crossed Ukinga and brought full employment. The military roads decayed after the cessation of hostilities, and the area reverted to isolation.[4] Frantic activity followed

[1] D.O. Rungwe to C.S., 1923 (T.N.A. S.M.P. 0273).

[2] Mackenzie to Ashcroft, 12 Aug. 1924 (N.L.S. 7818). Gemuseus, O., 'Lebensbild Ulisibisya Kibona aus Isoko' (Herrnhut, Nachlass Gemuseus).

[3] See U.F.C., *Foreign Mission Report 1924*, p. 95.

[4] *B.M.B.* (1919), 73. Northey Diary, 1 Jan. 1917 (W.O. 95/5329).

by rapid decline in 1919 stimulated a spiritual movement which influenced the Church. In another response to the transitional mood, a prophetess achieved a great following, part of which entered the Christian camp when Mackenzie called upon authorities to deport the leader as a troublemaker. Nyasuru had to contend with a very lively religious situation with only periodic European backing, carried out by the circuits made by Dr. Brown from Itete to perform the sacraments. Brown baptized a hundred and seventy-three Kinga at Bulongwa in 1922 and two hundred and fifty-three people of Buwanji at Magoje in 1923.[1] In that year, consistent with the plans to form a presbytery, the Bulongwa and Magoje congregations elected church sessions and looked forward to this advance in church government.

In the Berlin fields, Anderson declared that the people of his area were 'much afraid' of the prospect of the return of their old missionaries and stated that the congregations immediately concerned were cool. The Kinga and Wanji church sessions made plain their preference: their delegates petitioned the Presbyterians to remain. When questioned, the Kinga declared that they did not object to the Germans as individuals in Livingstonia service, implying that personalities could be subordinated if there were constitutional security; but the Wanji were uncompromisingly opposed.[2]

In Iringa, Anderson was always inclined to mix politics and religion and it is hard to extract from his reports a sense of what Africans actually thought. His own opinion was clear and the threat of some Berliners returning to the Southern Highlands revolutionized his relations with officials, who suddenly became part of his common front against the greater enemy. As he said: 'Frankly, I see *great danger*, and would not be afraid to tell the Authorities, in the proposed placing of Germans in a place like Milow so absolutely in the hinterland of Tanganyika Territory. The Germans have their eye on Kidugala and to have them at both our elbows would be unsafe.'[3] Anderson was prepared to have a showdown with the Livingstonia Mission in this matter and had support from Hetherwick.

The Berliners also proved to be adamant in their grievances. As the Lutheran–Presbyterian attitudes hardened, Mackenzie looked on with dismay and regret.

[1] U.F.C., *Foreign Mission Report 1921*, p. 41. Ibid., *1923*, p. 108.
[2] Mackenzie to Ashcroft, 15 Oct. 1924 (N.L.S. 7818).
[3] Anderson to McLachlan, 29 Jan. 1924 (N.L.S. 7607).

1924 was a year of mounting uncertainty in the matter of missionary occupation in Berlin fields. In May, the Leipzig, Herrnut, Bethel, and Berlin Directors had met at Edinburgh House, London, to discuss with Oldham the next moves towards their desired return to East Africa. From that time, it became increasingly obvious that they would be able to return, even if it meant sending individual missionaries under the guarantee of allied missions, because of the continuing statutory disabilities on ex-enemies. All of this negotiation left out the German Moravians, for the British Province held their property, not the Tanganyika Trust, and the consistent position had been one of encouragement of Livingstonia. At the end of 1924, it was proposed to lease the property to the Scots for a period of years, much as the Tanganyika Trust had done with the stations in its charge. Meanwhile the intention of employing Gemuseus came to fruition, and he returned to a triumphal reception in Rungwe in March 1925. As Mackenzie departed on leave by the same steamer that brought the old schoolmaster, the impression of a larger transfer was probably created. Hoping to bring the Jansa family back to the field, Gemuseus unearthed a cache of silver, 11,000 rupies, buried by Meyer in 1916. This action made the sensitive Mackenzie uneasy and 'morally challenged'.[1] Even before the German Societies meeting at Bethel in 1925 pledged to give one per cent of their income to enable the Herrnhuters to resume work in the Nyasa Province, therefore, the Livingstonia Supervisor and some of his missionaries had begun to reconcile themselves to stepping back.

The opening of the door to the Germans swiftly resolved the stalemate between the Blantyre and Berlin Missions. The home authorities of the Church of Scotland Mission withdrew from the embarrassing position of seeming to usurp the Iringa field, stating that the occupation had always been accepted as temporary. The order to withdraw in favour of the Germans stunned Anderson, who took a number of steps to forestall its execution. In an open letter to ministers in Scotland, he appealed over the head of the Committee, justifying his action by suggesting that the Berliners could not effectively take care of the field.[2] He also petitioned Governor Cameron to reserve at least the newly developed areas around Iringa in eastern Uhehe, where the English school had been a success and the town offered a base

[1] Gemuseus, *Sakalija Mwakasungula*, p. 16. Mackenzie to Ashcroft, 30 Sept. 1925 (N.L.S. 7819).

[2] Anderson to McLachlan, 29 Aug. 1925 (N.L.S. 7608).

for serving migrant Presbyterians from Central Africa.[1] By this time, local administrators had come to regret the prospective reversion of Kidugala and end of Anderson's effective activities, but Cameron refused to interfere in matters to be regulated by the missions themselves.

No open split between Christians and missionaries occurred in the Southern Highlands as it did in Buhaya, where Methodist practices offended members who turned first to the C.M.S. and then to the Bethel Mission in preference.[2] Whereas in Buhaya a referendum had to be resorted to, in the Berlin area the opposition in the Livingstone Mountains was smoothed over, and elsewhere there were only a few protests against the retransfer of the churches. The most poignant of these, from the 'Christians of Kidugala', displayed personal loyalty to Anderson rather than opposition to the Germans.

> To your excellency we would address a few words. Our words are these. We, Christians, are all very greatly surprised to hear that our minister here has to go away from Kidugala. We have great grief since we heard he must leave us. Yes, now we tell you, Sir, surely it is not fitting that a man should leave his child before he is able to walk by himself alone. This truly describes our state to-day. See, how we are like a man whose father has died. He just sits down dejected (jijiji) with his heart dried up. We are like this in our hearts. Great and small children—all are the same. From every direction, North, South, East and West our eyes are turned to Kidugala.
>
> We received our Minister and welcomed him in that time when it was dark in all the Bena country. Then the darkness was taken away and the hidden things became clear. What are we to do now? Who will give us what we require as Christians? We rejoice always to receive the Word of God and the Sacrament.[3]

Two other documents were submitted anonymously in 1927 by discontented people in the Konde Synod, requesting the return of the Livingstonia missionaries, but by then the moment for an effective African reaction had passed.[4]

The decade of war and Presbyterian influence in the Southern Highlands, 1916–26, may be regarded as a time in which an effort was made to reorient the area towards Central Africa. This shift

[1] Anderson Memorandum [Oct. 1925] (T.N.A. S.M.P. 3632).

[2] See Hellberg, C. J., *Missions on a Colonial Frontier West of Lake Victoria* (Lund, 1965), pp. 169, 178ff.

[3] Kidugala Christians to Governor [Oct. 1925] (T.N.A. S.M.P. 3632).

[4] For a different perspective, see Ranger, T. O., 'Christian Independency in Tanzania: The Negative Case', in D. Barrett, ed., *African Initiatives in Religion* (Nairobi, 1971).

began with the invasion from Northern Rhodesia and the semi-autonomous administration of Hector Duff in the South-western Zone which continued virtually until 1919. The subsequent endeavours to integrate the Lutheran and Moravian congregations with the Church of Central Africa, had they succeeded, would have furthered the tendency to look south rather than north and east. Opposing forces existed from the start, however, in the form of political distaste for the British administration as opposed to the Scottish missionaries. The ambivalence towards Central Africa could not have been better demonstrated than in the hesitation at making an irrevocable church alliance. Had the returning representative of the former times been someone other than Gemuseus, feelings might have been different. But it was the educator, the advocate of the legitimate aspirations of local leadership, who first appeared. However distinguished the service of the Nyasas and the Scots, the element of incipient nationalism, in the stress on local resources and in resentment against the new form of colonialism, played a part in these events.

The interregnum was not a time of violent internal change in the Christian communities. Temperance proved to be the major issue left behind as a discrepancy between Presbyterian and Moravian versions of the Christian ethic. Otherwise, the Presbyterians bowed out with grace, having established an excellent record in reconstructing and encouraging congregations towards self-government, rebuilding a flourishing central and bush school system, and setting a standard of medical work in the Livingstonia sphere which the Germans could not sustain. There had been a war, and inflamed nationalist feelings had tended to exaggerate differences. Yet the Scots, with basically similar religious values, responded very much as had the Germans to the character and needs of the situation in the Southern Highlands.

CHAPTER VIII
German Restoration

THE Southern Highlands in 1925 were in the midst of an economic and political transformation. With self-conscious rhetoric about its special trust in the mandated territory, the British administration instituted the full system of Indirect Rule, under which African tribal authorities received both a defined jurisdiction and supervision far more uniform than in German times. Some chiefs used their powers to impose observance of traditional rituals upon Christians and for a time enjoyed the support of enthusiastic administrators who dabbled in ethnography. Eventually, however, the prerogatives of the Native Authorities and Native Courts became regularized in such a way as to uphold freedom of conscience and none attempted to reverse the process of change associated with Christianization. Many other changes belied the notion that African life continued in a primordial fashion. The economic situation was permanently altered at this time by an influx of European enterprise. With the prospectors coming to try their luck on the rediscovered Lupa goldfield near Lake Rukwa, and the strategists of European settlement eyeing the Southern Highlands as a piece of the 'white back-bone' of Africa, the region was involved in new complexities. No longer did missionaries and officials alone vie for ascendancy. Both African and commercial white interest figured as never before.

In religious terms, too, the Rungwe–Mbeya area was more open than it had been before the war. The older churches had experienced a very large increase in membership in the early 1920s and continued to expand rapidly after 1925, being challenged but by no means giving way, either to the sectarian missions that succeeded in establishing a foothold or to the independent church leaders from Nyasaland and Northern Rhodesia who achieved a certain following. Social diversity, labour migration, and political adjustments stimulated a flurry of witch-finding and prediction, as well as heterogeneous Christian associations.[1] Oskar Gemuseus perceived and investigated these diverse elements in the local religious situation in his attempt to guide the responses of the Moravian Church. To be sure, the

[1] Kootz-Kretschmer, E., 'Safwa Texts', *Z.f.E.S.* xxiv (1933–4), 187ff.

Moravian province contained striking examples of the new fluidity, but the quality of missionary leadership could still have considerable effect. As an exponent of the progressive view that the Church must move forward to meet modernity, Gemuseus instinctively in his relations with Africans preserved a dynamic outlook which was especially remarkable in contrast to the style of Martin Priebusch and Schüler, under whom the Berlin Mission reverted to parish paternalism.

In the year or so between his arrival in Rungwe and the final withdrawal of the Livingstonia missionaries in mid 1926, Gemuseus became thoroughly attuned to the educational values of the Scots and the new Government's expectations. Notwithstanding the more than doubled membership and the absence of many of the faces, he naturally worked well with the leaders who had survived from the pre-war cadre of teachers. When Yoram Mphande left the Safwa area to return to Nyasaland, Gemuseus acted on the suggestion of a Scottish colleague and designated Sakalija to take charge of the work based on Utengule. Although not fully ordained, Sakalija was authorized to perform most spiritual functions including the administration of sacraments. Such an appointment might have gone unquestioned earlier, but in 1926 the Utengule church council raised a protest which demonstrated that they would assert their rights under a Presbyterian constitutional formula to make decisions as to who should be their minister.[1] The issue was complicated by a form of intertribal sensitivity that troubled the Moravians throughout the inter-war period because the Nyakyusa settled in significant numbers in the rift corridors. Sakalija, although a Nyakyusa, managed to be personally accepted by the Safwa and Nyiha, but the general jealousy remained.

The first General Church Conference after the departure of the Livingstonia men, took place at the end of January and beginning of February 1927. The desire of the elders and deacons to continue in their offices as understood in the Presbyterian order made it expedient that the Conference should be as similar as possible to a Presbytery meeting. All elders were therefore invited to come to Kyimbila to participate in making church policy. The whole tone differed from that of the previous Moravian Conference in 1913 when African delegates had tended to speak only when spoken to. The agenda contained many of the old questions of social regulation,

[1] Gemuseus, *Sakalija Mwakasungula*, p. 18.

which were quickly resolved, leaving the passionate debate focused on one matter, drink.[1]

From the earliest contacts between Christians from Nyasaland and the Southern Highlands, the matter of whether *pombe* drinking was sinful had been a significant point of dispute. Both Blantyre and Livingstonia missionaries had made the campaign against drink a principal cornerstone of their social and religious teaching, commenting that the war had encouraged excessive indulgence and criticizing the Germans for having been too loose in their attitude towards alcohol.[2] In Ubena, the councils had voted for prohibition and carried it through. Rungwe endorsed the same restriction with more dissent. The congregations of the Mbozi parish, however, had been torn apart by the rival pro- and anti-*pombe* factions.

Prohibition of *pombe* was fully identified with the Presbyterian era, and had been subscribed to by the elders who had achieved enhanced authority in that time. The discussion at the 1927 Conference, therefore, involved a constellation of sentiments. Three congregations, Rutenganio, Kyimbila, and Rungwe, had most completely implemented prohibition, and some early converts had thereby been excluded. 'The further from these centres, the stronger the disinclination or factionalism in the congregation. Below on the lake among the self-consciously pure Nyakyusa, in Mwaya and Ipyana, the restriction was not generally recognized or at least not the cause of exclusion of those who did not comply.'[3] The missionaries had invited a few old-timers as well as the new elders in order to have the several sides represented, but they seem to have been neutral about the outcome so long as it could be the basis of general agreement. Interestingly, the open debate indicated a majority for prohibition, while a secret ballot went 39 to 36 in favour of toleration. A hand vote again went in favour of prohibition, demonstrating a public disinclination to go against the stronger principle. As an admittedly unsatisfactory solution, put across with the close advice of Sakalija and Ambokile, it was agreed to advise every Christian against beer, but to make drinking a subject of discipline only for those holding offices or employment in the church and mission.[4]

In another, related, area of revision after the Presbyterian

[1] Gemuseus, *Sakalija Mwakasungula*, pp. 20ff.

[2] Mackenzie to Ashcroft, 12 Nov. 1923 (N.L.S. 7817). Ibid., 17 Apr. 1924 (N.L.S. 7818).

[3] Gemuseus, *Sakalija Mwakasungula*, p. 21.

[4] Gemuseus, *Sakalija Mwakasungula*, p. 21.

interlude, Gemuseus attempted to restore the personal conference or confession as a means of spiritual counselling, in order to stress the personal condition of the believer and to get closer to the real opinion of the majority in the church.[1]

These adjustments with regard to congregational life progressed with far greater ease than did relations with local officials, who became troubled in 1927 at the apparent connection between schemes of German settlement in the Southern Highlands and the Moravian lands. F. D. Bagshawe, the Provincial Commissioner of the Southern Highlands, was very disturbed by supposed German machinations and with some encouragement from Anderson, he objected to the commercialization of mission lands.[2] Rutenganio had been leased by the Moravians in 1926 to a settler named Pfeiffer who intended to develop it as a coffee estate. The financial difficulties of the Herrnhuters, unresolved by the assistance voted by other German missions, had led the Mission Board to resort to this expedient, allowing Pfeiffer an added option for a coffee plantation at Utengule as well. Knowing the hostility of local officials to German settlement, Gemuseus and Jansa revised the terms of the lease, confining Pfeiffer to Rutenganio and adding clauses to represent him, on paper at least, as a mission agent rather than as a free tenant. This whole turn of events annoyed the arrogant Pfeiffer, who did not have spiritual inclinations and felt himself to be too well connected in Germany to be toyed with by a few poor missionaries.[3]

The German settlement scheme in the Southern Highlands became involved in this private affair between Pfeiffer and the Brethren. The Foreign Office in sponsoring the emigration of small farmers had assumed that the open door to German nationals was all that was needed to establish them economically. Land regulations devised for the specific purpose of restricting alienation had the effect, however, of making it difficult for the would-be farmers to get the property they expected. So large numbers of Germans arriving with capital of about £1,000 and demands for up to 500 acres on which to cultivate coffee, had no alternative but to become squatters. They clustered in Dabaga, Mufindi and elsewhere but had no guarantee that the land of their choice would be available.[4] Consul Speiser of

[1] Gemuseus, '50 Jahre'.

[2] Anderson to Bagshawe, 25 Nov. 1926 (T.N.A. S.M.P. 0419).

[3] Eric Reed (D.O. Tukuyu) to P.C., 4 May 1928 (T.N.A. S.M.P. 11534).

[4] Scott Minute on Bagshawe to Scott, 29 Dec. 1926. Memo of Scott-Speiser interview, 8 Feb. 1927 (T.N.A. S.M.P. 0419).

the Nairobi German Consulate was desperate when he visited Pfeiffer at Rutenganio in mid 1926 and learned that the Moravians owned their land outright. The solution to his problems seemed to be the settlement of his protégés on these lands. While he cabled the Foreign Office to approach the Herrnhuters on this matter, he also appointed Pfeiffer as a kind of agent to help acquire property in the Mbozi–Rungwe area.[1]

When F. S. Joelson got wind of the Rungwe mission land manoeuvres, he published reports in *East Africa*, his settler periodical which kept critical watch on all matters relating to the former colonial power. The first stories alleged only that German missions were disposing of property to their countrymen in areas closed to white settlement. With a stringer like Eric Reed, the equally suspicious District Officer in Rungwe, these reports became more specific. The issue of 1 March 1928, reported that a German and three Swiss were exploiting Moravian lands, supposedly of immense extent, and that the German Consul had procured a subsidy for the mission on the condition that he could nominate the farmers.[2] The news fell like a thunderbolt upon Edinburgh House in London, where Oldham and others, labouring to ease the restrictions on German missionary activities, feared that the involvement with politics might cause a set-back. The Berlin and Leipzig Missions disclaimed any such land manipulation, and the Moravians, while confessing their relations with Pfeiffer, denied that they were obligated to German officials. They also announced that two companies provided with capital in Switzerland had been set up to develop land.[3] A degree of dissimulation may have existed in this statement. The Herrnhuters seem in fact to have accepted a loan of 10,000 marks for the development of Kyimbila and Mbozi, agreeing for their part to employ German nationals where possible and to purchase all necessary equipment in Germany.[4] They were not, however, bound to accept any personnel not chosen by themselves, and the farmers who became associated with the Mission after the Pfeiffer episode had clear religious motivation.

The international fuss subsided, but in Tanganyika Pfeiffer was intent on embarrassing the missionaries as much as possible and the

[1] D.T.G. to Pfeiffer, 11 Apr. 1927 (T.N.A. Deutsche Tanganyika Gesellschaft).

[2] C.O. to Maclennan (Tanganyika Trust), 1 Mar. 1928 (E.H. 7).

[3] See file 'Attack on German Missions, 1928' (E.H. 7).

[4] Agreement of 11 Feb. 1927 enclosed in Gunzert to A.A., 17 Feb. 1927 (B.A. R2/688).

feud led the administration to block loopholes in regulations concerning alienation. Pending investigation of titles, all missions were prohibited from disposing of their lands to third parties. The Charitable Lands Ordinance subsequently stipulated that land acquired from the State for philanthropic purposes could not be commercialized and if sold must be auctioned publicly. Much Moravian property was freehold and thus outside this measure, but the entire episode had a chastening effect.[1]

The influx of settlers and the prevalence of squatting created a situation which tested the authority of chiefs as well as the intentions of missions. Under the Indirect Rule arrangements, chiefs had been assured of their right to dispose of land within the tribe according to custom. White intruders did not come within this rubric and the administration felt the need to reassure the Africans that their rights would not simply be forgotten. When beacons marking land claims sprouted in the Mbozi area, for example, a *baraza* was conducted to guarantee publically that no alienation would take place without the consent of the Nyiha. At Mbozi and elsewhere including Lupembe, Dabaga (Pommern), and Mufindi in the proximity of long-established Evangelical stations, tribal authorities acquiesced in the leasing of land, although the extent was sometimes reduced at their request.[2] In terms of the missionary situation, the development of white settlement did not lead to an immediate crisis. The social patterns it engendered, however, had their eventual consequences in the troubled 1930s.

The sensitivity of the land question did affect relations in certain marginal areas where white missionaries had not earlier resided. A Safwa chief wanted a village school, but jibed at the establishment of a full mission station, until it became clear that Africans alone would live on the land. In this case the Moravians had acquired the land before the war, misplaced the deed, and would have found the officials reluctant to acknowledge the claim. The chief's council did not wish to see Christians benefit from a desirable agricultural plot, especially alien Christians. The origin of this jealousy lay in the Moravians sending no less than seventeen evangelists to develop homesteads, since the spot had been chosen as a base for missionary

[1] Cameron Minute, 19 Dec. 1927 (T.N.A. S.M.P. 11584). Gemuseus to D.O. Tukuyu, 29 June 1928 (Rungwe 4).

[2] P.C. to C.S., 24 Feb. 1928 (T.N.A. S.M.P. 11584). Reports 25 May, 30 May, 1 June 1930 (T.N.A. S.M.P. 10393).

work on the Lupa goldfields. This larger strategic consideration made the Brethren tenacious, and after strenuous negotiations the Christians' rights were sanctioned.[1]

The Konde Synod had its own history of the years following the return of the Berliners. In the Livingstone Mountains, enthusiasm for the retransfer was in any case lacking, and Martin Priebusch, impatiently awaiting the opportunity to get back to Ilembula, seriously misread the situation at Magoje. The Berliners would have been pleased if Nyasuru had accepted the invitation to stay on, but when he refused, Priebusch quickly singled out a local man to serve as his deputy in Buwanji and endowed him with considerable powers. Throughout his career Priebusch had been precipitous in selecting African assistants and had both good and bad results. Most recently, his ordination of Martin Ganishya had had highly successful consequences. Ganishya had been entrusted with the Supervision of the Usaramo–Dar es Salaam area when the Germans were deported in 1920. He was a freedman of Yao origin who had been Klamroth's leading helper in earlier years and had the qualities and experience to carry on as the chief Lutheran in Dar es Salaam from 1920 to 1926.[2]

Benjamin Buwanji did not have the same stature, in spite of the fact that his position gave him a certain local status and reports glorified his leadership. He was introduced to the visiting missionary leaders as a possible candidate for ordination and the preserver of the Wanji congregation during the war. When the young missionary Wolff, who had grown up in the region on his father's mission station, came to Buwanji to set up a bush school system, he soon discovered from the congregational council that Benjamin was a fraud. The charges were at first put down to jealousy. When a special committee consisting of Priebusch and several members of the congregation made a full investigation, however, they concluded that Benjamin had indeed been appointed on the basis of misrepresentation.[3] The council reasserted its authority by sentencing the culprit to exclusion from communion and seemed to have won their struggle to be recognized as a ruling body.

The largest cluster of problems in the period of adjustments by the restored German mission related to education, again an area of great

[1] Gemuseus to Land Officer, 18 Oct. and 1 Dec. 1928 (Rungwe 4). Gemuseus to Bandert, 19 Oct. 1929 (Rungwe 3).

[2] *B.M.B.* (1921), 91. *B.M.B.* (1928), 3.

[3] *B.M.B.* (1928), 82. Berlin *Jahresbericht 1931*, pp. 44f.

emphasis by the Scots. As in other respects the Moravians accommodated to the changed conditions far more successfully than did the Berliners. On the official side, appreciation for the German system of State schools caused the Director of Education, Stanley Rivers-Smith, to be far more critical than were colonial educators elsewhere in Africa, of the premises expounded by Thomas Jesse Jones during the tours of the Phelps-Stokes Commission.[1] The reservations of a few people in Tanganyika had but scant hearing. Missionary circles in Britain and Germany welcomed the adaptive line with its stress upon morality and the systematic co-operation between missions and Government. Sir Donald Cameron discussed educational priorities with Oldham before taking up his duties as Governor of Tanganyika in 1925 and intimated that he would implement a programme of grants-in-aid.[2] Following closely upon the publication of guide-lines for imperial policy in the White Paper entitled Education in Tropical Africa, a conference convened in Dar es Salaam to present the educational goals and plans for co-operation to be pursued in Tanganyika. Cameron opened the proceedings with a statement fully identifying his policy with that of the 1925 White Paper, which had been so comprehensive that his so doing could disturb no one. Rivers-Smith in his turn pledged to use education to achieve 'a social system suited to Africa and the African psychology, in which the individual will be guided to develop on lines suitable to his natural environment, with only such Western influences as may be necessary to replace the abuses which civilization demands must be abolished.'[3] While he thus publicly associated himself with the modish philosophy of African education, the Director continued also to push for English standards and aspired to upgrade the entire system so that its élites could compete in the urban and modern sector.

The criteria for receiving grants included adoption of the official curriculum, employment of qualified teachers, and acceptance of inspection. Missionary enthusiasm was unanimous.[4] Anderson

[1] Rivers-Smith Memorandum, 3 May 1924 (E.H. 15).

[2] See Oliver R., *The Missionary Factor in East Africa*, 2nd edn. (London, 1965), pp. 265ff.

[3] *Proceedings of the Education Conference in Dar es Salaam, 1925* (Dar es Salaam, 1926), p. 6.

[4] The Germans had been informed of the policy at the High Leigh Conference in September 1924, and it was one of the factors which made them eager to return to Tanganyika. For Diedrich Westermann's report, see *B.M.B.* (1925), 55.

attended the conference and became a member of the Territorial Advisory Committee. His own Nyasa teachers already followed a curriculum very like that proposed by the Government and he foresaw little difficulty in converting Kidugala immediately into a grant-earning Central School, as he was himself a qualified schoolmaster. Yet this rosy picture was clouded, for African teachers lacked the required competence in the Swahili language and interest in education seemed to be declining in the Iringa District, because the officials, in comparison with the progressive Germans, seemed indifferent to it. Moreover, Anderson predicted that things might not be easy for the Germans: 'Of course the Education policy is being laid down: the Berlin Mission in taking over the field or part of the field will have to conform.'[1]

The ability of the Berliners to conform rested in part upon the attitude of Anderson towards them, for if he had chosen to stay as headmaster for the Berlin Mission at Kidugala, as he was invited to do, the educational hierarchy in Ubena would have been maintained. To accept such a proposition would have been a volte-face impossible for Anderson, however, and he insisted on retiring.[2] Following this decision, no educational personnel with the specified qualifications served the Berlin Mission in the Southern Highlands during the entire inter-war period. The lack of staff from the Mission itself did not worry Schüler, who after eighteen years in South Africa had been recalled to East Africa as the Superintendent of the joint Konde and Bena Synods. He made one appearance at a Provincial Education Committee meeting, in 1927, declared the Lutheran preference for character training, and withdrew from any further discussion with officials or fellow missionaries about the territorial educational system.[3]

Although Schüler remained hostile to secular education, the men at Berlin Mission headquarters continued to look for ways to provide educational staff. Ludwig Weichert and Diedrich Westermann came to London to discuss the situation with Oldham and officials at the Colonial Office. The scheme they presented was essentially that of Axenfeld before the war, with added touches of Phelps-Stokes adaptationism. An education secretary would be sent to England to

[1] Anderson to McLachlan, 11 Oct. 1925 (N.L.S. 7608). Tanganyika Territory, Education Department, *Annual Report, 1926*, pp. 15f.

[2] Berlin *Jahresbericht 1927*, p. 31.

[3] See Southern Highlands Provincial Education Committee Minutes, 1927 (T.N.A. Iringa 17/16).

acquire the requisite training in English methods and would then set up a conforming central school, perhaps in co-operation with other missions, and would lay stress upon the training of itinerant village school supervisors.[1] But the inability to liquidate property in Dar es Salaam meant that finance for this plan could not be found.

The Moravians enjoyed better timing and personnel in the area of education. Gemuseus came back in the first instance as Education Secretary for the Livingstonia Mission and therefore kept abreast of all developments in the early stages of co-operation with the Government. The boarding-school at Kyimbila continued and the Moravians received a building grant to reconstruct the central school at Rungwe Station. Jansa's wife was English and had been for many years a teacher in England, so that in adjusting to the new administration's demands, the internationality of the Brethren once again rendered concrete advantages.[2] In 1929 the Nyasa Province became qualified for a full grant for the Rungwe School because of the arrival of Walter Marx, an education specialist trained in England.

The other school establishment of significance in the Southern Highlands in the late 1920s was developed at Malangali. At the time of its foundation in 1927, the motive for having such a school was political, based on anxieties about the overwhelmingly non-British citizenship of both Catholic and Protestant Missions.[3] The Malangali School contained a variety of sections, including one following the English language central school course, another concentrating on industrial training, and a third characterized as a tribal school which used traditional forms of education to prepare the aristocracy for their positions within the 'traditional' sector. The tribal school dominated all the other sections during the tenure of W. Bryant Mumford as Headmaster, 1928–31. Mumford had earlier been in charge of the Bukoba Government School, where he experimented with secular moral training through the Boy Scout movement and concluded that the Scout format was insufficiently African in character. Mumford was more satisfied with the application of his principles in leadership training in Bukoba, where the sense of tribal allegiance, he claimed, had reached such a level that the sons or near relatives of chiefs were elected to head the ethnic divisions, rather than the

[1] Memorandum of Conference of Rivers-Smith, Vischer, Westermann, and Weichert at the C.O., 19 Sept. 1927 (E.H. 12).

[2] Gemuseus, '50 Jahre'.

[3] Bagshawe to C.S., 27 May 1927 (T.N.A. S.M.P. 10835).

strongest personality, as in other schools. It was Mumford's ideal to design an education wholly to complement Indirect Rule, interpreted as an ideology committed to social conservation.[1]

Malangali became a social laboratory, with two aims, 'the assimilation by simple steps of those elements of European culture as are necessary for happy interracial relations and the development of indigenous culture so as to build up an educational system which is truly African.'[2] As Malangali was centrally located for the Hehe, Sangu, and Bena peoples, these tended to predominate in tribal adaptation, especially when it was discovered that they had all had similar forms of court training of youths in the past, when elders had been mentors, indoctrinating the proper customs and virtues. To reconstruct this system, old men were selected as the moral tutors of the students, and the setting included traditional toga-like wraps as uniforms, dormitories built in *tembe* quadrangles, spear throwing, tribal dancing, and tribal lore in lieu of other forms of athletics and entertainment. Academic courses took their examples from the immediate environment.

Enthusiasm carried Malangali through its first year and more, and Mumford then departed to write a thesis and to lecture on his tribalized approach to education. During his absence, Gemuseus attended his first Provincial Education Committee meeting and delivered his maiden speech, a prudent balance of favour towards native customs, pragmatism about the relation of tradition and administration, and a plea for respect for the bush school as the place where literacy and elementary subjects as well as religion were introduced. In a concluding remark, he revealed his progressive inclination by stating that old beliefs were being supplanted by Christianity partly because they had proved inadequate in the face of modern conditions.[3] As the Moravian leader became more and more concerned about the effects of the Malangali approach upon youths from his area, it became evident that he would collide with the 'tribalist' headmaster.

Mumford returned to the Southern Highlands to find the morale at his school very low, owing to criticism from many directions, primarily because of its social policy. After some frowning, Rivers-

[1] *Education Conference, 1925*, pp. 79ff. See also Mumford, W. B., 'Native Schools in Central Africa', *Journal of the African Society* (1926–7), 237.

[2] Mumford, W. B., 'Malangali School', *Africa* iii (1930), 268ff.

[3] Southern Highlands Prov. Ed. Com. Minutes, 6 Nov. 1929 (T.N.A. Iringa 17/16).

Smith promised to continue to support the enterprise, and late in 1930 Mumford embarked upon a second stage of experimentation and asked for anthropologists to be attached to the institution to explore the possibility of basing education on initiation ceremonies.[1] His exploration of the 'religious problem', with the express aim of bringing together traditional beliefs and the spirit of Christianity, led directly to differences with Gemuseus. 'I spoke [with the elders] of how we are all aware of the Supreme Being', reported Mumford, 'and of the Spirits of those who have passed on. I suggested that before we start school in the mornings we should meet together and call upon the Spirits of our races to guide and help us.' The absence of sacrificial rituals presented a problem, but Mumford thought he could make up in good intentions: 'I do want to help them to keep a belief in themselves and to feel they can be people of whom their ancestors would be proud.'[2]

Gemuseus preserved a degree of tolerance until he attended the Provincial Conference in November 1930. At that time, owing to the climate of criticism, some 40 per cent of the students had not returned from vacation and the paramount chiefs of Uhehe and Usangu were conspicuously absent from the meeting. Mumford conceded the need for greater consistency in personnel and programme, then launched into a description of the religious exercises he had introduced. The Catholics preserved a discreet silence, but Gemuseus, wishing privately that the Berlin Mission had sent someone to reinforce the Evangelical ranks, declared that it was impossible for Christian students to participate in communal prayers at which pagans invoked the spirits of their ancestors. Stirred to find out the whole situation, he interviewed discontented teachers who complained that tribal singing and dancing made serious inroads into academic and industrial instruction time. Christians from Rungwe complained of the whole system and later refused to inform the experimenters about any aspect of their tribal rituals.[3]

The apparent encroachment by the State in the religious sphere, and its syncretistic tendency, worried Gemuseus. Although on closer acquaintance he judged Mumford to be Utopian but sincere, the Malangali experiment became symbolic for him of the mistaken

[1] Rivers-Smith to Oldham, 1 Aug. 1930 (E.H. 12).

[2] Mumford, circ. letter, 1 Nov. 1930 (E.H. 12).

[3] Report on Prov. Conference of 5 Nov. 1930 (Rungwe 2). Official Minutes (T.N.A. Iringa 17/16).

attitude of many groups in Tanganyika, including some German missionaries, who had come to treat Africans as museum pieces rather than human beings.[1] The old tension between progressives and conservatives that had nearly ruptured the Moravian fraternity at the outbreak of war had come to assume heightened ideological overtones in Tanganyika. Progressives like Gemuseus based their opinions upon the demands and potentialities of some of the people for full participation in the wider world, and for the Nyakyusa in particular no opportunities were to be lost. They retained a certain smugness bred in the relative affluence of Rungwe, but traffic to and from mines and migration due to the land shortage in their home country widened their horizons, placing the old order under severe strain. Yet traditional institutions also assisted the thrust towards modernity. Individualism and age-villages and princely factionalism assimilated innovations more easily than some other forms of social and political organization. The younger generation of Nyakyusa showed frank impatience to earn the educational qualifications offered by the English curriculum. Even Gemuseus seemed a little conservative in this light, for he was not so prepared as his colleague in the Bethel Mission, Ernst Johanssen, to convert wholly to the English medium, and believed that enriched Swahili was the key to unity and healthy relations between the educated and uneducated. Nevertheless, he felt that the desires of his students could not be denied.[2]

The leaders of the Berlin Mission at this time reverted to the practice of subordinating East Africa to South Africa, and wrote much of the need to buttress tribes against change. Director Knak entirely subscribed to Gutmann's elaboration of the divinely-ordained difference between races and nations. He accepted the view that bush schools and rural community development deserved the brunt of the educational effort and that the best energies of the Mission must be expended on the congregation, not on the school.[3] Weichert, although he considered the English curriculum to be absolutely perilous to the education of 'good Africans', at least realized that Europeanization would make its mark. As the East African Inspector for the Berlin

[1] Report 5 Nov. 1930 (Rungwe 2).

[2] See particularly Gemuseus, O., 'Gedanken zur Erziehung des Afrikaners', *E.M.M.* lxxv (1931), 298ff., and Gemuseus's paper on Improved Elementary Education, Dresden Conference, 1932 (E.H. 12).

[3] Knak, Siegfried, *Zwischen Nil und Tafelbai* (Berlin, 1931), pp. 180ff.

Mission, he was aware of the frustrating inadequacies of the work in the Southern Highlands, but could do nothing, and tended to gloss over them with a political rationalization: the missionary situation shared the disabilities imposed upon the German nation as a whole.[1] Weichert, at the Marangu Conference of Protestant Missions in 1928, referred to the Southern Highlands in the following terms: 'We have in one of our districts 250 schools with about 15,000 students. We have no training course for new teachers, only a few trained teachers, three missionaries, and one missionary candidate. How could we give the full number of hours (of secular course work) in that case? It is totally impossible! In any co-operation with the administration we must expect it to understand this situation.'[2] But the Education Department then and for several years thereafter did not attempt to come to a sympathetic understanding. The Berliners, for their part, did not actively solicit it and if any students went beyond their bush schools, they proceeded to the Rungwe School, to Malangali, or to the several local government elementary schools.

As the economic retrenchments caused by the Great Depression began to affect all institutions dependent upon Government grants, Gemuseus again regretted the lack of support from his Berlin neighbours. Towards the end of 1930, Rivers-Smith warned of impending cuts in funds and advised the postponement of normal expansion. All capital grants for construction were suspended, with the consequence that the Brethren were caught at a critical moment in the enlargement of the Rungwe School.[3] Gemuseus complained of the turn of events and concluded: 'One is really on a treadmill with the grant. Certainly the position of the Berliners is much more comfortable, just to take no grant. But then one sacrifices the relationship with the whole school programme of the colony. This is just opposition for opposition's sake. Schüler and Weichert are unanimous in this—everything English shall be rejected!'[4]

Without underestimating the financial and personal factors contributing to the Berliners' neglect of advanced education, it is useful to look at the policy assumed by the German missions in concert, by which Weichert and others justified inactivity. It is worth noting that the Bethel, Leipzig, and Moravian Missions, while protesting

[1] Weichert, L., 'Memorandum on British Colonial Policy' [1930] (E.H. 3).

[2] Marangu Conference, Sept. 1928, Protokolle (Leipzig Archives).

[3] Rivers-Smith to C.S., 24 Dec. 1930. Draft circular, 10 July 1931 and minutes (T.N.A. S.M.P. 10993).

[4] Gemuseus to Baudert, 3 Feb. 1931 (Rungwe 3).

some of the social consequences of the standard education requirements, none the less conformed; both Bethel and Leipzig opening central schools and teacher-training centres in 1927 that earned full grants. They spoke, therefore, as agencies operating within the system. Although enthusiastic about various policy statements made between 1924 and 1927, the German missionaries concluded that instead of favouring vernacular and community education, the specific details of the Education Ordinance and Regulations issued late in 1927 tended to discriminate against popular education.[1]

At that time, the recognized schools fell into three divisions, the elementary vernacular school or village school consisting of two Sub-Standards plus Standards I and II, in which Swahili replaced the local vernacular at Standard I, the central schools consisting of Standards III to VI with English as the nominal medium of instruction, and the teachers' training schools divided into two categories, of vernacular or Grade 2 teachers and English or Grade 1 teachers. The vernacular teachers received an elementary education plus two years of training, and the English teachers received four years of training after completing Standard IV. In time, the Grade 2 category was to vanish, as the entire teaching staff achieved Grade 1 or better status. By these regulations, the bush school was regarded as a pre-elementary school which was not to be included in the recognized system, except in as far as it might be elevated in the future to meet elementary school standards.[2]

To combat this attack upon the bush school and the concomitant 'exaggeration' of English, and in order to formulate a common Protestant position with regard to the official school programme, the Leipzig and Bethel missionaries sponsored a conference held in September 1928 at Marangu.[3] This meeting was heralded as the long-delayed successor to the 1911 meeting and again all societies were invited regardless of nationality. When the conference assembled, there were three Germans to each English speaker, and the necessity of having an interpreter to translate from German hindered spontaneous exchanges, although Canon Hellier of the U.M.C.A. and other Englishmen participated quite fully. There were conspicuous absences. The C.M.S. did not send a missionary delegate, being

[1] Raum, J., 'Educational Problems in Tanganyika Territory', I.R.M. xix (1930), p. 567.

[2] For regulations, see Oldham, J. H., and Gibson, B. D., *The Remaking of Man in Africa* (London, 1931), pp. 163f.

[3] Raum to Gemuseus, 1 May 1928 (Rungwe 2).

instead represented by the Anglican priest resident in Moshi. Neither Moravians nor Berliners from the Southern Highlands attended.

The two announced items on the agenda called for adoption of a Protestant attitude towards the Education Ordinance, and measures to amplify Swahili literature. Other matters also arose, but the prime concern for the basis of co-operation with the Government predominated. In effect, the Germans objected that the 'co-operation' had been inaugurated by the handing down of regulations which had not been reviewed and agreed to in advance. The English had indeed seen the drafts and both the U.M.C.A. and Oldham at Edinburgh House had approved. While they confirmed their confidence in English sympathy for mission efforts, the Germans attempted to regain a voice in the legislative process in education by a series of resolutions advocating revisions in the Ordinance and Regulations. Especially as the U.M.C.A. representative seemed so much of one mind on the social and evangelical ends of education, there was a sense of hope that officials would give heed.[1]

In the Marangu Resolutions, the conference petitioned for a period of grace during which schools could be brought to the prescribed standards, and for more latitude in accommodating religious instruction in the syllabus. More forcefully, they went on to protest that vernacular teachers were best suited to vernacular schools and ought not to be alienated from a popular orientation by English studies, but trained to a higher standard by a prolonged course and enrichment of the Swahili syllabus. Again, flexibility rather than uniformity was stressed in the recommendation that elementary schools might be modified with the consent of the respective Provincial Educational Committee, taking into account local language and environment. English, in these resolutions, ranked as a subject to be thoroughly taught without being adopted as the medium of instruction until the higher standards. To prolong the Swahili segment of the curriculum, the conference proposed the insertion of two extra years as a supplement to elementary school and a bridge to the central school.[2]

Rivers-Smith and his deputy, Isherwood, assured the Lutherans that some latitude could be given in the transitional period before the system operated fully, and pointed to their leniency in issuing provisional licences pending the graduation of teachers from the

[1] Marangu Conference Protokolle (Leipzig Archives).

[2] Marangu Conference Resolutions, Sept. 1928 (Gibson Papers).

training course as laid down. But Rivers-Smith would not forego the requirement of English as the medium in central schools. Uniformity at that point assured an effective overall system, and if the Lutherans wanted to prolong the vernacular course, the Director warned, they would be creating a new kind of central school for which grants would not be made.[1] Rivers-Smith and others were concerned about deviations among the non-British missionary societies, who had to suffer not only because of his preference for English standards, but also because of political discrimination. In 1929, German missions were secretly excluded from access to increased grants for both recurrent and capital purposes, owing to their ex-enemy status.[2]

The German missionaries in Tanganyika, and their Directors who formed a special 'East African Commission' in Germany, enjoyed the facilities available through Oldham and the International Missionary Council in their endeavours to lobby for a greater emphasis upon Swahili in education. Their tenacity contrasted markedly with the line of wholehearted conformity taken by the Catholics, who left 'no stone unturned to understand what is wanted and to do it in the right way'.[3] In a second post-war conference, a much more exclusively Lutheran affair, the range of matters for negotiation was narrowed. All hopes were placed on the recognition of a new type of central school, with Swahili as the medium to Standard IV, after which the school would break into two streams, one following the regulation 'English' course and the other a Swahili curriculum; on leaving, students in each were to receive certificates of equal value.[4]

As the Lutheran Memorandum of 1930 pointed out and German missionaries constantly reiterated, examples of vernacular primary schools already existed in Tanganyika. In the various Tribal Schools, such as Malangali, the Government itself deviated from the Ordinance. More important as a prototype for the Lutherans was the Bishop of Masasi's Swahili Central School. Bishop Lucas believed that the central school syllabus did not meet the needs of his diocese, where people with an 'English' education had little possibility of employment. As a substitute, he had proposed to build a modified syllabus around the theory and practice of agriculture and animal husbandry,

[1] Rivers-Smith to German Evangelical Missionary Conference (draft), 19 Apr. 1929 (T.N.A. S.M.P. 13323). Memorandum, Jan. 1930 (E.H. 14).

[2] Isherwood to C.S., 19 Nov. 1934 (T.N.A. S.M.P. 15692).

[3] Rivers-Smith to Oldham, 28 May 1929 (E.H. 12).

[4] Dar es Salaam Evangelical Mission Conference, Oct. 1930 Memorandum (E.H. 12).

offering as well a range of subjects similar to that of the standard syllabus but taught through the Swahili medium, laying stress upon the principles of citizenship and arithmetic as a requisite for commerce. This format gained recognition in 1928 and the U.M.C.A. received both building and salary grants.[1]

Many other aspects of missionary practice in Masasi attracted the Lutherans, and the Leipzigers especially. They too, under the leadership of Bruno Gutmann, had discussed the possibilities of basing a Christian moral education on an adaptation of initiation rites. Bishop Lucas in fact went further than the Leipzigers in Christianizing circumcision.[2] Other U.M.C.A. men, particularly Canon Broomfield of Zanzibar, agreed in advocating that Swahili be employed as the language of African education although Broomfield did not care for the two-stream arrangement.[3] Notwithstanding some differences, and in spite of the fact that they enjoyed privileges and latitude not extended to ex-enemies, the U.M.C.A. served as a highly significant ally, having influence and working on lines similar to those of the Lutherans. Only such an outsider as Weichert would suggest that the education issue be taken to Geneva to be arbitrated by the Mandates Commission. For the leading figures in Tanganyika, solutions were to be sought through less contentious means, in some confidence that ideological positions were not national, and that the missionary lobby would succeed in bringing the desired changes.

In the reconciliation of the Germans, especially in the matter of social-educational policy, the role of Edinburgh House cannot be overestimated. Oldham had been behind the policy statements of 1925 which anticipated that the whole range of educational activities, from grass-roots to university, would be comprehended in the future programmes of colonial governments. The Advisory Committee on Education which met in London turned its attention successively to the particular aspects.[4] While sweeping statements of intention continued to be made as to the desire to preserve the organic societies of Africa and integrate and adapt education, local policy such as that in Tanganyika was allowed to move in other directions. Looking

[1] Education Department, *Annual Report, 1928*, pp. 23f.

[2] Lucas, W. V., 'The Educational Value of Initiatory Rites', *I.R.M.* xvi (1927), 192ff. See also Raum, J., 'Educational Problems', 565ff.

[3] Territorial Advisory Committee, Nov. 1930, Minutes (E.H. 12).

[4] The language problem was always thorny. See C.O. African 1110, *The Place of the Vernacular in Native Education*, 1927.

back on the international missionary conference at Le Zoute in 1926 as a time when colonial policy had been in apparent accord with their own social thinking, the missionaries often invoked the 'spirit of Le Zoute'. The good faith of the ecumenical party thus came into question and the Edinburgh House team acknowledged that a significant part of the comprehensive programme, namely the recognition of bush schools and vernacular teachers as important constituents of the system, had not been put into practice in Tanganyika. When the matter was raised, officials proved to be wary. Rivers-Smith held out for a complete separation of religious and secular schools and as a signal that the tide was also against bush schools in metropolitan circles, Hans Vischer in the Colonial Office wrote that they probably retarded the progress of 'real education'.[1]

Challenged by the impasse between progressives and conservatives in educational policy, and desiring to launch a Christian Council in Tanganyika which might be a more effective lobby with the Government, Oldham arranged meetings in London in June 1930 where officials, Germans, and Anglican bishops from East Africa could all be present.[2] The initiative bore fruit in several ways. The Tanganyika Advisory Committee on Education resolved in 1930 that the Swahili medium should continue through Standards III and IV, so that those entering the vernacular teacher-training course need never spend time in a course taught through English. Typically, the Education Department regarded this resolution as inconsistent with the aspirations of Africans, and doubted whether the boys qualified to enter the English Standards would really prefer to remain confined to the vernacular.[3]

The Leipzig and U.M.C.A. strategists both hoped in 1930 that upon Rivers-Smith's retirement, which was imminent, Isherwood with his known interest in vernacular education would be named his successor. At the same time, depression economies required a shift of emphasis away from the expensive boarding-schools and towards a more elementary level. Anticipating and fully approving of this switch, Oldham and some others, including Dougall, the Education Secretary from Kenya, travelled to Dresden late in 1932 to discuss the Lutheran position and how it could be presented for consideration when the Education Ordinance was revised. The Dresden

[1] Rivers-Smith to Oldham, 28 May 1929 (E.H. 12). Vischer to Gibson, 25 Jan. 1928 (E.H. 14).

[2] Conference on Christian Education, 16–17 June 1930, Minutes (E.H. 9).

[3] Education Department, *Annual Report, 1930*, p. 7.

resolutions recapitulated the main points in favour of vernacular schooling and concluded with a bid for 'an explicit recognition of the substandard or bush schools when under effective mission control and supervision, to secure for them a place in the system of education even though they may not receive grants from the central education authority.'[1] The apotheosis of the bush school as an educational institution, heralded by Victor Murray in 1929 and supported by Oldham and B. D. Gibson in their *Re-making of Man in Africa*, had effects in Tanganyika in 1932–3: the Armitage–Smith Report on Retrenchment then singled out mass education as a perennial responsibility, as opposed to English education which served only the few, and did not always find outlets in employment. Isherwood's appointment as Director of Education guaranteed the wholehearted co-operation of the Department in this development.[2]

By 1932, the German missionaries in Tanganyika were reaching an accommodation with the British regime on adaptive education. Africans exerted by far the greater pressure in the direction of progressive and Western values. In response or reaction to their demands, factions began to become increasingly evident in missionary discussions, the educators moving into a position identified with their protégés and the pastoral missionaries adhering to a conservative, organic social outlook. As the official policy became one of sympathy with bush schools, the younger Leipzig missionaries also yielded a little, observing that scholars coming out of the English course had not been so alienated from their society as theory supposed.[3] The Chagga themselves mounted an agitation for the ordination of 'national pastors', which the Leipzigers again proved willing to grant, overriding the objections of Bruno Gutmann who believed that the office could not be legitimate because it had no precedent in Chagga social institutions.[4] Without doubt, the progressives were also pragmatists who could see that Christianization had already taken place extensively among the Shambala, the Chagga, the Haya, and the Nyakyusa. Alternatives might be sought by Africans in these areas if missionaries could not respond to their needs and aspirations.

Nowhere were such alternatives offered more invitingly than in the

[1] Conference in Dresden, July 1932, Memorandum (E.H. 12).

[2] Isherwood Memoranda, 13 Feb. 1932 and 21 Sept. 1933 (T.N.A. S.M.P. 18680).

[3] Fleisch, *Hundert Jahre*, p. 444.

[4] ibid., pp. 418f., 444. Interviews with Josephu Merinyo and Bishop Stefano Moshi, Oct. 1964.

Nyasa Province. The locus of classic independent church activities lay in the Nyakyusa lake plains, where George Ngemela headed the 'Last Church of Christ', offering a brand of Christianity which filled part of the institutional vacuum between Christian and tribal moralities. Ngemela baptized polygamists, permitted drink, and declared that his church would raise money by free offerings, not by assessing a tax. Ngemela himself had moved out of the Church of Scotland Mission to join the Watch Tower movement, from which he had separated in 1925 to found his own church. Being from Ngonde, he moved easily among the related Nyakyusa, and probably benefited from the reaction against the temperance movement introduced by the Livingstonia Mission. At least one chief and many commoners in Rungwe District joined the 'Last Church'.[1] According to Moravian observation, these adherents came from those unwilling to make or sustain the sacrifice of traditional wealth and prestige to become monogamous Moravians or Lutherans. The community of practising Christians did not respond to this proffered licence.[2]

The Pentecostal Holiness Mission at Igali had a greater effect. As part of his anti-German measures, Bagshawe had in 1927 directed the American Pentecostals to the former administrative post at the Igali Pass. In an attempt to establish a co-operative arrangement, the Moravians offered to recognize the Malila area as a Pentecostal preserve. The repercussions none the less shook Rungwe as ecstatic worship services and rebaptisms took place. Of the forty-five people baptized in 1930, Gemuseus judged that only three were former pagans. The attraction of the Pentecostals lay in novelty, emotionalism, and above all in the speedy promotion Africans received. Ordinations were common and teaching posts carried greater autonomy and salaries than they did in the Moravian mission.[3] Adjustments were made by the Moravians to fend off defections and woo back their members. They included extension of semi-ordination to four men in addition to Sakalija, all five of whom received full ordination in 1933, and arrangements for periodic re-elections of elders. The elections provided for the installation of a new generation, much as the 'coming out' did in traditional Nyakyusa society.[4]

[1] Wilson, *Communal Rituals*, pp. 172, 195f.

[2] Gemuseus, O., 'Notes about the Religious Situation', May 1933 (T.N.A. S.M.P. 15330).

[3] ibid. Interview with Lazarus Mwangisi, 10 Dec. 1964.

[4] *H.M.B.* (1931), 85. *P.A.* (1932), 130f. Gemuseus, '50 Jahre'.

During the period of adjustment from 1925 to 1932, the Moravians and Berliners clearly responded differently to the new situation in Tanganyika. Yet in social terms, the Christian pattern had already been established. Monica Wilson concluded after her field-work in the 1930s that among the Nyakyusa, Christian morality had achieved a stable effectiveness equal to that of traditional morality; there were two rituals but not two distinct communities.[1] Of course missionaries were quick to report incidents of friction, as when the refusal of a Christian widow to be inherited by her polygamist brother-in-law led to the burning of the huts of three elders who supported her position.[2] On the whole, however, coexistence and peace reigned. This compatibility must be attributed to war experiences, Scottish emphasis on off-station work, and the popularity of the progressive education available through the Livingstonia and the Moravian schools. In Rungwe the balance had in fact moved towards the ascendancy of Christian values, even if certain ethical strictures kept some people from formal association with the older churches. The heir to the priesthood of Pali-Kyasa explicitly stated that he would be a Christian but for a sense of obligation to keep up the functions of his forebears; the cult of Lwembe had not had an incumbent since before the war and its surviving rituals clearly belonged to the aged.[3]

At the same time as the Wilsons worked in Rungwe, the Culwicks conducted anthropological research among the Bena of Ulanga, in a mood far more hostile to Christianity and Islam, which they admitted were influential with the progressive, but had not really supplanted older values. In the early 1930s, the following conclusion was possible for researchers whose sentiments were even more conservative than those of the headmaster of Malangali.

> At the present day, ceremonies vary somewhat from family to family and person to person, owing to the exotic influences to which the tribe has been, and is being, subjected. Many people perform rites which represent a strange admixture of Bena, Moslem, and Christian practices. The tribal religion is, however, very far from being superseded by any other, and though many a man has changed his name to Saidi or Musa or Emanuel or Johanni, . . . he will seldom be found to have done more than overlay the still living old with a thin veneer of the new.[4]

[1] Wilson, *Communal Rituals*, p. 172. See also Wilson, M., 'An African Christian Morality', *Africa* x (1937), 290.

[2] *P.A.* (1932), 132.

[3] Wilson, *Communal Rituals*, pp. 29, 47.

[4] Culwick, *Ubena of the Rivers*, p. 130.

Ulanga still continued to be a frontier on which different religious impulses converged, but to label them exotic at that stage was to misjudge the Africanization of Islam and indeed of Lutheran values. In the highland strongholds of the Berliners, the absence of central schools under mission auspices reduced the leavening effects of the Christianization. But other factors of change were at work and encouraged association with the Church. At Ilembula, where Priebusch re-established his pre-war pattern, a great expansion took place. By 1931 Priebusch reported that four hundred and fifty people had been baptized during the year and that a staff of fifty-two teachers and helpers were at work. The inability of the Berliners to supply extra services may well have been conducive to a growing sense of self-reliance in the Bena Church. The extent of its popular base became strikingly apparent in the years following 1932.

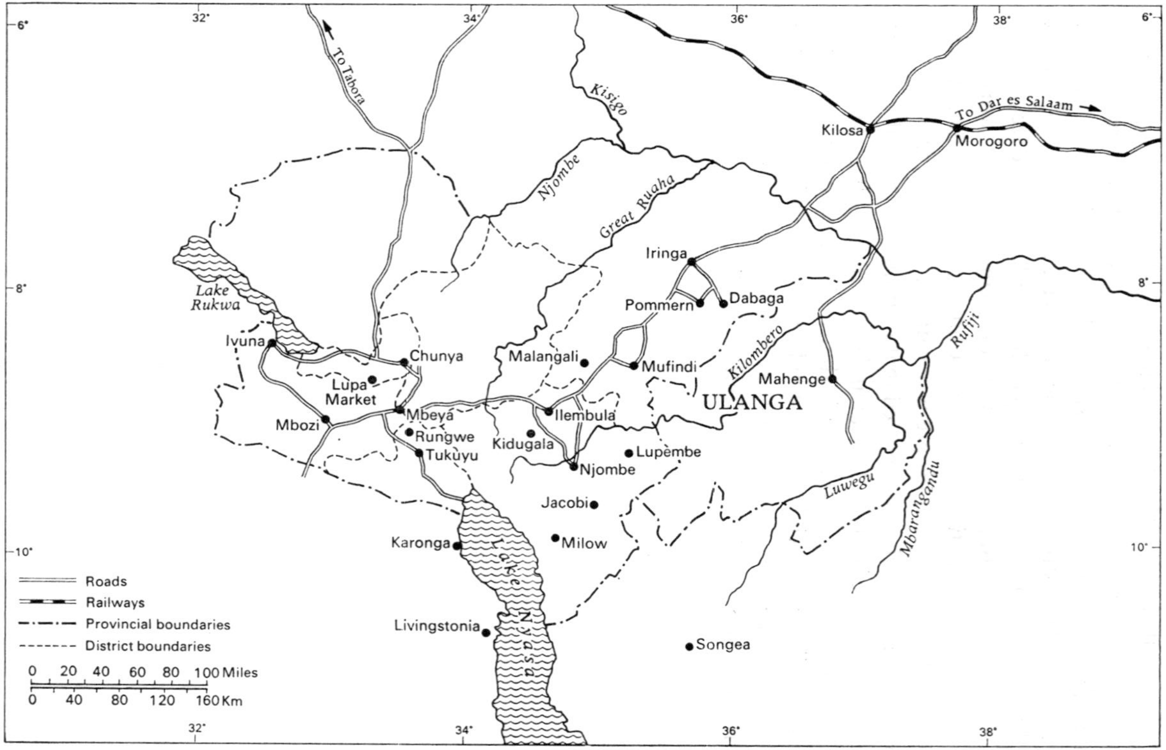

Map VIII Southern Highlands Province [*c.* 1930]

CHAPTER IX

Crisis Years, 1933–1939

THE year 1933 may be regarded as the beginning of a new chapter in the history of the Lutheran and Moravian churches. A number of Africans were ordained then and in following years, the prevalent philosophy of education from 1933 to 1939 led officials to be positively engaged in helping rudimentary school and community efforts, and the matter of church union began to be a vital and controversial concern. Furthermore, the world significance of 1933 as the year of Hitler's coming to power and the proclamation of the Third Reich, exerted a decisive influence in marking a new period because German missionaries were not immune from the totalitarian mobilization of the Fatherland. Both ideology and economic controls affected the missions profoundly, by raising ecclesiastical questions through the effort to bring into being a nationalized church, and by imposing constraints on all overseas Germans to toe the line politically and commercially. The national inclinations of the German missionaries therefore came to the test.

One consequence of the First World War had been its legacy of nationalism, particularly in the Berlin Mission. Whereas during the nineteenth century the Germans concentrated upon cultural nationalism, the years just before the war had seen them relaxing from the controversies of the early colonial period and working within a colonial framework which in German East Africa, at least, was deemed propitious. The Berlin Mission had at that time made special efforts to influence the higher officialdom of the capital and more than ever became the mission of the 'Establishment'.[1] Its battles for the return of the Southern Highlands had been conducted with the furious righteousness of those who felt morally wronged. J. H. Oldham, on the occasion of a visit to Berlin in July 1920 had encountered the full force of this sentiment and heard Julius Richter's commentary.

> There is one aspect of the matter which can be stated, though it is by no means the whole. Practically all those whom we met were Monarchist in sympathy. Richter told us that this is the attitude of almost the whole

[1] Committee Minutes, 26 Aug. 1913, 8 Jan. 1914 (Berlin I 1 9).

of German Christians. He explained it historically. Many of the Hohenzollerns have been religious men and strong supporters of the Church to which they looked in return for sympathy and support. Liberalism in Germany has never shown itself a constructive force. The labour movement has been almost entirely Marxist and therefore materialistic and atheistic. As a result of these historical developments, Kaiser, Kultur, and Kirche have become inseparably associated in the consciousness of German Christians. . . . The result of this way of looking at things is that the minds of those whom we met, and if Richter is right, of German Christians generally, are turned towards the past rather than the future; they are looking for support (as it seems to us) to earthly props rather than launching out to face the new and unknown future with trust in God.[1]

The diplomacy of Oldham, Ashcroft, and others succeeded generally in restoring the spirit of international co-operation between Continental and Anglo-Saxon missions, but the Berliners always remained prickly and ready to see discrimination in the colonial situation. Ludwig Weichert became intimately connected with a movement of 'German Christians' which aspired to nationalize churches and use them to support the cult of the State. Weichert was one of the more idealistic German Christians who stepped back from this association after 1933, but by that time had influenced many seminarians and others in its favour. As an arm of the Nazi Party, the German Christians endeavoured to impose a central administrative authority over the Lutheran, Prussian Union, and Reformed Churches. 'Positive Christianity' required conformity to the doctrine of racial purity and separation as contained in the 'Aryan Clause'.[2] For a few months, some moderate nationalists who did not subscribe to this ideology, but saw some merit in the concept of a national church, attempted to collaborate. Friedrich von Bodelschwingh, the figurehead of the Bethel Mission, became provisional *Reichsbischof* for a brief period until the tactics of German Christian and Nazi militants caused him to resign, opening the way for Hitler to designate his own candidate.[3] About the time of Bodelschwingh's resignation, Weichert withdrew from the Central Committee of the German

[1] Oldham, Notes on a Visit to Berlin, 1–4 July 1920 (Gibson Papers). For details of national feelings of the German missionary movement in the early 1920s, see Wright, 'German Evangelical Missions', pp. 282ff.

[2] Cochrane, A. C., *The Church's Confession under Hitler* (Philadelphia, 1962), pp. 90ff.

[3] Koechlin to Oldham, 20 Sept. 1933 and Koechlin Report, 2 Nov. 1933 (E.H. 5). Koechlin, an I.M.C. committee member and official of the Swiss branch of the Basel Mission, was a valuable observer-participant in the German mission crisis.

Christians and Siegfried Knak publicly qualified his former support of the movement. By October, 1933, the Berlin Committee was free of German Christians, notwithstanding the fact that the themes of nationalism and *Volksmission* still dominated the Society's publications, with good effect upon subscriptions.[1]

After capturing the *Reichskirche*, the German Christians attempted to make inroads upon the independence of the missionary organizations. Again, some people believed that centralization might benefit the movement. One of them, Julius Richter, was empowered with Knak to negotiate on behalf of the Committee of German Missions with representatives of the German Christians. The result of this bargaining effort was so compromising that the *Missionsbund* at its meeting at Barmen in October 1933 rejected it totally. Feeling compelled in some way to respond to the call for centralization, the missionaries resolved to form a nationally comprehensive, loose association called the *Missions-Tag*, with a *Missionsrat* as the executive or continuation committee. Thus reformed, the body dissociated itself from the *Reichskirche*, from politics, and from the Aryan Clause.[2] Among mission leaders, Knak alone preserved an ambiguous attitude towards the *Reichskirche*. Director Ihmels of Leipzig regarded a closer relationship with the Saxon Church to be unavoidable, but the Church itself remained defensively Lutheran as against the bastard national church. The Basel Society upheld its ecumenical, international character in repudiation of the 'heretical, illegitimate Church leadership' of the *Reichskirche*. Koechlin took a strong line that mission men must defend their independence on grounds of inner conviction, not out of fear of the British Colonial Office or other external considerations. The *Reichskirche's* formation also deepened denominational differences, especially on the part of Lutherans whose long-standing hostility to union became thoroughly aroused.[3]

Economic difficulties rivalled theological tensions as the main subject when the venerable Continental Missionary Conference met at Bremen in 1934. Overall, the member societies reported that income was reduced by 25 to 30 per cent; the Moravians were worst off with a decline of 62 per cent. All had been required to cut salaries,

[1] Ruth Rouse, memorandum of interview with Knak, 24 Oct. 1933 (E.H. 6).
[2] Koechlin Memorandum, Oct. 1933 and Report, 2 Nov. 1933 (E.H. 5).
[3] Koechlin to Oldham, 15 Aug. 1933 (E.H. 5). Ihmels to Schlunk, 17 Aug. 1933 (D.E.M.R. Ihmels).

reduce native staff, and curtail programmes, with many grave effects in Tanganyika and Sumatra where expansion was rapid, and Catholic competition severe.[1] The Berlin Mission Director, still confined within nationalist preconceptions, was 'shaken' by a solicitous message brought to the Bremen Conference by a staff member of the I.M.C., William Paton. This stated that in addition to doing everything possible to release emergency education funds to help the Germans in Tanganyika, Isherwood had also written to Oldham that the Berlin Mission must improve teacher training or risk the loss of their religious influence. Knak promised to urge his Committee to do more.[2]

The financial crisis did not reach its peak until July 1934, however, when the Foreign Exchange Regulations took effect. Acting quickly and exploiting his position as a known sympathizer with national renewal, Knak succeeded in negotiating on behalf of the Missions the release of up to 172,000 marks per month, or 75 per cent of the salaries of German personnel in the field, accepting an absolute prohibition of use of these funds for other than the support of German nationals.[3] The *Reichsbank* had still to give its approval to this disposition of foreign exchange and the regimes' control was complete. As if to demonstrate this fact, the *Reichsbank* immediately added a further condition on the release of funds: German consular officials should make a monthly report affirming that German missionaries were 'essential for the propagation of German cultural values and of real importance to the Reich'. The Basel Mission gave leadership to other missions when it promised to uphold the prestige of Germany but refused to be inspected.[4]

The appeal by the Basel Mission to Oldham to help Knak resist the temptation to agree to 'fatal' political surveillance is a commentary both upon the influence wielded by him and the extremity of the situation. In the event, Knak decided himself against such a condition and turned to the I.M.C. for relief. To estimate how much aid would be required, leaders from Herrnhut, Basel, and Leipzig met with secretaries of British societies in London. As a consequence, the

[1] Notes on Hartenstein Report to Bremen Conference, May 1934 (E.H. 5). Knak, S., 'Die Geschichte der Berliner Mission, 1924–1950' (MS., Berlin Mission Library).

[2] Note of Paton–Knak interview (E.H. 8). Knak, 'Die Geschichte'.

[3] Memorandum of Oldham–Knak meeting, 26 Sept. 1934 (E.H. 5). Knak to Vertrauensrat, 1935 (D.E.M.R./Knak).

[4] Koechlin to Oldham and Hartenstein to Oldham, 6 Oct. 1934 (E.H. 5).

societies and the I.M.C. together pledged to raise £50,000 per annum to credit against marks deposited in the Deutsche Bank.[1] So strengthened, the German missions could negotiate for foreign exchange in Berlin under less pressing circumstances.

A side effect of the exchange crisis was the growing sensitivity of Knak to the full range of actions by the State to interfere with voluntary contributions and to ride rough-shod over privacy by searching mission offices. Because it became impossible to send money overseas, there was no longer any point in supporting national themes as a fund-raising device. Finally, the conspicuous paganism of the Nazi ideology made him give up his attempt to serve as a bridge between the regime and the missionary movement. In 1935 he informed the Executive Committee of his intention to suspend all collaboration with the *Reichskirche*, and the next year he had the courage to make his opposition known publicly, and earned the ire of one subscriber who described him as the saboteur of German law and justice.[2]

In Tanganyika, the nationalist mobilization made itself felt in the white colonial community. A German *Bund* had been formed shortly before Hitler came to power. As a special German party, it advocated the enfranchisement of all colonists, and representation in the Legislative Council. After the organization of the Nazi Party later in 1933, the adoption of the principle of militant political separation heightened suspicion about the designs of the German community. Because of the close association of the Berlin Mission with the sponsored German settlement in the Southern Highlands, Phillip Mitchell called for a closer scrutiny of its potentially political activities among Africans, and argued for the retention of the distinction between centres of evangelization such as bush schools, and the regular schools, so that the former could be controlled by the provincial administration. Suddenly it seemed desirable to use religious competition to thwart German activities: 'Nice tidy plans for a solid German settlement in the S.W. cared for by a nice tidy and recently satisfactorily Hitlerised national church will obviously be seriously interfered with by the entry on the scene by a body with so pronounced and international an outlook as the Church of Rome.'[3] Oldham informed Mitchell of

[1] Oldham to Torm, 28 Nov. 1934 (E.H. 6).

[2] Knak to Vertrauensrat, 1935 (D.E.M.R./Knak). *B.M.B.* (Special Number, 15 Aug. 1936) and *B.M.B.* (1937), 20.

[3] Mitchell Minute, 6 Oct. 1933 (T.N.A. S.M.P. 15330).

the opposition by missions to the totalitarian state, but he and other officials remained sceptical. With his usual effective presentation of the position he advocated, Mitchell made scathing attacks upon the Berliners, whom he accused of having slumbered for years doing a little evangelizing and rudimentary education

> in perfect good faith that they have a fundamentally different point of view from ours, since they aim at no more than a people resembling in a general way the submissive European peasantry. In complete good faith they feel that it is Rome they are struggling against, but it is not really that, it is the invasion of modern conditions generally and the distraction of their peaceful enclave: they are afraid of new forces.[1]

In 1931, at the behest of the German Foreign Office, the Berlin missionaries had begun to serve as pastors to the settlers. Neuberg at Dabaga, Priebusch at Mufindi, and Sehmsdorf at Lupembe added this task to their already heavy obligations. Priebusch was successful, having the greatest experience of Africa, and acted as Chairman of the German School Committee for the Lupembe German School, as well as the favourite preacher on national days.[2] Priebusch took it all in his stride, but young Georg Sehmsdorf did not content himself with superficiality. He criticized his German congregation for their sins, especially the abuse of their labourers, with the same zeal that led him to remonstrate with his African parishioners for their Europeanized dress and style of dancing. When Sehmsdorf turned all African residents off mission land in 1933, with the agreement of the elders, and readmitted only those who would obey the rules, his stern measures were accepted.[3] The settlers, on the other hand, had much grief already with their marginal, depression-struck farms, and proceeded to boycott the church where they received such tongue-lashings. Damnation meant little to these settlers, but political sanctions did, tied as they were for economic survival to the sponsorship of the German Government. Sehmsdorf therefore affected a *coup* by being appointed Nazi Party leader in the area. At the cost of time devoted to party duties, he secured his ascendancy over the German nationals and could execute his moralistic reforms:

> In Lupembe I am now, so to speak, the 'strong man', thanks to the iron

[1] ibid. See also Oldham to Mitchell, 16 Oct. 1934 (E.H. 5).

[2] Berlin *Jahresbericht 1931*, p. 46. See also the periodical of the German community, *Das Hochland* (1932), pp. 81 f.

[3] Berlin *Jahresbericht 1933*, p. 46.

party discipline. Attacks against the mission, as were formerly possible, cannot now occur at all. The Party is a true blessing for Lupembe. There is at last a force that compels respect. It was possible before for every vulgar man to defame others without punishment; the Germans will never submit cases to the English. Now peace and quiet reigns in Lupembe.[1]

The new Superintendent in the Bena-Hehe Synod, Julius Oelke, had no jurisdiction over his missionaries in their function as European pastors and he nearly resigned when disputes originating in this sphere caused crippling dissension. Knak alone had the power to redirect missionary energies, and his awakening to the damage of Nazism came all too slowly. In 1934 he had even protested when the Bethel Mission severed relations with an ardent Nazi. By August 1936, however, he turned to a missionary of the Bethel Mission who was a patriot but not a Nazi, to mediate in the Southern Highlands.[2] The task had to be finally carried out by a new East African Inspector, Braun, when he visited in 1936–7. At that time Sehmsdorf returned to Germany, leaving one of the major Bena stations without a white missionary.

Owing to the curtailment of funds for missionary work, the Moravians and Berliners both looked to African congregations for a greater degree of self-support. In this respect, the Bena Church became a virtual prodigy. Its fast growth had caused it to be designated as one area where British substitute funds would be spent, but there is no evidence that economies were any less stringent in the Southern Highlands than elsewhere in Tanganyika.

Luckily, the Director of the Berlin Mission had been forced in 1932 to recognize the inadequacies of Schüler as an executive capable of managing the united Konde and Bena-Hehe Synods. Knak came to Tanganyika in 1932 because the unfortunate situation in Buwanji did not end with the demotion of Benjamin. The investigation had unnerved the congregation, and trouble persisted. Depression due to unemployment, fire, and smallpox, and the departure of the sympathetic Wolff, was not alleviated by the character of the missionary, a man named Schmidt whose practical training under Schüler had been in the tradition of high paternalism. Schmidt lacked the basic benevolence that saved the old Superintendent. As head of the teacher training school which should have been one of the bright lights in the minimal occupation of the Berlin Mission, he failed to establish

[1] Sehmsdorf, Report for 1935, 10 Jan. 1934 (Berlin III 9 1).
[2] Knak to Ronicke, 8 Jan. 1935 and 19 Aug. 1936 (Bethel/Scholten).

confidence and as leader of the Magoje Station he acted dictatorially in imposing absolute moral standards. The Wanji council finally sent a delegation to Bulongwa to appeal for relief from his ruthless regime. Their honest concern and the incapacity of Schüler to bridle Schmidt, brought home to Knak the inertia of leadership in the field.[1] In 1932, during his tour, Knak also realized that there had been no genuine communication between the missionaries and headquarters.[2] And although suspicion of white missionaries continued to blight church development in the Livingstone Mountains, Knak's decision to separate the Bena Synod had good effects in that area.

At the end of its protracted effort to reclaim all former territory, the Berlin Mission succeeded in 1931 in re-acquiring Jacobi from the U.M.C.A. The reconstituted Bena Synod once again attempted to comprehend all the Bena, as well as some Sangu and Hehe. The able former missionary, Julius Oelke, who had been persuaded to return to the Bena Synod as education inspector, was suddenly catapulted into the position of Superintendent, to the immediate disadvantage of the school programme, but to the overall advantage of the Bena Church.

From the time of his arrival in 1933, Oelke devoted himself single-mindedly to building up the Bena Church in a broad cultural sense in tune with the classic continental ideology, as distinct from the narrow, absolutist morality of the young missionaries Sehmsdorf, Schmidt and others. The natural materials for this task were plentiful. Anderson, in the middle 1920s, had noticed that the institution of Indirect Rule conveyed a 'new sense of unity and cohesion' to the tribe.[3] Before that time, the Berliners had been instrumental in re-inforcing the Bena identity and had established Kibena as the vernacular for literature, education, and synodical meetings. As his first act after assuming the Superintendency, Oelke assured the Paramount Chief Pangamahuto that the Church would support tribal authority. The renewed Bena-Lutheran alliance was quickly turned to advantage, for when the Roman Catholics managed to purchase an alienated

[1] Berlin *Jahresbericht 1931*, p. 45. Ibid., 1932, p. 79. Knak to East African Missionaries, Oct. 1932 (Maneromango 12).

[2] From 1930 to 1932, better reporting from the field was regularly solicited. On the other hand, the general content of circulars reaching East Africa was pre-occupied with commentary on the political and spiritual situation in Germany that missionaries probably felt their work to be of secondary interest. See Maneromango files.

[3] Education Department, *Annual Report*, 1926, p. 15.

plot of land in Ubena in order to gain a foothold, Oelke could protest in the name of the people and the paramount and received the support of the District Officer, who attested that popular support was solidly behind the established Lutherans.[1]

One of the innovations of this period was the Bena *Volkfest*, a celebration of the Bena heritage. At the central point in the day, before Pangamahuto and other chiefs as well as a large assembly of ordinary people, missionaries and African preachers spoke on the theme of Christian morality and conservation of the tribe. Having recognized that Pangamahuto and other authorities among the highland Bena functioned because of Indirect Rule rather than 'traditional' legitimacy, the Berliners deferred to them without glorification, and still aimed at direct influence with commoners, arguing that the Church represented the true source of morality to help uphold the character of the people, especially their peasant self-reliance and home life, against pernicious foreign influences. The *Volkfest* became an event attracting Muslims, other non-Christians, and tribal dignitaries, notwithstanding the outspokenness with which the Bena pastors took the chiefs and others to task for their toleration of witchcraft and immorality.[2]

The Church moved into its position as a central institution in the Ubena highlands in part because Oelke decided to ordain pastors as soon as the African representatives at the Synod of 1933 agreed to support them. A generation of tried teachers and evangelists offered a reservoir of leadership capable of fulfilling the duties of pastors; most had been associated with the Berliners before the war and had continued on their own initiative to be teachers and community leaders in the absence of missionaries. The most obvious generalization about the eight men ordained after a four-months course in early 1934, was their identification with the Germans. Ludzabiko Nato and Johani Nyagava were former askaris both of whom had been taken prisoner. Ananidze Kyungu and Alatunvanga Musitu were long-standing mission teachers who had attended the Kidugala Seminary and entered mission service before 1914. Kyungu had lived with Oelke during his boyhood in Ubena and then at Pommern in Uhehe before entering mission boarding-schools from which he had proceeded to the Government School in Dar es Salaam in 1914. Lutengulo Melele had been in the process of advanced education

[1] Acting D.O. Njombe to P.C., 11 Aug. 1933 (T.N.A. S.M.P. 15330).
[2] Berlin *Jahresbericht 1933*, p. 94. *B.M.B.* (1937), 38.

under Nauhaus at Schlesien when the school closed in 1915, and the last two new pastors, Ludzabiko Kihupi and Mutendzi Kyelula, had been schoolboys in 1916. All the civilians except Mutendzi Kyelula had been detained or imprisoned by the British as part of the dangerous pro-German élite.[1]

A second feature common in the pastors' background was their debt to Anderson. Some who had been catechumens before the war had been baptized by him; all had served as teachers in his time. Anderson had succeeded in conveying a sense of the present and future importance of African church leadership, even if at the time of the let down in 1925 some had left the mission service for more lucrative posts. Financial dependence on the mission did not figure much in the relationship of these men to the Church, however, and all of them had been self-supporting to some degree if not as completely as Musitu, who worked entirely without a subsidy in Ulanga from 1923 to 1926.[2] It would be hard to imagine a cadre of leaders more ideally prepared to transcend the stresses and impoverishment of the mission in the 1930s.

After their ordination, the pastors immediately undertook parish responsibilities without close supervision. In 1935, they received a short course to supplement their brief training and to muster enthusiasm for a campaign to improve standards for baptism. With remarkable similarity to the style of their mentors, the African clergy seem to have operated as strongmen not subordinated to councils. Sehmsdorf reported with pride how Ludzabiko Nato, a *jumbe*'s son, exploited his hereditary and military background to maintain stern discipline in his congregation and school. Mutendzi, also in charge of a parish near Lupembe, served an area in which he had been a teacher even before the war and had acquired a venerable image, and he consciously attempted to make his headquarters an approximation of one of the central stations with a large school and a clinic staffed by Africans trained by the mission doctor at Lupembe. For the power of his preaching, Mutendzi was described as 'the best hated man by witch-doctors and Catholics'.[3]

Lutangilo's position at Jacobi required him on occasion to represent the church in disputes with the Catholics. In arguing before the Paramount Chief in a matter of the occupation of a village where

[1] *B.M.B.* (1934), 167ff., 185ff. *B.M.B.* (1935), 8f.
[2] ibid.
[3] Sehmsdorf circular letter, Mar. 1936 (Berlin III 9 1). *B.M.B.* (1936), 78.

teachers of the two denominations conflicted, a priest was exposed for having stated that Oelke bribed Pangamahuto to favour the Lutherans. Although untrue, the allegation served as an indication of the exasperation of the Catholics at the alliance of the Bena Church and local authorities who controlled the licensing of bush schools.[1] The administration was on the lookout for propaganda, but during the mid 1930s judged rumours in the Southern Highlands of the imminent return of German rule to be the product of misunderstanding fed by the Lutheran–Catholic rivalry, in which the Berliners, the 'German' party, protested against intrusion into 'inchi yetu', or their country.[2] By 1937, on the recommendation of the Njombe District Officer, the Central Government stopped worrying about political intrigue and recognized the Bena Church to be an indisputably popular institution worth a degree of protection from Catholic encroachments.[3]

On the Moravian side the ordination of pastors also took place, but with less haste. Sakalija at Utengule, Aswile at Isoko, and Kaisi at Ipyana, all knew in the early 1930s that they would soon acquire full clerical authority and meanwhile proved themselves as *de facto* pastors. Like the Bena Church, the Nyasa Province saw a rapid increase in membership, to the dismay of the missionaries who spoke of an 'almost over-rich harvest' in reporting of the nearly 1,500 baptisms that had taken place in 1934.[4] To prepare financially for more pastors, some congregations doubled or trebled their income from dues and voluntary contribution, and the way formally opened when the General Church Conference of 1934 promised to double church dues across the board. As Gemuseus had been made a bishop in 1932, he had authority to ordain, and proceeded to give a short course to five men who became full pastors during 1935. Their number, of course, included Sakalija, Aswile, and Kaisi, and in addition Wamasamba was ordained for Mbozi and Msatulwa for the express task of ministering to Presbyterians and Moravians in the Lupa region.[5]

A premium upon experience rather than formal education prevailed in the Nyasa Province too. Many of the pastors had been Gemuseus's scholars before the war but the senior of them, Sakalija, exemplified the possibility of advancement in the Church for a man

[1] *B.M.B.* (1934), 166ff. [2] P.C. to C.S., 24 Oct. 1934 (T.N.A. S.M.P. 15456).
[3] Isherwood Memorandum, Sept. 1937 (T.N.A. S.M.P. 15692).
[4] *P.A.* (1934), 29. [5] *P.A.* (1935), 32.

without any central school education at all. Sakalija had other credentials for leadership, however, having already become the elected head of his age-village by the time the missionaries first appeared in 1891.[1] His subsequent career as a teacher and trusted advisor had demonstrated an acute political sense and stable religious commitment. Sakalija and the other twelve men ordained before the outbreak of war all accepted the values stressed by the Brethren, which included a conspicuous degree of humility in their office and a willingness to regard it as the work of the Lord not rewarded in worldly and material ways.

The discrepancy between Nyakyusa attitudes towards the Church and towards secular education was epitomized by the career of Lazarus Mwangisi, intellectually the most gifted of the pastors ordained before Gemuseus retired in 1939. Mwangisi had attended the Rungwe School from 1913 to 1915 and taught between January and May 1916 when owing to the invasion he chose to become an inconspicuous person. From 1917 to 1919, in co-operation with Yoram Mphande, he became an evangelist and thereafter began teaching under Mackenzie in the English boarding-school. In 1928, he received a vernacular teacher's certificate and two years later qualified for the Grade I English certificate. Always the principal African teacher in the Central School, Mwangisi remained at Rungwe until 1935 when he resigned to take a better paying position in the Malangali School. The motives involved in Mwangisi's move to a Government school were in part material. He did not believe that teaching in the territorial education system should be confused with church work and objected to the missionaries' practice, in financial straits, of reducing the salaries of such teachers, asking for sacrifices in the name of conscience.[2]

Other issues also influenced the situation at the Rungwe School in 1935, however. The long-awaited revisions in the Education Ordinance opened the way for a far greater vernacular emphasis. Central schools following the English syllabus were permitted to transform themselves into vernacular teacher-training schools because a large number of central school leavers could not, during depressions, find employment and were regarded as potential agitators. Furthermore, Isherwood promised more attention to bush schools as

[1] Gemuseus, *Sakalija Mwakasungula*, p. 5.

[2] Gemuseus and Busse, *Ein Gebundener*, pp. 92f. Interview with Lazarus Mwangisi, 10 Dec. 1964.

recognized educational institutions, and the terms of qualification for grants were eased. A new category of 'village primary schools' followed a Swahili syllabus up to Standard IV. Grants went to those 'likely within a reasonable period to provide the full course' and the supervisor of a certain number of these village schools could receive a salary grant at the discretion of the Director of Education.[1] The Catholics lamented that Isherwood was prejudiced against them: it was true that the structure of Evangelical education lent itself better to the resurrected slogan of the 1925 White Paper, that the first task of education was 'to raise the standard alike of character and efficiency of the bulk of the people'.[2] Under the new regulations, the Bena Synod could earn an initial grant of £150 for the Kidugala Teacher Training School, although it had not yet instituted the whole curriculum.

For progressive Africans and missionaries in Rungwe, however, the new policy seemed to permit a compromise in educational goals. The decision to convert the Rungwe School into a vernacular Teacher Training centre came as a result of votes by newer missionaries whose concern was to retard westernization.[3] As the grant earned under both arrangements was equal, financial considerations did not favour English, as they had before. Lazarus Mwangisi would not accept the reduction of pay offered to teachers once the English branch was closed, and generally aligned himself with the progressives. In 1936, the major reaction against the new regime took place. Protesting against the limitation of their opportunities, students and teachers both departed for Malangali, which had by then been reformed as a regular 'English' central school with muted African overtones. Gemuseus appealed to Isherwood for additional aid to enable him to offer at least some English Standards, but received only sympathy in reply.[4]

Gemuseus confided to Isherwood that the young missionaries took nothing but a tribal approach to evangelization. They invoked Bruno Gutmann as their apostle and undoubtedly felt that their racialism was also the proper ideology for missionaries in the time of the Third Reich. The new Headmaster of the Rungwe School, rather than being the leader of the progressive party as education specialists were in other missions, was a student of Carl Meinhof,

[1] Isherwood Memorandum [Jan. 1933] (E.H. 34).
[2] Echoed consciously by Isherwood.
[3] Gemuseus to Isherwood, 17 Sept. 1936 (Rungwe 4). [4] ibid.

the linguist who by the 1920s had become an extreme racialist and German nationalist. This Headmaster would not suffer English on either nationalist or ideological grounds. For his undisguised sentiments, he became known to the schoolboys of his day as Hitler's nephew.[1] With this ideologue in a vital position, and with the devaluation of the Swiss franc and harrassment of the Moravians by the German Government, the financial position of the Nyasa Province reached its nadir. The racialists drove home their attack upon the idea of offering higher standards of education in the province, writing off the demand for English as the agitation of a faction motivated by materialism, and emanating from troublesome elements in the congregations. The Leipzig Mission became a model to be followed in apportioning resources, because it seemed to lay relatively greater stress on pastoral rather than educational work. Moravian missionaries favouring the Leipzig ratio, proposed that education should be made available only in so far as the schools were paid for by the congregations themselves, and they invoked the theoretical tenet that this measure would encourage the autonomy of the Church.[2]

In the Konde Synod, a group of younger missionaries held views similar to those of the racialist Brethren. The Konde Synod had continued to be weak in church development well into the 1930s. The duty of Weichert's successor as East African Inspector was to introduce self-government, since the African Church had to become independent of foreign aid. This process was helped by the decline of racial–national elements in Knak's policies. Walter Braun met with the Konde Synod in 1937, when he urged the congregational delegates to vote for a new system of increasing church revenues. In reply, the elders demanded the ordination of African pastors. When Braun yielded, Schüler resigned protesting that local men were too immature for pastoral responsibility. A Kinga helper was ordained at Bulongwa at the end of 1937 and the way to greater Africanization of church leadership at last seemed to be open.[3] Yet the last years before the war did not see the progress that the retirement of Schüler might have made possible. White management did not decline, especially in the Nyakyusa area, where a missionary named

[1] Gemuseus to Isherwood, 23 Oct. 1936 (Rungwe 4). A. Nsekela, interview, 10 Sept. 1964.

[2] Nyasa Provincial Conference, 8 June 1937, Minutes. Memorandum on the English School at Rungwe, 31 May, 1937. Memorandum, 'Gemeinde und Schule' [1936] (Runge 5).

[3] Knak, S., 'Geschichte', p. 257. *B.M.B.* (1937), 94.

Rudlaff was determined to apply Gutmann's methods of congregational development. To this end, he adopted age groups as confirmation units and looked towards a union with the Nyakyusa on the Moravian side to complete the tribal unit for an 'organic church'.[1] The effect was hardly devolutionary. With Schnabel at Rutenganio as his principal Moravian collaborator, Rudlaff pushed for the tribal approach and managed to advance the planning in 1936 and 1937, when the two missions authorized a committee to carry the project forward under the chairmanship of Gemuseus. Thereafter, the matter went to Germany to be regulated and finalized by the Directors. The idea of a united church in Rungwe had been favoured by Mackenzie, but as he appreciated, it had to be carried through with careful regard for African opinion. Rudlaff's and Schnabel's theories opposed that opinion, for leading Christians recognized the regressive mood of their proposals. But given the fact that authority rested in Berlin and Herrnhut rather than in congregational councils, Gemuseus could only hope that Braun's appreciation of Nyakyusa aspirations would make him realize that the venture was unrealistic. He still feared that the approach would appeal to Knak.[2]

In the middle and later 1930s, the Moravian Church in the Southern Highlands certainly suffered by the 'pay as you go' attitude, especially in education. By doubling and trebling church taxes, the charge for maintaining their own elementary schools was met by African congregations by 1938.[3] The concomitant to this self-support was not, however, greater self-government. More stringent discipline was imposed by missionaries bent upon control and greater tribalization. Elders protested against the tinkering with Christian communal sanctions, but licence for tribal dancing and beer drinking was pushed through. The younger missionaries now in charge of the province noted some African antagonism, but failed to see this as an explanation of the decline of catechumens and the fact that, increasingly, church discipline did not bring repentance and a return to the fold.[4]

Gemuseus might have enlightened them, had he not decided after the Provincial Conference of 1936 that he was too out of tune with

[1] Berlin *Jahresbericht 1936*, pp. 93f. See also Schnabel, H.,'Gemeindeaufbau in Ostafrika', *H.M.B.* (1936), 73ff.

[2] Gemuseus to Herrnhut, 12 Jan. 1939 (Rungwe 3).

[3] *H.M.B.* (1938), 111f.

[4] *H.M.B.* (1937), 116.

his colleagues to remain as their chairman. Taking up the duties of Station Missionary at Utengule, he worked for the good of the Church as he understood it. From Utengule, in association with Sakalija Mwakasungula and Mwashitete, he tackled the difficult problems arising from resentment against large-scale Nyakyusa colonization of Usafwa and the semi-industrial complex of the gold-fields, where small returns perpetuated the day of the individual prospector. To aid them, Lazarus Mwangisi returned from his sojourn in Iringa where he had resumed religious work serving among migrants from Rungwe and Central Africa.[1]

Gemuseus retained the office of bishop and when released from other missionary work in 1938 and 1939, he trained and ordained another group of pastors. During this semi-retirement, he also collected linguistic and historical materials, some of which bore fruit immediately in a celebration of the fiftieth anniversary of the 'liberation' of the Safwa, when German officials had recognized Mwalyego as the paramount chief in the stead of Merere. The ancient Mwalyego attended as a guest of honour, but like the Bena *Volkfest* the occasion served primarily to identify the mission and Christianity with the progress and change of the tribe, not with a static past.[2]

With all the troubles accompanying the Third Reich, it is ironic that German nationalism also promoted a co-operative movement among Lutheran and German mission churches, which permitted a practical influence to be exerted by the relatively healthy, balanced leadership of the German missions in the northern part of Tanganyika, upon church development in the south-west. The Mission Church Federation on a Lutheran Basis emerged as a contingency organization in case Tanganyika should be retransferred to Germany as part of appeasing Hitler, and it reflected the theological defensiveness revived in the Lutheran Church by the *Reichskirche*. The national theme was tempered by practical concern arising from a knowledge of local conditions, for the M.C.F. came about as an alternative to other schemes of church union, and gained the support of Americans and some old-time German missionaries for whom fear or approval of European nationalism did not interfere with a clear practical judgement of the Tanganyikan situation.

Ernst Johanssen of the Bethel Mission had been the first German

[1] *P.A.* (1937), 57. [Gemuseus], *Mission und Gold* (Herrnhut, 1936), pp. 11f. Mwangisi, interview, 10 Dec. 1964.

[2] *H.M.B.* (1939), 74ff.

to call for some sort of church union. In an article entitled 'Heraus aus der Isolierung' he demanded the recognition of an African desire for union. While conceding that the good in tradional culture ought to be upheld and Christians ought not to be cut off from their pagan relatives, he nevertheless warned against creating the impression that missionaries wished to confine the people to their old style of life. He contended that the Church should be openly engaged in the process of equipping Christians for the new times by teaching English and earning Government grants through its provision of standard education. In this presentation, the isolation from non-German missionaries and churches was to be regretted as much as the disunity among the Germans themselves. Johanssen nevertheless considered a union of German mission churches to be preliminary to closer ties with the Anglicans.[1]

This call for union was premature. Johanssen himself gave up the approach, preferring to press a related campaign against the Gutmann doctrine of tribalized Christianity. Due to the popularity in Germany of the romance of a pristine national cultural heritage, critics of tribalism could not expect general applause. In mission circles, they crossed swords with Knak in the early 1930s when he was still a vehement advocate of the Gutmann method as an antidote to communism, Europeanism, secularism, and a whole host of other demoniacal agencies of world assimilation spoiling both German and Bantu cultures.[2] Johanssen and others opposing such a reactionary view pointed out that clans, age groups, and other social ties did not constitute a basic Christian relationship. They reverted to the pietistic tradition in claiming that the primordial spiritual relationship was between God and individual souls. Referring to the process of Christianization, Johanssen argued that the nuclear family formed the essential unit of religious practice and that conversion meant a change of heart causing an irreparable breach with tribal culture. In 1933, he persisted in leading the progressive group, insisting that Christianity would spread only with the lowering of tribal and national barriers.[3]

[1] Johanssen, E., 'Heraus aus der Isolierung', *N.A.M.Z.* (1930), 75ff.

[2] Walter Freytag in a review (*Africa*, 1931, p. 519) called Knak's *Zwischen Nil und Tafelbai* the most complete expression of the special German attitude towards nationality. For a review article critical of Knak and Gutmann see Nitsch, W., in *E.M.M.* lxxv (1931), 346–8. Knak's rebuttal was 'Bantuvolkstum, Evangelium, Pietismus', *E.M.M.* lxxvi (1932), 139ff.

[3] Johanssen, E., 'Das Evangelium in seiner Auseinandersetzung mit Afrikanischem Volkstum', *E.M.M.* xxvii (1933), 138–9, 145.

The practical impetus to church union came from the Anglican side. Bishop Chambers of the C.M.S. seized the moment before the Tanganyika Missionary Council was founded to call an ecumenical conference of Protestant missionaries at the Mvumi School near Dodoma, where he proposed an ecclesiastical union in Tanganyika on the basis recently adopted in Kenya, anticipating the eventual formation of a single church in East Africa. The Chambers Plan allowed for government by an episcopal executive, reconizing bishops outside the Apostolic Succession, and a representative assembly of African and missionary delegates. Reciprocal rights of communion and similar patterns of worship were to be instituted. The African demand for a more universal and self-governing church was expected to accelerate the evolution of a full Union.[2] The Moravians faced a serious conflict of loyalties. The British–Danish Moravian Province in Tabora co-operated closely with the C.M.S., and the Chambers Plan appealed to the ecumenical convictions of Gemuseus as well. On the other hand, traditions of German and Continental co-operation were also strong and alive in the German Directors' East African Commission, which caused Herrnhut to think in more German terms.

Not unexpectedly, the U.M.C.A. and Leipzig Society by their absence expressed their antipathy for ecumenical unions. Johannes Raum on behalf of the Leipzig missionaries submitted a memorandum explaining that as orthodox Lutherans, they rejected any exchange of the rights of communion with other denominations. Harking back to the Reformation, the statement also claimed that the Anglican hierarchy of church offices gave undue power to the clergy to the neglect of the primary religious body, the congregation. Their Lutheran converts, the Leipzigers believed, would not wish to compromise their beliefs. Finally, it was objected that the Anglican Church ought first to unite within itself and that the Chambers Plan, as an unhappy echo of territorial Closer Union in East Africa, was open to suspicion as religious imperialism.[2] More positively inclined Germans attended the Mvumi Conference. Roehl, the linguistic specialist of the Berlin and Bethel Societies, Krelle and Tscheuschner of the Berlin Usaremo Synod, and Gemuseus—all responded to the prevailing atmosphere of evangelical brotherhood and idealism. After intro-

[1] *P.A.* (1934), 34–5.

[2] Raum, J., 'Erklärung auf der allgemeinen Konferenz zur Union der Kirchen in Ostafrika' [1933] (Rungwe 2).

ducing semantic moderations in the 'Basis' to remove the bad connotations of union and priest, the Germans came away convinced that the movement was in the best interests of the future African Church and that it could be put across to the Leipzigers.[1]

When Raum issued invitations to attend the German Evangelical Missionary Conference to take place in Dar es Salaam in January 1934, the usual agenda carried two extra items, the Chambers Plan and the church situation in Germany. When the conference convened, the question of local union swamped all others: 'The question dominated the day to such a degree as to be dragged in by the Leipzigers again and again, even into subjects that had no relationship to it. It was such an irritant that a consensus, even mediation of the two standpoints, was completely impossible. One may at least be thankful that this question has been discussed with complete frankness. . . .'[2]

The ecumenical party at first seemed to be the stronger. Even the American leader of the orthodox Augustana Synod favoured territory-wide union from the African point of view, although he thought that a Lutheran Church should come before a broader ecumenical fusion. The Leipzigers were not yet prepared to follow this compromise, remaining rigidly exclusive in reserving communion. They criticized Roehl for advocating the Mvumi union plan in the pages of the 'Lutheran' magazine *Ufalmi wa Mungu* and for his unauthorized offer of the magazine as the joint Swahili periodical for the Union Church. The Leipzigers regarded the Tanganyika Missionary Council as a sufficient vehicle for co-operation. The initial drive of the ecumenical party exhausted itself against this intransigence, for while Roehl and Oelke remained firm, Scholten and Krelle looked for compromise in a closer association of German missionaries. The decision to change the name of the gathering to the 'German Lutheran Conference' demonstrated the direction of events, and a committee was instructed to study union in light of the domestic situation in Germany.[3]

After the foreign exchange crisis enforced a certain practical centralization, and all Directors united in opposition to the *Reichskirche*, the M.C.F. began to take shape. The Directors of the

[1] Gemuseus, 'Besuch der Konferenz für Church Union in East Africa', Report [1933] (Rungwe 2).

[2] Minutes of German Lutheran Mission Conference, 18–22, Jan. 1934 (Bethel/Scholten). Report by Dr. Müller, Jan. 1934 (Bethel/Personn).

[3] German Lutheran Conference, 18–22 Jan. 1934 (Bethel/Scholten).

Bethel and Leipzig Missions in May 1934 resolved to move towards a fusion of the Usembara and Pare-Kilimanjaro churches, agreeing that the Chambers Plan meant hopeless Anglicanization and that union could only be achieved in Lutheran terms, but unhurriedly.[1] When this project was referred to East Africa, the Bethel Missionaries and church leaders in Usambara reacted against the proposals for exchanging secondary education in their schools for theological training at Machame, fearing that the Shambala would be swamped by the more aggressive Chagga.[2]

Heinrich Scholten, of the Bethel Mission in Buhaya, became the leading promoter of Union. As Secretary of the Tanganyika Missionary Council, head of the Bethel Mission in Buhaya, and heir to Johanssen's attitudes, he was acutely aware of the political and religious opinions of Africans. Suspicions roused by the issue of political Closer Union had already stirred the Haya when the collapse of the coffee market and the build-up of Anglo-German rivalry agitated them further. When Scholten returned from leave in early 1934, it was rumoured that he prefigured the restoration of German rule.[3] Experience of the complex of European and African politics that drove the Evangelical Church in Buhaya on to the defensive, especially in the face of anti-German propaganda by the Catholics and their 'fishing' for evidence of disloyalty on the part of the Bethel missionaries, made Scholten aware of the delicacy of the church situation.[4]

He rested his case for a German mission church union on the changed conditions of the war and post-war periods, during which Africans travelled more widely, realized the political and religious differences among Europeans, rejected the old paternalism, and were sophisticated in assessing European motives. The war, he asserted, had dramatized the greater stability of the Roman Catholic Church, and the evangelical Christians wished an analogous church association to attain greater universality and immunity from ties to a particular belligerent in case of a renewed European struggle. A larger union was also considered to be in the interests of the German Societies should the retransfer of the Tanganyika Mandate to Germany occur, for failing such a voluntary centralization, one would

[1] Ronicke to Bethel Superintendents, 24 May 1934 (Bethel/Scholten).
[2] Personn to Ronicke, 30 June 1934 (Bethel/Personn).
[3] Scholten to Ronicke, 18 Mar. 1934 (Bethel/Scholten).
[4] Scholten to Ronicke, 24 Aug. 1936 (Bethel/Scholten).

then be dictated.[1] Here, in sum, was an argument assuming that political crisis compelled church union.

It is worthwhile to note in connection with the possible transfer of the Mandate, that Nazi colonial policy as formulated for international and humanitarian consumption paralleled the contemporary British line. The Germans demanded a territorial settlement by 'peaceful change'. The German colonies would be developed for mutual benefit of the home country and the native populations. The militaristic or imperialistic settlement of large European populations in African areas was abjured; European communities would be supported only to fulfil responsibilities to the native peoples. On the question of race, the policy promised respect for the different mentality of African tribes and educational measures which would help them to cope with their environment and to develop within their racial character.[2] Under the slogan of 'preparedness', transfer was expected in Tanganyika between 1936 and 1938, during which time a German shadow administration was appointed.[3]

In July 1936, amid all these confusing contingencies, the German Lutheran Conference took Scholten's memorandum as the starting-point for discussions. With some dispatch it was agreed in principle to form a Mission Church Federation on a Lutheran basis. Prospective constituents were invited to form a constitutional committee of which Scholten was to be Secretary. Some months later, after approval came from the home base, this committee came up with an organizational structure, comprised of a *Bundeswart* or President as the executive, a missionary committee, and a representative assembly including African delegates. The Lutheran question then became critical, for the Leipzigers insisted that only those who subscribed to the full confessional creeds and catechism could be included in reciprocal rights of communion. That qualification would have created an inner circle comprised of the American Augustana Mission, the Berlin Society, and the Leipzig Society, leaving the Moravians and Bethel Mission in a second-class category. Confessional rigour

[1] Scholten, Memorandum on the Church Situation in East Africa (extracts), and Proposal for a Collective German Missionary Organization in East Africa [1936] (Bethel/Scholten).

[2] 'Richtlinien für einheitlichen Grundton der deutschen Referate zu den colonialen Untersuchungen der internationalen Studienkonferenz', 18 Nov. 1936 (Africa-Verein A II/12).

[3] Memorandum on Tanganyika Government attitude towards Germans [Jan. 1947] (E.H. 13).

was also to be guaranteed by Leipziger control of the proposed Union Theological School.[1]

When the matter was referred back to Germany, the Directors proved to be much more willing to agree on a compromise constitution permitting all to participate as equals. Dr. Baudert of Herrnhut suggested that a more ecumenical arrangement might spare Africa the agonizing theological disputes of Germany, and Knak proposed that Luther's smaller catechism be taken as the Lutheran basis, for to this Moravians and Bethel missionaries could both subscribe. Dr. Ihmels of Leipzig had already on occasion seen danger in excessively rigid orthodoxy in Africa and agreed to the modified basis, whereupon the final arrangements were entrusted to the men on the spot.[2] In Tanganyika, parochialism and the desire for a non-denominational union reasserted themselves when Scholten pressed for action in April 1937. Gemuseus still wanted to follow the Chambers Plan, but he came around, brightened by the prospect that the federation would provide for migrant Christians, and encouraged by the arrival of Swedish Lutherans who added a welcome element of internationality.[3]

The Mission Church Federation finally came into being in September 1937 on the basis proposed by Knak, with Augustana, Berlin, Bethel, Leipzig, and the Herrnhut Moravians, as charter members. The structure was not exclusive; each had the right to make or continue relations with non-Lutheran churches, so that the Nyasa Province, for example, retained its exchange agreements with the Central African Church. By agreement the position of *Bundeswart*, reserved for an orthodox Lutheran, went up to the progressive Leipziger, Paul Rother.[4]

There had been no formal consultation with Africans in the negotiations for constituting the Mission Church Federation. In all four major German Evangelical missions, however, churches had, by the later 1930s, regular congregational councils, representative

[1] Minutes of the German Lutheran Conference, Dar es Salaam, 5–8 July 1936 (D.E.M.R./O.A.K. Minutes). Kommission zur Vorbereitung des Lutherischen Missionskirchenbundes . . . , 23–4 Nov. 1936 (Kidugala 3). The Herrnhuters at this stage were very sceptical about this project. Ronicke to Scholten, 3 Sept. 1936 (Bethel/Scholten).

[2] Minutes, East African Commission, 26 Jan. 1937 (D.E.M.R./O.A.K.).

[3] Scholten to Mission Heads, 14 June 1937, Gemuseus to Scholten, 24 Aug. 1937 (Rungwe 2). Scholten to Ronicke, 23 Aug. 1937 (Bethel/Scholten).

[4] Minutes, Federal Assembly, Kidugala, 19–24 July 1938 (Kidugala 3). *B.M.B.* (1938), 166ff. Scholten to Ronicke, 14 Mar. 1937 (Bethel/Scholten).

synods including leaders from several tribal areas, and a growing number of ordained African pastors. Seven Africans participated in the first Church Assembly held in July 1938 at Kidugala. Their most obvious contribution came in their favouring of the widest possible scope for union. Only the Roman Catholics, the Adventists, and the Pentecostals were beyond inclusion. Stefano Moshi, then a teacher, indicated that the Chagga Church would not be dogmatic when he spoke for a purely Biblical foundation of beliefs. The Assembly also took up church discipline, the joint theological school, and liturgy; but what breathed life into the Federation as a future African Church was the informal contact of leaders from opposite ends of the country who for the first time exchanged ideas, experiences, and aspirations.[1]

For the improvement of conditions in the Southern Highlands, the biennial inspection by the *Bundeswart* was the most significant innovation associated with the Federation. Paul Rother used the occasion of the Assembly meeting to tour the southern Lutheran and Moravian areas, and in a penetrating report enumerated a variety of basic weaknesses. He observed that the Bena Synod was overstrained by efforts to evangelize Uhehe and Ulanga and that the failure to give adequate material support to helpers caused suffering. The missionary staffing of the Kinga–Buwanji parishes was judged to be disproportionately high for the returns, and the Nyakyusa tribal church scheme seemed to Rother a Utopian folly, especially in view of the crying need for attention to education. Even Utengule came under fire for the inefficiency of holding services in three different languages, Kisafwa, Kinyakyusa, and Kiswahili.[2]

The depressed condition of education shocked Rother most. In this area, the Federation offered much to the Southern Highlands, especially when a number of Grade I Chagga teachers were employed to prime the pump in developing standard education in the Berlin Synods. The theological schools on Kilimanjaro and in the Usambaras promised to equip candidates professionally as briefer local training could not.[3] Gemuseus explained the absence of candidates from the Nyasa Province at the first seminary course as due to the reactionary missionaries then in charge. He noted that the Tabora

[1] Minutes, Federal Assembly, Kidugala, 19–24 July 1938 (Kidugala 3). Interview with Bishop Moshi, Oct. 1964.

[2] Rother, Report of the Bundeswart [1938] (Rungwe 2).

[3] Gemuseus to Rother, 2 Mar. 1939 (Rungwe 2).

Moravians had sent representatives, and hoped that the local Christians could 'bring their missionaries round'.

For African churches associated with German Evangelical missionaries in 1939, the future was full of promise and peril. The Mission Church Federation promised a new scope for development; the flexibility of manpower and resources achieved through it gave some relief from what appeared to be the perpetual material disabilities of the German Societies. There was as yet no prospect of being rid of missionaries. Promise of this, however, lay in metropolitan pressure for devolution and union, and in theological revisions which militated against racialism and paternalism.

Inspector Braun in the Berlin Mission led the way in proposing that the missionaries be fully instructed in regard to theological changes,[1] but it remained to Knak to make the telling reassessment. In addressing the Continental Conference and the International Missionary Conference in 1938, Knak acknowledged that the old idea of a special German 'charisma' in missionary work continued, but pietism counted heavily once more; individuals, not nations, were to be the objects of salvation. The concept of Divine revelation working through time in a process of organic evolution was shattered, as illusions about the German State were shattered. Gutmann received credit for illuminating the interrelationship of the individual and society, but his assumptions of racial isolation were declared to be neither realistic nor Biblical.[2] Had dialectical theology continued to influence Knak, had the war not intervened, and in so far as doctrine affected missionary behaviour, the next generation of missionaries representing the Berlin Mission would surely have adopted the style of Klamroth, Johanssen, and Gemuseus, rather than that of Gutmann.

The perils in early 1939 loomed high. Ever since Munich, the whole territory had been alive to the probability of war. Expectations of peaceful transfer of the Mandate faded and everyone suspected the existence of the top-secret 'Z Scheme' for the arrest of German nationals.[3] To the permanent damage of the Berlin

[1] Minutes, Meeting of the 'Heimischen Rates' (the East African Commission's title after formation of the Mission Church Federation), 28 Sept. 1938 (Rungwe 2).

[2] Knak, S., 'The Characteristics of German Evangelical Missions in Theory and Practice', pp. 367–9, 374–5. Knak, S., 'Die geistlichen Kräfte zum Aufbau der Heidenchristlichen Gemeinden', *E.M.M.* lxxxii (1938), 244ff.

[3] Plans for the Z Scheme started in September 1938 and in the same month German leaders approached the Government with a proposal that in the event of war, the German community should surrender arms, pledge not to engage in

Mission, the crisis caused Depersdorf in Dar es Salaam to disobey the orders of Inspector Braun and resume his leadership of the Nazi Party. Because Depersdorf realized that his askari parishioners might soon be his gaolers, he was cautious to avoid political propaganda among them, but for the Germans he presided as High Priest at meetings held in the chapel of the *Missionshaus* under the portrait of Hitler. Africans no longer attended services in the chapel, and proceedings to discipline Depersdorf were underway within the local missionary hierarchy, but neither of these facts availed to blunt the scandal raised by the discovery of the 'Hitler Alter' and the consequent indictment against German missionaries as a body.[1]

The function of European politics, ideology, and financial distress before the Second World War must be regarded as both positive and negative in affecting church development. Racial theology in the hands of some missionaries in Unyakyusa tended to become hardened paternalism in the late 1930s, but on the whole, the crises promoted local responsibility and accelerated progress towards a larger and broader Lutheran Church.

---

propaganda, and be allowed to continue in their occupations. By the spring of 1939, the Southern Highlands settlers were reported to be avoiding Party functions and conforming in general only out of fear of reprisals to relatives in Germany. P.C. to C.S., 29 Apr. 1939 (T.N.A. S.M.P. S 41 and S.M.P. S 26).

[1] Depersdorf, Report for the first half, 1938, and Annual Report for Dar es Salaam, 1938 (Berlin III 10 1). Gibson to Scott, 7 Jan. 1946. Braun, Memorandum on Depersdorf, 21 May 1946 (E.H. 13).

CHAPTER X

Tests of Church Autonomy

WITH the removal of the last Berlin missionary from the Southern Highlands in 1940, fifty years of German influence came to an end. The Berlin Mission never rebuilt its position, and where Lutherans and Moravians received missionaries from abroad, they came predominantly from Scandinavia rather than Germany. A fitting epilogue to the era of German evangelization may be found in the transient 'independence' of the Evangelical Lutheran Church of Southern Tanganyika (the Southern Church) between 1939 and 1941, for the events of these years afforded an opportunity to measure the results of missionary tutelage and the qualities of the indigenous church.

The experiment of independence was almost unavoidable, due to the exceptional thoroughness with which the Germans of the Berlin and Moravian Missions were rounded up and removed at the outbreak of war. Internationality once again came to the aid of the Moravians, for they could quickly shift a Danish subject from Tabora to supervise the Nyasa Province and their property was exempted from the 'enemy' category with its rigid controls. To the north, three-quarters of the Bethel missionaries and half of the Leipzigers enjoyed parole because the demands of security were mitigated by the fact that missionary reactions to militantly hostile settlers were relatively non-political and, more importantly, because both societies sponsored subsidized educational and medical institutions which the administration wished to keep running. The uninstitutionalized missions of the Southern Highlands received no concessions and only the elderly Martin Priebusch was permitted to remain to advise in the Berlin sphere. From November 1939 when he renounced executive authority until August 1941, the Southern Church was independent in the sense of having no formal missionary supervision.[1]

Pastors and elders of the Konde and Bena Synods met at Kidugala

[1] Memoranda on Germans and German missionaries in Tanganyika, Dec. 1939, 2 July 1940; supplied by Colonial Office (E.H. 13).

on 11–14 November 1939, to consider the future. Priebusch declared that he no longer possessed powers of supervision and that the Synods ought to unite as an autonomous Evangelical Lutheran Church within the Mission Church Federation. A self-supporting church with ordained pastors had, he felt, even before the war reduced missionaries to the position of advisers. He assured the Synods that the affirmation of independence, and election of a president would enable them to do without missionaries altogether.[1]

The action of Priebusch in relinquishing his authority was probably more instinctive than reasoned. His trusting delegation of it had been many times apparent during his career. Besides having confidence in the church, he almost certainly acted as a nationalist determined not to let enemy missionaries supplant the Germans. This motive was rationalized and toned down by Knak, who stated that the intention of Priebusch in warning the church against European missionaries had been to strengthen it to decline non-Lutheran missionaries. From the official Berlin Mission viewpoint, Martin Nordfeldt, the Swedish Lutheran who had settled at Ilula in the eastern part of Iringa District just before the war, was a satisfactory supervisor.[2]

Meanwhile, the new Southern Church took up the challenge of independence and elected Johani Nyagava as President. Senior pastors were designated to look after various ethnic divisions, Alatunvanga Musitu in the Mahenge-Bena and Wadamba country, Kabale at Pommern in Uhehe, Mpogolo at Brandt in Usangu, Sifike Mganyilo at Magoje in Buwanji, Tupeliwe Sana at Bulangwa in Ukinga, and Ambonisye Sana at Manow for Unyakyusa. Thanks to the war emergency, Rudlaff had ordained two helpers at Manow, so that Lutheran Nyakyusa at last had their own pastors, bringing the total number in the Southern Church to sixteen.[3]

Because Nyagava attempted to exercise extensive central control over the Church, a few additional biographical details may be a helpful preface to his Presidency. After an introduction to Christian ways as a catechumen and student at Ilembula, Nyagava had joined the German forces just at the time they went on to the defensive in 1916. His service was remembered as a happy time of association

[1] Priebusch to D.O. Njombe, 7 Jan. 1940. S.M.P. 28439. Priebusch to Gibson, 24 Feb. 1940 (E.H. 13).

[2] Priebusch to D.O. Njombe, 7 Jan. 1940. S.M.P. 28439. Knak to Warnshuis, 27 Apr. 1940 (N.L.C. W.M.).

[3] Priebusch to D.O. Njombe, 7 Jan. 1940 (T.N.A. S.M.P. 28439).

with a well-ordered, European-type unit of some five hundred askaris commanded by only one or two German officers. After being released from prison camp he had married the daughter of the leading helper Jesikaka at Ilembula and achieved a prominent place in the community. He was baptized by Anderson and became a mission helper until the period of retrenchment in 1925, when he went off to Dar es Salaam in search of work. While employed as a medical attendant in Government service, he had also attended the Lutheran Church and had been impressed by Martin Ganishya who in this period from 1925 to 1927 was an outstanding example of African achievement as a pastor and influential community leader.

It is said that Martin Priebusch noticed his former pupil in Dar es Salaam and persuaded him to return to Ilembula to work for the mission again. Certainly Nyagava was promoted quickly by the missionary, becoming a prominent lieutenant stationed at the strategic and multi-tribal centre of Malangali both before and after his ordination in 1934. For his identification with Priebusch, whose somewhat autocratic manner he adopted, Nyagava earned the nickname 'son of Priebusch'. Orthodox mission attitudes were loyally upheld by him, especially in speaking for strict discipline at Bena Synod Meetings and at the Federal Assembly, in 1938.[1]

Just after his election and while Priebusch was still present to advise, Nyagava established contact with the Government and with the International Missionary Council for the purpose of obtaining financial and other assistance to maintain schools. His petition for a continuation of the grant for the Kidugala School first brought the autonomous church to the attention of officials:

> As the aim of this school is to train scholars who will be needed in teaching and preaching, the community would not like to leave off the work, but the great obstacle is money.
>
> Being in such a difficulty the community has decided to ask the government for help (money-in-aid), and it trusts that its Government will have sympathy with its citizens that they may get out of the darkness and come to the light of civilization.[2]

Faced by this 'new African Religious and Educational movement', the Provincial Commissioner became worried by the lack of European supervision and rejected the idea of paying a grant to Kidugala as a

[1] *B.M.B.* (1937), 58. *B.M.B.* (1938), 167f. Eli y. Nyagava (son of Johani), in an interview, 12 Dec. 1964. Further details courtesy of James Graham, letter 24 Mar. 1966 and John Iliffe, personal communication.

[2] Nyagava to D.E., 31 Dec. 1939 (T.N.A. S.M.P. 28439).

boarding-school directed only by a Chagga teacher, but agreed to continue African salary grants for a (day) village primary school under the auspices of the Native Authority, in the same fashion as the Rungwe school was being treated.[1]

The Education Department smiled upon the African initiatives to prevent the disintegration of the Church pending its adoption by a British or neutral foster-mission. All officials assumed that church independence was temporary during the awkward time of reorganization and assignment of the custody of German missionary property in the Southern Highlands. The Provincial Commissioner urged the appointment of a Presbyterian supervisor of education because of the happy memories within the Christian community of the former era of Scottish missionaries.[2]

The kind of supervision to be exercised became the major issue for Miss Gibson of the I.M.C. who wrote to Nyagava after receiving a letter from Priebusch describing the self-government of the Church. With great tact, she offered to find someone to help in technical matters: 'I have thought that if we could find someone with medical or educational qualifications, that might be the most useful for you—a man on whom you could rely to give you such help and backing as you wanted but who would realize the importance of the step you have taken and respect the independence of the African Church.'[3]

At this point, the Southern Church was following a conventional course and held a joint synod in May 1940 to make policy decisions collectively. The delegates, thirteen pastors and thirty-one elders, were asked to state whether the Church could manage without missionaries. Their answer was affirmative, on the condition that the pastors retained the respect of the congregations. If they did not, then it would be wise to solicit outside help. Following this decision, Nyagava wrote to Miss Gibson that though the Church could cope with religious and social aspects of the Christian community, it needed a man qualified in education; but he warned that the funds must be supplied externally as it was a struggle even to meet daily expenses from local revenue.[4]

Much as the Southern Church may have hoped to maintain its

[1] P.C. to D.E., 16 Feb. 1940 (T.N.A. S.M.P. 28439).

[2] Davidson to P.C., 26 Feb. 1940, P.C. to D.E., 16 Feb. 1940 (T.N.A. S.M.P. 28439). The British Societies left trusteeship entirely in the hands of Lutherans, but the Government would have preferred otherwise.

[3] Gibson to Nyagava, 1 Apr. 1940 (E.H. 13).

[4] Nyagava to Gibson, 10 June 1940 (E.H. 13).

independence, officials of the Mission Church Federation were sceptical of the practicality and wisdom of it. Paul Rother made his doubts known locally and internationally.[1] His general statement covering Lutheran churches throughout the territory, regarded supervision by one or more white missionaries as essential to 'church discipline, educational and medical work, and last not least the question of finance'.[2] Accordingly, Richard Reusch, the Leipzig missionary who was free to travel on account of his Russian nationality, became the agent of the larger Lutheran concern, charged with regularizing the relationship of the Southern Church to the Federation.

Reusch arrived in the Southern Highlands in July 1940 just in time to nip Nyagava's budding schemes for a more far-reaching independence. According to Reusch, Nyagava was very much influenced by the ideas of Archbishop Alexander of the African Orthodox Church, who had given ordination to members of separatist churches in Uganda and Kenya. Whether Nyagava ever met Archbishop Alexander personally is very doubtful, but certainly he did use information about the movement as the core of his scheme to consolidate his position as head of the Church. His strategy hinged upon the ordination of elders as pastors in sufficient numbers to dominate the Synods, whereupon he would be elected Bishop for life. He had already started a 'training course' for some of these candidates.[3]

The bubble of separatism was quickly pricked. Neither the existing pastors nor the Provincial Commissioner favoured 'wildly ordained Pastors'. The former saw that they would not be able to hold out against sectarian movements and the Provincial Commissioner stated that they would not be recognized by the Government. A convincing argument for orthodoxy was the access it gave to outside money, which everyone realized was important for the Church. Nyagava withdrew from his vulnerable position and gave assurances that his was a pre-seminary course only and that he had no intention of ordaining on his own authority. Having quashed Nyagava's 'fantastic scheme' to become Bishop, Reusch took steps to limit his financial powers as Treasurer by appointing Nordfeldt to receive and dispense

[1] Gibson to Warnshuis, 25 Apr. 1940 (N.L.C. W.M.).

[2] G. N. Anderson and Rother to P.C. Northern Prov., 15 Aug. 1940 (N.L.C. W.M.).

[3] Reusch to Wright, 12 June 1966. For the activities of Archbishop Alexander and the A.O.C. see Welbourn, F. B., *East African Rebels* (London, 1961), pp. 79–81, 148.

all external funds.[1] This power of the purse varied in importance with the amount of financial aid. Between December 1939 and August 1941, the Southern Church received external funds through the M.C.F. and the Augustana Mission amounting to 4,652 shillings, and larger amounts followed later.[2]

The President attempted to reassert his authority after Reusch departed by ordering all pastors to have nothing to do with Nordfeldt except by permission. Unquestioning obedience, if it ever existed, was less easy to exact after the recent chastisement, and because Nyagava's leadership became suspect in certain areas. All Church revenue went to him as Treasurer, but it seemed to some churchmen that no disbursements were made. Volunteer work by evangelists and teachers during the 1930s had been tolerable because the missionaries were also impoverished and generally shared authority in return for self-support. Criticism was inevitable when the President built a new, pretentious house while the rest of the staff went unpaid. Nyagava was further weakened by other charges which the pastors, as the moral prefects of the community were unwilling to condone.[3]

The process of divesting Nyagava of his powers began at the Church conference of November 1940. With the encouragement of Nordfeldt, the delegates dismissed him as Treasurer. The Konde Synod delegates refused to continue to recognize his Presidency, causing a split into the old divisions, the Konde Synod reverting to collective leadership. The precedent of withdrawing recognition was followed in July 1941 in the Bena Synod, which dismissed Nyagava as President and rusticated him to Pommern. Thereafter no one assumed the office of President.[4]

Nordfeldt remained during this period at his own station in the far east. He observed that the problem of leadership in 1940 had to do with a failure in the Berlin Mission training, in that the pastors had no notion of accounting procedures which might have clarified financial matters both for Nyagava and for his critics. Yet at the time, he may have been less than objective as a rival of Nyagava and one who helped to focus resentment against the President's 'dictatorship'. It may have been in view of the upset in the Church that the Augustana Mission as trustees opted at first to bring in a new man as the

[1] Reusch to Wright, 12 June 1966. Dean Bernander in interview, 6 Sept. 1965.

[2] Olson to Long, 8 Aug. 1941 (N.L.C. W.M.).

[3] Nordfelt to Visser 't Hooft, 23 Sept. 1942 (N.I .C. W.M.). Nordfeldt in interview, 3 Sept. 1965.

[4] Nordfeldt to Visser 't Hooft, 23 Sept. 1942 (N.L.C. W.M.).

formal supervisor of the Berlin fields. Manpower was certainly short, for even before the war the Americans had been chronically understaffed and the ship bringing four recruits in 1940 was torpedoed. As a consequence, Lutheran missionaries already in Africa were asked to meet the emergency. By their response, the Scandinavians became a significant factor in Tanganyika, albeit under American auspices.[1]

The Supervisor in the Southern Highlands for a brief period in the last half of 1941 was Gustav Bernander, formerly a missionary in Southern Rhodesia. But Bernander, hamstrung by his inability to speak either Kibena or Kiswahili, was forced to communicate on every occasion through the English-speaking Chagga teacher at Kidugala, the Church leaders being completely ignorant of a European language. Recognizing the ineffectiveness of his supervision, he resigned, making way for the appointment of the obvious candidate, Nordfeldt.[2]

The tendency towards decentralization and caution in the Southern Church was typical of the Lutheran Churches throughout the territory at this time. Morale everywhere had been rudely shaken by the outbreak of war, although like the Southern Church, the others tended to stabilize in 1941. The war had also caused Africans to be elevated to important positions in congregations and schools which they did not wish to see downgraded by any change in the *status quo*. African views became plain at a meeting in September 1941 in Singida District to discuss the future of the Lutheran Church as a whole. The Augustana Mission wanted to enlist Anglican help in education, but the delegates rejected the proposal on the grounds that headteachers must be Lutheran in order to avoid recurrence of interdenominational strife. Non-Lutheran doctors were acceptable so long as they did not interfere with local church affairs.[3]

The wide latitude advocated by the African delegates at the Kidugala Conference of 1938 was not necessarily belied by this retreat into denominationalism. The ideal of a pan-Christian church took second place, however, to the desire to retain the degree of real responsibility which the war had suddenly caused to be shifted to African teachers and pastors and which would certainly have been jeopardized by the calling in of Anglicans, i.e. white men.

[1] Nordfeldt in interview, 3 Sept. 1965. *I.R.M.* xxxii (1942), 90. Danielson to Long, 22 July 1941, and Warnshuis to Long, 31 Dec. 1940 (N.L.C. W.M.).

[2] Dean Bernander in interview, 6 Sept. 1965.

[3] Committee on the Care of the Former German Missions, Meeting, 11–13 Sept. 1941 (N.L.C. W.M.).

This defence against white control was matched by jealousy of parochial autonomy, a feeling aroused by a plan for centralized financial management and the projected circuit of peripatetic preachers. Outside interference in evangelization was especially discouraged: 'The African pastors, elders, teachers, and evangelists within their respective areas are sufficient for the task of awakening their congregational areas, and for reporting any situation to their superintendents and to the President of the Augustana Mission.'[1] Elmer Danielson, the American in charge of the co-ordinating committee, was disappointed that Church leaders were so unwilling to envisage and undertake active co-operation beyond their localities. The principal common denominator in the Mission Church Federation continued to be the joint seminary, especially after 1944 when it was resolved that no pastors would be ordained within the Federation without having taken the course.[2] The controls of the wartime situation, the recession of the financial and political imperatives of the 1930s, and resurgent parochialism brought about a tendency to allow the M.C.F. to deteriorate as the nucleus for a united church. Nordfeldt well expressed this caution when he wrote, 'I fully agree . . . that the M.C.F. is ONLY an advisory body and NOT legislative.'[3]

Particularly in the political sphere, the Americans and most Scandinavians did not comprehend the subtleties of attitudes within their 'foster' mission churches.[4] The Augustana missionaries, anxious to stand well with the Government and aware of the continuing restlessness of the Christians and the population generally, ran to a facile conclusion that some misguided missionaries had been solely responsible: 'Some of the German missionaries were strong firebrands for Nazism instead of Christ. In one native church the picture of Hitler was even hung over the altar. Thus the Government too is anxious that there be missionaries of the right type . . .'[5] Danielson, too, was fearful of official judgement against all Lutherans: 'For some uncomprehended reason so very many of the

[1] Committee on the Care of the Former German Missions, Meeting 11–13 Sept. 1941 (N.L.C. W.M.).

[2] Danielson to Long, 23 Sept. 1941 (N.L.C. W.M.). Mission Church Federation, Meeting 9–13 Sept. 1944, Minutes (T.N.A. S.M.P. 25812). Reusch retained considerable powers during the war, but by 1951 these had diminished.

[3] Nordfeldt to G. N. Anderson, 21 May 1951 (Kidugala 3).

[4] See Bernander, G., *Lutheran Wartime Assistance to Tanzanian Churches, 1940–1945*, (Lund, 1968).

[5] De Lany to Reed, 30 Sept. 1941 (N.L.C. W.M.).

German missionaries, whether knowingly or unknowingly, became chiefly Nazi Propagandists, and the African Christians under their care were gradually becoming politically minded rather than Christ minded.'[1] To blame the missionaries for the political mindedness of African Lutherans, especially in the Chagga and Haya areas, was surely to misread the whole colonial situation, in which African Christians tended to channel their hostility to the authorities in their own identification with the enemy. Bishop Moshi has explicitly noted the African feeling of opposition by vicarious identification.[2] The Tanganyika Government recognized such sentiments, but like the Americans, could not see them in an African and colonial context. Again, the Germans were made out to be the initiators of all 'disloyal' thoughts. According to the official summary on the subject, the Nazis schemed 'to subvert the Africans by the belief in an early German reoccupation bringing prosperity for all, this last activity being carried out largely by German missionaries.'[3]

The Southern Highlands were politically less alert than the North, but as the war went on, the Church became a focus for suspicion of fifth-column activities. The authorities were not loved for the uprooting of mission coffee plantations as 'diseased', or the conversion of Kidugala into a Polish prisoner of war camp using the church for Catholic services, or the frequent detention of pastors and teachers.[4]

Church affairs in the Moravian sphere were more placid. Hansen from Tabora received a warm welcome from twelve of the thirteen pastors when he arrived in the autumn of 1939. Sakalija Mwakasungula made a point of praising Gemuseus as the kind of missionary the Church desired. Upon convening a meeting to agree on emergency measures to defend orthodoxy by giving prior notice of all baptisms of adults and undertaking to maintain unaltered forms of services and administration of the sacraments, Hansen soon realized that the Province's problems lay not merely in dangers of ecclesiastical irresponsibility. The questions of drink, the strained Safwa–Nyakyusa relations at Utengule, and education, were as urgent as ever.[5]

Nordfeldt and Hansen inevitably put education at the top of their lists of priorities. The minimal literacy required before baptism in the Konde Synod had been noted in the late 1930s, but only when

[1] Danielson to Long, 22 July 1941 (N.L.C. W.M.).

[2] Interview, Oct. 1964.

[3] Memorandum in Tanganyika Government attitude to Germans [Jan. 1947] (E.H. 13).

[4] Nordfeldt in interview, 3 Sept. 1965.

[5] *P.A.* (1940), 35ff.

Nordfeldt explored the situation in the Bena Synod was it generally realized that the great expansion of the Church had taken place without the Bible, the Kibena version having been out of print for some years before 1939.[1]

Taking a long-range view, the conservatism and withdrawal into parochial bases which characterized the Lutheran Churches in 1941 may be considered to be in part a fruit of German missionary cultivation of Christianity in ethnic terms. In the parochial strongholds, especially the Nyakyusa and Bena cores of the evangelical mission churches in the Southern Highlands, Christian communities were stable and self-possessed. But, reflecting the local societies, they were not uniform. Historical circumstance had created special relations between the Christian and non-Christian communities within these tribes; in Ubena the Christians tended to be the upper class advantaged by an extended world view and easier access to rudimentary education,[2] whereas in Unyakyusa the communities tended to remain in balance, each with its tight morality, the Christian educational opportunities being weighed against material and spiritual values tied to tribal rituals. Nevertheless, in both areas the Lutheran–Moravian fashion of Christian religion and behaviour had become the appropriate one, to the disadvantage of other denominations.[3]

This assimilation occurred because of historical conditions forcing the German missionaries to modify their conventional patterns and adopt the more sensitive social doctrine of the *Volkskirche* formula. The interruption of white missionary supervision and the reduced circumstances of the 1930s also contributed to devolution. Socially, the evangelical churches in the Southern Highlands had received their most critical tests in the First World War, at which time the Nyiha experiment had collapsed and primary church areas emerged. Once the Nyakyusa became colonizers and labourers on the coffee farms around Mbozi, the Nyiha lost forever the sense of the limelight which Bachmann had conveyed, and in modern times have warmly resented the Nyakyusa cast of the Church.

[1] Wilson, *Communal Rituals*, p. 170. Nordfeldt to Visser 't Hooft, 23 Sept. 1942 (N.L.C. W.M.). Nordfeldt in interview, 3 Sept. 1965.

[2] A similar Christian-tribal 'social affiliation and cultural outlook' has been noticed among Lutherans in rural Transvaal. Hans Florin, *Lutherans in South Africa* (Durban, 1965), p. 51.

[3] A field study of the Christian community in Ubena or of the Southern Church as a whole would be a valuable contribution to match the work done by the Wilsons.

The extremes of tribalism, whether that of Bachmann or the racists of the 1930s, have not become part of the Christian scene. The very fact that these experiments had taken place, however, served as a kind of immunization against Zionist forms. For the Nyakyusa progressives, at least, syncretism appeared to come from missionaries and had little appeal under these or other auspices. The conservative mood of the Moravian and Lutheran congregations existed in spite of the fact that labour migration had been going on at a modest rate for decades. A certain alarm had been expressed by the Berliners before the First World War, when Priebusch was granted funds to build a large church at Ilembula in hopes of keeping Bena from seeking wage labour at a distance. After the war, comment on migrating Christians subsided, except in the context of church union discussions. The churches obviously did not suffer any dramatic demoralization because of the coming and going of members.[1]

Nevertheless, as religious and social institutions, the church-communities had weaknesses. Low standards of education for leadership prevailed and effective helpers and intelligent candidates for ordination were not Divinely provided. The First World War deepened the commitment of the first generation but the 'second growth', always a difficult one, was not forthcoming. Together with the background of rivalry between tribal-paternalist and progressive missionaries, the special circumstances in Tanganyika and the drive for self-support account for failure to rear an élite. Gemuseus bemoaned the long-term effects of the unwillingness of his colleagues to pay their teachers the sums promised during training. The first graduates of the Rungwe School continued to be loyal, but the next crop recognized the material disadvantages of mission service. The status of Rungwe as a grant-aided Central School between the wars absolved the students of the sense of obligation imbued by Meyer before 1916 and, as in German times, greater wealth was available through State employment. The Church remained a career for the spiritual rather than the ambitious. Although the development of the Christian community and the prestige of ordination offered increased

[1] Although the documents are relatively silent about responses to migratory patterns, the Nyakyusa in South Africa and the Bena in the Tanga area retain a communal grouping. Religious attitudes in this setting deserve study. For Bena migration, see Graham, James D., 'Changing Patterns of Wage Labor in Tanzania: A History of the Relations between African Labor and European Capitalism in Njombe District, 1931–1961' (unpublished Ph.D. diss., Northwestern, 1968), p. 74.

inducement, Lazarus Mwangisi stood out as the intellectual among candidates in Gemuseus's last course of pastor-training.[1]

The Berliners allowed their reservoir of talent to shrink after the First World War by postponing the reopening of seminaries at Kidugala and Manow. Apart from non-participation in standard education, this failure to provide centralized religious training had a grave effect on leadership. Nordfeldt toured stations giving month-long refresher courses to bush school-teachers, introduced standard education, and was determined to raise the level of literacy, but these measures could not produce the 'strength of leadership' he found wanting in 1941 and which continued to plague the Church executive offices.[2]

Warneck declared that 'only when Christianity has been so planted in the foreign soil of heathen nations that it becomes naturalised there as a domestic growth, can a really independent native Christian Church be brought into being'.[3] In the nineteenth century this ideal stimulated a healthy expansion of German missionary horizons. The third and fourth decades of the twentieth century proved, however, that a Christianized people could not exist in isolation, but required far-sighted leadership, interdependence with territorial and world Christianity, and material support, in order to achieve its aspirations and to consolidate its gains in the parochial setting.

[1] Gemuseus, 'Mittelschule, 1914–1916'. Gemuseus to Vogt, 23 Feb. 1939 (Rungwe 3).

[2] Berlin *Jahresbericht* 1933, p. 95. Nordfeldt to Visser 't Hooft, 23 Sept. 1942 (N.L.C. W.M.). Nordfeldt in interview 3 Sept. 1965.

[3] Warneck, *Outline* (1906), p. 404.

Appendix A

Church Growth—Statistical[1]

Moravian Nyasa Province

	Baptized Christians	*Day School Students*[2]
1900	141	329
1905	434	1,268
1910	1,087	4,238
1913	1,955	7,931
1927	5,653	6,279
1931	10,656	11,389
1935	15,410	11,565
1939	19,153	13,074

Berlin Mission
Southern Highlands Synods Combined

1900	131	63
1905	706	756
1910	2,227	2,664
1913	3,654	11,101
1927	5,183	16,343
1931	9,565	14,732
1935	14,095	19,489
1938	17,695	15,512

[1] Irregular series due to breaks in mission tenure.

[2] Numbers include those enrolled in bush schools. Actual attendance frequently fell far short of these numbers. They can be used, however, to illustrate relative growth.

Appendix B

Bena-Hehe Synod, Platzordnung[1]

I. Conditions for settling on the estate.

1. It is not required that people settling on the property of the Berlin Mission shall already have been converted to Christianity or have given notice of the intention to become Christian. Pagans and Muslims will also be admitted. Polygamists, as a rule, are not to be taken on, exceptions being permitted by the missionary of the estate with the agreement of the Superintendent.

   The estate resident shall submit in writing to the following contract, the *Platzordnung*, before his entry.

2. People who wish to join must bring evidence that their tax has been paid to the Government. Those who have been in the service of Europeans or have lived on another mission station shall bring with them a reference from their master or the respective missionary as to their deportment. If possible, their chief shall be asked about people who have lived under native chiefs.

II. Life on the estate.

3. On the plot supplied to him, which remains the property of the Society, the estate resident receives the right and duty to erect his huts and associated buildings, to plant and to cultivate. This right, with the approval of the missionary, is transferrable and shall be retained so far as possible within the family of the estate resident.
4. The fulfilment of these rights and duties comes under the supervision of the mission.
5. Huts and farms shall be kept clean, the cultivation being laid out in an orderly manner.
6. The estate resident shall dress respectably according to the customs of the country. The family head is responsible for the clothing of his dependants.
7. The estate resident must lead a moral life, avoiding adultery and whoring, fighting and nuisance, also those attitudes in general that are unworthy of the resident of a Christian mission station and may annoy the estate congregation.

   Pagan immorality is not to be tolerated from the estate residents, including pagans; in particular

   a drinking celebrations
   b dancing
   c puberty rituals—for either sex.

[1] *Platzordnung* source, Berlin Mission to Gov., Mar. 1909 (T.N.A. IX A 3a).

8. It is expected that all estate residents shall participate in Divine Service and morning prayers.
9. Sunday is to be kept holy.
10. Compulsory education is effective for all children of the appropriate age. Parents or employers, also pagans and Muslims are obliged to send their children regularly to instruction.
11. Contravening the *Platzordnung* may result in

   a warning from the missionary after consultation of the elders (see 15) and entry on a record
   b eviction from the estate.

   If, to prevent his exile from the estate, the resident declares himself ready to undertake an atonement for his offence against the *Platzordnung* (work, fine) and the missionary agrees, the penalty shall be applied to communal use. The kind and degree [of the penalty] shall be decided by the elders with the agreement of the supervisor of the estate.

   Offences against the civil law, even if resulting also in a warning or exile from the estate by the missionary, shall be heard before the regular state authority.

III. Estate fees and work.

12. As remuneration for the provision of land, each adult shall pay an annual fee, as fixed by the Synod, to the station treasury. As an alternative, the same can be supplied by work or provision of produce. In special cases, namely poverty, age, and sickness of the incumbent, the fee will be pardoned so far as it cannot be provided by his dependants.
13. Labour in the communal interest of all estate residents, especially the laying out and maintaining of paths, bridges, water courses and plantations of trees, defence against damage of all kinds (wild pigs, *rinderpest*, etc.) is to be rendered by all residents without compensation.

IV. Withdrawal.

14. Huts and cultivation of people who shall be excused or exiled from the station become the property of the mission. The mission, however, will allow the departed resident the benefit of a harvest, so long as there are no weighty reasons against it, and shall grant an emigrant compensation or credit in the station treasury for his planting and development.

V. Estate officials.

15. For maintenance of order on the estate and conciliation of disagreement between the estate residents, estate elders assist the missionary.
16. Estate elders are named from among worthy estate residents by the missionary after conferring with the estate congregation.

17. If elders do not succeed in making peace between the residents, it is the task of the missionary, as supervisor of the estate, and in extreme cases the Superintendent, to arbitrate.

Revisions[1]

Iringa District: Regulation of various questions regarding the coloured members of the mission stations, 12 Nov. 1910.

Issue	*Decision*
1. Regarding coloured authorities over the Christian community	The *jumbe* of the mission station will be appointed by the Military Station; functions as any other *jumbe*.
2. Taxation of coloured Christians	Tax collection is made through the *jumbe*. Each native pays the *jumbe* to whom he belongs.
3. Removal to the mission	People who move to or from the mission station shall report to the respective *jumbe*s of the station. A compensation is to be paid to the former *jumbe* by arrangement after acceptance on the station.
4. Movement of relatives	Relatives are subject to the foregoing, especially in matters of reporting and compensation.
5. Christians possessing cultivation at the old residence, which they wish to retain	If people still have cultivation, house, cattle with the old *jumbe*, they pay him the usual fee (for use of land, 14 days work or 1 sack of produce).
6. Transient labourers at the mission (i.e. not Christians and not regular labourers)	These remain under the administration of their chief, with duties to him *a* to pay government tax *b* to work 14 days or pay 1 Rupie *c* to participate in maintaining public paths, or provide a substitute, or pay compensation. These working at the mission must perform these duties or be prosecuted. No chief may excuse them.
7. Work of the chief	Each coloured male is obliged to work 14 days for his chief. The chief must support him during this period.
8. Women who leave their husbands for the mission	Divorces shall be judged in a legal fashion by the official administration.

[1] Revisions source, enclosure in Berner to von Rechenberg, 28 Mar. 1911 (T.N.A. IX A 3a).

Issue	Decision
9. Serious disputes among the coloured people	Both parties with their evidence shall be sent to the native court of the regular official.
10. Provision of voucher to coloured persons who go to the Military Station	Thoroughly unnecessary. Gives a feeling of legal insecurity and helplessness to those who do not have a chit. It is also disadvantageous if a European is the advocate of those who may be judged guilty.
11. Labour on paths	So long as neither the personnel nor the resources of the administration are available to maintain these paths, their clearance must be done by the residents under the supervision of the respective chief.
12. Manner of tax collection	Tax collection is made by the *jumbe*.

Appendix C

Questions posed at the Nyasa Province General Church Conference, 1913
Nyasa Province: Matters for discussion at the General Church Conference, Oct. 1913.

1. May Christians become betrothed in the customary fashion to immature girls, without being vulnerable to the dangers of this step recognised by the society? [The delegates in general conceded that betrothal might take place after puberty (*Bujufya*), but not before. They wanted a strict prohibition of sexual relations before marriage.]
2. How should Christians regard an inheritance, especially if they inherit women and girls?
3. Shall the custom of paying fines [or compensation] (*bonola, homba*) be retained as a measure of church discipline?
4. Do the congregations wish to see more of the unobjectionable customs of the country introduced at such services as baptism, marriage, and funerals?
5. What initiatives should the congregations and individual Christians take, to win back those excluded from the Church [under discipline]?
6. What should happen to such excluded members as turn away from God and practise magic?
7. What should happen to women who, without fault of their own, are deserted for years by their husbands? And what should happen to such men?
8. What ought we to do in order that Christians can cease to be indebted among themselves and to others? [A debt relationship according to tradition implied dependency and the inability of the debtor to be a witness or otherwise to be the civil equal of the creditor. The persistence of such rules in a time of increasing commercial activity and communal heterogeneity led to conflicts, especially with the Moravian values of individual freedom and openness.]
9. What should we do to strengthen the sense of community of Christians among themselves and of congregations with other congregations?
10. Should the congregations not come to the point of supporting one or another helper? What means to this end are to be recommended?
11. If necessary: Take up the question of church contributions, collections, school fees, etc.
12. Draft a greeting to the General Synod.

BIBLIOGRAPHY

ARCHIVAL SOURCES:

Listed abbreviations as they appear in footnote references.

Germany:

Auswärtiges Amt, Bonn (A.A.)
Files under the heading *Kolonialpolitik*. Some are available in London (P.R.O.) on microfilm. Records of the Nairobi Consulate, 1926–39.

Bundesarchiv, Koblenz (B.A.)
Reichsfinanzministerium (R2) files on war compensation and official investments in Tanganyika. Nachlass Solf—personal papers of Wilhelm Solf, Colonial official and Colonial Secretary.

Deutsches Zentralarchiv, Potsdam (D.Z.A.P.)
Kolonialamt Files on Missions, Files on Districts. Proceedings of the Kolonialrat, 1891–1907. Photocopies of the latter consulted in Oxford, courtesy of Hartmut Pogge von Strandemann.

Preussisches Staatsarchiv, Berlin
Schnee Archiv, personal papers of Heinrich Schnee, Colonial official and Governor of German East Africa, 1912–16.

Berlin Mission, Berlin
Committee minutes, 1911–39. Correspondence with Superintendents and selected stations, 1891–1939.
Records of Karl Axenfeld's visitation in East Africa, 1912–13.

Bethel Mission, Bethel bei Bielefeld
Correspondence with Tanganyika, 1925–39. Special file on the history of the Bethel Mission.

Brüdermission, Herrnhut
Correspondence with the Nyasa Province 1891–1914. Minutes of Provincial meetings. Nachlass (Private papers): Oskar Gemuseus and Elise Kootz-Kretschmer.

Leipzig Mission, Leipzig
Correspondence with the East African Conference, 1924–39. Minutes of the Marangu Conference, 1928.

Missionsrat, Hamburg (D.E.M.R.)
Files pertaining to pre-First World War creation of Missionshilfe, build up of wartime recriminations, and post-war activities, including the East African Commission (O.A.K.) and relations with the Reichskirche, Kirchliches Aussenamt (H.K.A.).

Afrika-Verein, Hamburg
Commercial and academic interests in Africa, especially East Africa, 1920–39.

Weltwirtschaftsarchiv, Hamburg

Files of clippings, both biographical and territorial, inherited in part from the Hamburg Kolonial Institut.

Great Britain:

Public Record Office (C.O., W.O.)

Colonial Office volumes on Nyasaland (1915–19) and Tanganyika (1916–22). War Office, War Diary for Norforce (1915–17).

Church Missionary Society, London (C.M.S.)

Files for fields in German East Africa. Committee minutes, 1890–1914.

Edinburgh House, London (E.H.)

Archives of the International Missionary Council (N.B. Some of these documents have been transferred to the World Council of Churches Archives, Geneva); Tanganyika Trust; and Education Advisory Committee. (Boxes unnumbered, key to references below):

EH 1 Germany, General Situation, 1915–20.
4 Germany, Correspondence.
5 Germany, Missionary Situation, 1933–45.
6 Germany, Church Situation, 1933–7.
7 East Africa, Tanganyika General.
8 East Africa, Tanganyika—Berlin and Scots.
9 East Africa, Tanganyika Missionary Council.
10 Africa General, Education, High Leigh.
11 Africa General, Education, Missionary Policy.
12 East Africa, Tanganyika, Education.
13 War and Missions, Tanganyika, C.O.
14 Africa General, Education, African Education Group.
15 Phelps–Stokes Commission, Central Africa.
20 Tanganyika Trust, C.O.
21 Tanganyika Trust, Berlin.
22 Tanganyika Trust, Maps, Schedules.
23 Tanganyika Trust, Correspondence, Memoranda.
25 Education Advisory Committee, Minutes I.
33 Education Advisory Committee, Tanganyika (1924–9).
34 Education Advisory Committee, Tanganyika (1930–9).

National Library of Scotland, Edinburgh (N.L.S.)

Church of Scotland Missions.

Correspondence regarding Blantyre Mission and Tanganyika, 1918–26.

United Free Church of Scotland Missions.

Correspondence and letter-books regarding the Livingstonia Mission, 1890–1926. Frank Ashcroft's ecumenical negotiations in Germany, 1923.

Universities Mission to Central Africa, London (U.M.C.A.)
Correspondence regarding the Dioceses of Zanzibar, 1890–1930.
Gibson Papers, Edinburgh
Personal papers of Miss B. D. Gibson, some to be filed later at Edinburgh House.
Oldham Papers, Nuffield College, Oxford
Correspondence regarding East African Federation, 1924–32.
Rhodes House, Oxford
Bagshawe papers and diaries.

Tanzania:

Tanzania National Archives, Dar es Salaam (T.N.A., S.M.P., D.T.G.)
German Official (Zentralburo) files on Missionswesen and Schulwesen (T.N.A. IX A, B), 1891–1916. British Secretariat Minute Papers: Secret (S.M.P. 01, S1, etc.), Confidential (15,000–18,000), Ordinary, 1919–40. Miscellaneous Provincial files, mainly about education, 1925–39.
Kidugala–Njombe District (Berlin Mission)
1[1] Correspondence with the Central Government, 1892–1906.
2[1] Correspondence with Iringa Stationschef, 1912–15.
3 Mission Church Federation, 1938–53.
Maneromango[1]–Dar es Salaam District (Berlin Mission)
Files of the Usaramo Synod, 1927–39.
Rungwe–Rungwe District (Moravian Mission)
Files of the Nyasa Province, 1926–39.
1. General Correspondence
2. Territorial Conferences
3. Correspondence with Herrnhut
4. Correspondence with District Commissioner
5. Provincial Conference
6. Annual Reports and Statistics

United States:

National Lutheran Council, New York (N.L.C.)
Boxes on World Mission (W.M.), and Lutheran World Conference (L.W.C.), 1920–45.

PERIODICAL AND SERIAL PUBLICATIONS:

Missionary Societies:

Berlin Mission
Jahresbericht.
Missionsberichte. (*B.M.B.*).

[1] Deposited in Lutheran Church of East Africa offices, Dar es Salaam.

Bethel Mission
Nachrichten der evangelische Mission zu Deutsch-Ost-Afrika, later, *Nachrichten der Bethel Mission.*
Church of Scotland
Reports of the Foreign Mission Committee
Leipzig Mission
Evangelisch-Lutherische Missionsblatt.
Jahresbericht.
Moravian Church (Brüdergemeine)
Missionsblatt aus der Brüdergemeine, Herrnhut (*H.M.B.*)
Moravian Missions, London
Periodical Accounts, London (*P.A.*)
United Free Church of Scotland
Report on Foreign Missions
Missionary Record

Official Publications

Deutsches Kolonialblatt, Berlin, Auswärtiges Amt. (*D.K.B.*).
—— *Beilage, Entwicklung der deutschen Schutzgebieten.* (Annual Reports to 1909.)
Die Deutsche Schutzgebiete in Afrika und der Südsee, Berlin, Reichskolonialamt. (Annual Reports, 1909/10–1912/13.)
Landes-Gesetzgebung, 2 vols., Tanga, 1911, Das Kaiserliche Gouvernment.
Proceedings of the Education Conference in Dar es Salaam, 1925 (Dar es Salaam, 1926).
Tanganyika Territory, Education Department, *Annual Reports.*

Periodicals—Other:

Africa, International Institute of African Languages and Cultures, London.
Afrika, Evangelische Afrika-Verein, Berlin.
Allgemeine Missionszeitschrift (*A.M.Z.*), after 1923, *Neue Allgemeine Missionszeitschrift* (*N.A.M.Z.*).
Deutsche Kolonialzeitung, Kolonialgesellschaft, Berlin (*D.K.Z.*).
East Africa and Rhodesia, London.
Evangelisches Missions-Magazin (*E.M.M.*), Basel Mission, Basel.
Das Hochland, Deutsches Wirtschaftsverband, Mufindi.
International Review of Missions (*I.R.M.*), International Missionary Council, London.
Journal of African History (*J.A.H.*), Cambridge University Press, London.
Koloniale Rundschau, Die Deutsche Gesellschaft für Eingeborenschutz, Berlin.
Tanganyika Notes and Records (*T.N.R.*), The Tanganyika Society, Dar es Salaam.
Zeitschrift für Eingeborenen Sprachen (*Z.f.E.S.*), Hamburg.

UNPUBLISHED THESES, MEMOIRS, AND HISTORIES:

ALTHAUSEN, JOHANNES, 'Kirchliche Gesellschaften in Berlin 1810 bis 1830', 2 vols. (unpublished Ph.D. diss., Halle, 1965).

BATES, MARGARET L., 'Tanganyika Under British Administration, 1920–1955' (unpublished Ph.D. thesis, Oxford, 1958).

EBNER, FR. ELZEAR, 'History of the Wangoni' (cyclostyled, Songea, 1959).

GEMUSEUS, OSKAR, 'Die Tätigkeit in der "Mittelschule" in Rungwe, 1914–1916' (MS., Rungwe School, 1940).

GRAHAM, JAMES D., 'Changing Patterns of Wage Labor in Tanzania: A History of the Relations between African Labor and European Capitalism in Njombe District, 1931–1961' (unpublished Ph.D. diss., Northwestern, 1968).

GUNZERT, THEODOR, 'Erinnerungen' (microfilm, Rhodes House, Oxford).

HARWOOD, ALAN, 'The Safwa before 1900' (unpublished paper presented at Columbia University, February 1969).

—— 'Witchcraft, Sorcery, and Social Classification in a Bantu-speaking Tribe of South-western Tanzania' (unpublished Ph.D. diss., Columbia, 1967).

ILIFFE, JOHN, 'The German Administration of Tanganyika, 1906–1911: the Governorship of Freiherr von Rechenberg' (unpublished Ph.D. diss., Cambridge, 1965).

KNAK, SIEGFRIED, 'Die Geschichte der Berliner Mission, 1924–1950' (MS., Berlin Mission Library).

MCCRACKEN, JOHN, 'Livingstonia Mission and the Evolution of Malawi, 1875–1939' (unpublished Ph.D. diss., Cambridge, 1967).

SHORTER, AYLWARD, 'Ukimbu and the Kimbu Chiefdoms of Southern Unyambezi' (unpublished Ph.D. thesis, Oxford, 1968).

ST. JOHN, C., 'Indigenous and Long-distance Trade in the Late Pre-Colonial Period: Kazembe and the Corridor' (M.A. essay, London, 1968).

WRIGHT, MARCIA, 'German Evangelical Missions in Tanganyika, 1891–1939, with Special Reference to the Southern Highlands' (unpublished Ph.D. diss., London, 1966).

BOOKS AND ARTICLES:

ANONYMOUS [ROTHER, P.], 'Ostafrikanisches Bantu-Volkstum', *E.M.M.* lxxvi (1932).

ARNING, WILHELM, *Deutsch-Ost-Afrika, gestern und heute* (Reimer, Berlin, 1936).

AXENFELD, KARL, 'Die Berliner Mission in Deutsch-Ostafrika', *A.M.Z.* xxxvi (1909).

—— 'Die Ausbreitung des Islam', *Verhandlungen des Deutschen Kolonial-Kongresses, 1910* (Berlin, 1910).

—— *Germany's Battle for the Freedom of Christian Missions* (German Evangelical Mission Aid Society, Berlin, 1919).

—— 'Die Dezemberversammlungen der Berliner Mission', *A.M.Z.* xl (1913).

—— 'Johann Christian Wallmann', *A.M.Z.* xxxviii (1911).

—— *Küste und Inland* (n.p., Berlin, 1912).

—— *Das Kriegserlebnis der deutschen Mission im Lichte der Heiligen Schrift* (Berliner Mission, Berlin, 1917).

—— 'Die Missionarische Aufgabe in Deutsch-Ostafrika', *B.M.B.* (1909).

—— 'Die Sprachenfrage in Ostafrika vom Standpunkt der Mission aus betrachet', *A.M.Z.* xxxv (1908).

—— *The Problem of Islam* (Student Volunteer Missionary Union, London, 1912).

—— 'Zum Gedächtnis Gustav Warneck', *E.M.M.* lv (1911).

—— *Eben-Ezer: bis hieher hat der Herr geholfen* (Berliner Mission, Berlin, 1907).

BACHMANN, TRAUGOTT, *Ich Gab Manchen Anstoss*, ed. H. W. Jannasch (Appel, Hamburg, n.d.).

—— *Ambilishiye: lebensbild eines eingeborenen Evangelisten aus Ostafrika*, ed. Paul Hennig (Missionsbuchhandlung, Herrnhut, 1917).

BENZ, ERNST, 'Pietist and Puritan Sources of Early Protestant and World Missions', *Church History* xx (1951).

BERLIN MISSION, *Missions-Ordnung der Gesellschaft zur Beförderung der evangelischen Missionen unter den Heiden zu Berlin* (Berliner Mission, Berlin, 1882).

BERNANDER, G., *Lutheran Wartime Assistance to Tanzanian Churches, 1940–1945* (Gleerup, Lund, 1968).

BEYERHAUS, PETER, AND LEFEVER, HENRY, *The Responsible Church and the Foreign Mission* (World Dominion Press, London, 1964).

BROCK, B., 'The Nyiha', in A. Roberts, ed., *Tanzania Before 1900* (East African Publishing House, Nairobi, 1968).

BRÜDERGEMEINE, *Die Kirchenordnung der evangelischen Brüder-Unität in Deutschland* (Missionsbuchhandlung, Herrnhut, 1897).

BURTON, RICHARD F., *The Lake Regions of Central Africa* (Longmans, London, 1860).

BÜTTNER, C. G., 'Die Kulturarbeit der Heidenmission', *D.K.Z.* i (1884).

CHARSLEY, S. R., *The Princes of Nyakyusa* (East African Publishing House, Nairobi, 1969).

COCHRANE, A. C., *The Church's Confession under Hitler* (Westminster Press, Philadelphia, 1962).

CONNER, J., 'Count Zinzendorf and Mission Work', *P.A.* (1900).

COXHEAD, J. C. C., *The Native Tribes of North-Eastern Rhodesia* (Royal Anthropological Institute, London, 1914).

CULWICK, A. T. and G. M., *Ubena of the Rivers* (Allen & Unwin, London, 1935).

DAMMANN, ERNST, 'C. G. Büttner, der erste Berliner Afrikanist', *Wissenschaftliche Zeitschrift der Humboldt-Universität zu Berlin* (1958/59).

DEPPERMANN, KLAUS, *Der hallesche Pietismus und der preussische Staat unter Friedrich III* (*I*) (Vandenhoeck & Ruprecht, Göttingen, 1961).

DERNBURG, BERNHARD, *Zielpunkt des deutschen Kolonialwesens: Zwei Vortäge* (Mittler, Berlin, 1907).

DRUMMOND, HENRY, *Tropical Africa* (Hodder & Stoughton, London, 1888).

DU PLESSIS, J., *A History of Christian Missions in South Africa* (Longmans, London, 1911).

ELTON, J. FREDERIC, *Travels and Researches among the Lakes and Mountains of Eastern and Central Africa*, ed. H. B. Cotterill (Murray, London, 1879).

FABRI, FRIEDRICH, *Bedarf Deutschland der Kolonien?* (Perthes, Gotha, 1879).

—— *Fünf Jahre deutscher Kolonialpolitik* (Perthes, Gotha, 1889).

FAGAN, B. M., and YELLEN, J. E., 'Ivuna: Ancient Salt-Working in Southern Tanzania', *Azania* iii (1969).

FLEISCH, PAUL, *Hundert Jahre Lutherischer Mission* (Evangelisch-lutherischen Mission, Leipzig, 1936).

FLORIN, HANS, W., *Lutherans in South Africa* (Lutheran Publishing House, Durban, 1965).

FOTHERINGHAM, L. MONTEITH, *Adventures in Nyasaland: A Two Years Struggle with Arab Slave-dealers in Central Africa* (Low, Marston, Searle & Rivington, London, 1891).

FREE CHURCH OF SCOTLAND, *The Livingstonia Mission of the Free Church of Scotland in Nyasaland: Third Quinquennial Narrative* (Glasgow, 1891).

FÜLLEBORN, FRIEDRICH, *Das deutsche Njassa- und Ruwuma- Gebiet, Land und Leute* (Reimer, Berlin, 1906).

—— *Atlas* (Reimer, Berlin, 1906).

GEMUSEUS, OSKAR, and BUSSE, JOSEPH, *Ein Gebundener Jesu Christi, Fiwombe Malakilindu* (Appel, Hamburg, 1950).

GEMUSEUS, OSKAR, *Sakalija Mwakasungula* (Appel, Hamburg, 1953).

—— *Mission und Gold: Bericht aus den Goldfeldern des Lupaflusses in Ostafrika* (Missionsbuchhandlung, Herrnhut, 1936).

—— 'Gedanken zur Erziehung des Afrikaners', *E.M.M.* lxxv (1931).

GENSICHEN, MARTIN, *Bilder von unseren Missionsfelder in Süd und Deutsch-Ostafrika* (Berliner Mission, Berlin, 1902).

GOLIN, GILLIAN L., *Moravians in Two Worlds* (Columbia University Press, New York, 1967).

GÖTZEN, GUSTAV ADOLF VON, *Deutsch Ostafrika im Aufstand, 1905/6* (Reimer, Berlin, 1895).

—— *Durch Afrika von Ost nach West* (Reimer, Berlin, 1895).

GROESCHEL, P., *Zehn Jahre christlicher Kulturarbeit in Deutsch-Ostafrika* (Berliner Mission, Berlin, 1911).

GRÜNDLER, D. 'Die Seminare der Berliner Mission in Deutsch-Ostafrika', *A.M.Z.* xliv (1917).

GULLIVER, P. H., *Land Tenure and Social Change among the Nyakyusa* (East African Institute of Social Research, Kampala, 1959).

—— 'Nyakyusa Labour Migration', *Rhodes–Livingstone Journal* xxi (1957).

—— *A Report on the Migration of African Workers to the South from the Southern Highlands Province*, with special reference to the Nyakyusa of the Rungwe District (Tang. Prov. Admin. Sec. Research, February 1955).

GUNN, D. L., 'A History of Lake Rukwa and the Red Locust', *T.N.R.* 42 (1956).

GUTMANN, BRUNO, 'The African Standpoint', *Africa* viii (1935).

—— 'Aufgaben der Gemeinschaftsbildung in Afrika', *Africa* i (1928).

—— 'Christianisierungsprobleme eines Bantustammes im Spiegel der Heidenpredigt', *A.M.Z.* xxxviii (1911).

—— *Dichten und Danken des Dschagganeger* (Evangelisch-lutherischen Mission, Leipzig, 1909).

—— *Das Dschaggaland und Seine Christen* (Evangelisch-lutherischen Mission, Leipzig, 1925).

—— *Die Stammeslehren der Dschagga* (Beck, München, 1932–8).

HAMILTON, J. TAYLOR, *History of the Missions of the Moravian Church during the 18th and 19th Centuries* (Times Publishing Co., Bethlehem, Pa., 1901).

—— *Twenty Years of Pioneer Missions in Nyasaland* (S.P.G., Bethlehem, Pa., 1912).

HARWOOD, ALAN, 'A Case of Sociocultural Adaptation to Food Scarcity in a Safwa Community', *Proceedings of the East African Institute of Social Research Conference*, January 1964 (E.A.I.S.R., Kampala, 1964).

HELLBERG, CARL J., *Missions on a Colonial Frontier West of Lake Victoria* (Gleerup, Lund, 1965).

HENNIG, PAUL C., 'Ein Besuch in Livingstonia', *A.M.Z.* xxxiv (1907).

—— *Hopes and Ideals of Missions with reference to the World War* (n.p., n.d.).

—— 'Die Mission der Brüdergemeine in Deutsch-Ostafrika', *A.M.Z.* xxxv (1908).

HOGG, WILLIAM RICHEY, *Ecumenical Foundations: A History of the International Missionary Council and its Nineteenth Century Background* (Harper, New York, 1952).

HUXLEY, ELSPETH, *White Man's Country*, 2 vols. (Chatto & Windus, London, 1953).

ILIFFE, JOHN, 'The Organization of the Maji-Maji Rebellion', *J.A.H.* viii, 3 (1967).

ILONGA II, M., 'The Story of Wawungu', trans. F. G. Finch, *T.N.R.* 52 (1959).

JOHANSSEN, ERNST, 'Das Evangelium in seiner Auseinandersetzung mit Afrikanischem Volkstum', *E.M.M.* lxxvii (1933).

—— 'Heraus aus der Isolierung', *N.A.M.Z.* (1930).

—— *Führung und Erfahrung*, 3 vols., vols. 2–3, ed. Gerhardt Jasper (Bethel Anstalt, Bethel, 1934–8).

KERR-CROSS, DAVID, 'Crater Lakes North of Lake Nyasa', *The Geographical Journal* iii (1895).

—— 'Geographical Notes on the Country between Lakes Nyassa, Rukwa, and Tanganyika', *The Scottish Geographical Magazine* vi (1890).

KLAMROTH, MARTIN, *Auf Bergpfaden in Deutsch-Ostafrika* (Berliner Mission, Berlin, 1907).

—— *Ein Christ* (n.p., Berlin, 1910).

—— 'Die erste deutsch-ostafrikanische Missionskonferenz in Daressalem', *A.M.Z.* xxxviii (1911).

—— *Der Islam in Deutschostafrika* (Berliner Mission, Berlin, 1912).

KNAK, SIEGFRIED, 'Bantuvolkstum, Evangelium, Pietismus', *E.M.M.* lxxvi (1932).

—— 'The Characteristics of German Evangelical Missions in Theory and Practice', *Tambaram Reports* iii (1939).

—— 'Die geistlichen Kräfte zum Aufbau der Heidenchristlichen Gemeinden', *E.M.M.* lxxxii (1938).

—— *Mission und nationale Bewegung* (Kommissionsverlag, Leipzig, 1932).

—— *Säkularismus und Mission* (Bertelsmann, Gütersloh, 1929).

—— *Zwischen Nil und Tafelbai* (Heimatdienst-verlag, Berlin, 1931).

KOOTZ-KRETSCHMER, ELISE, 'Abriss einer Landesgeschichte von Usafwa in Ostafrika', *Koloniale Rundschau* 4–6 (1929).

—— *Die Safwa, ein ostafrikanischer Volksstamm in seinem Leben und Denken*, 3 vols. (Reimer, Berlin, 1926–9).

—— 'Safwa—Texte in Kleinen Erzahlungen und Briefen', *Z.f.E.S.* xxiv (1933–4).

—— 'Safwa und Nyihatexte', *Z.f.E.S.* xxii (1932).

—— ed., *Stories of Old Times*, trans. M. Bryan (Sheldon, London, 1932).

KRÜGEL, S., *Hundert Jahre Graul Interpretation* (Lutherisches Verlagshaus, Berlin, 1965).

LANGHANS, ERNST, F., *Pietismus und Christenthum im Spiegel der äusseren Mission* (Otto Wigand, Leipzig, 1864).

LINDEQUIST, F. VON, *Deutsch Ostafrika als Siedelungsgebiet für Europäer unter Berücksichtigung Britisch-Ostafrikas und Njassalands* (Duncker & Humblot, Leipzig, 1912).

LIVINGSTONE, D., *Last Journals of David Livingstone in Central Africa* (Harper, New York, 1875).

LIVINGSTONE, W. P., *Laws of Livingstonia* (Hodder & Stoughton, London, 1921).

Q

LUCAS, W. V., 'The Educational Value of Initiatory Rites', *I.R.M.* xvi (1927).

LUGARD, F. D., *The Rise of Our East African Empire*, 2 vols. (Blackwood, London, 1893).

MACKENZIE, DUNCAN, R., *The Spirit-Ridden Konde* (Seeley, Service & Co., London, 1925).

MALENG, F. *et al.*, *Zum Gedächtnis August Hermann Franckes* (Waisenhaus, Halle, 1927).

MERENSKY, ALEXANDER, *Deutsche Arbeit am Njassa* (Berliner Mission, Berlin, 1894).

—— 'Die deutschen Missionsunternehmungen im Njassa-Gebiet', *Petermanns Mitteilungen* (1892).

—— *Erinnerungen aus dem Missionsleben in Transvaal, 1859–1882* (Berliner Mission, Berlin, 1899).

—— 'Der Mohammedanische Gegenstoss gegen Christliche Einflusse in Zentral-Africa', *D.K.Z.* v (1888).

—— *Wie erzieht man am besten den Neger zur Plantagen-Arbeit?* (Kolonial Abhandlung, Berlin, 1887).

METHNER, WILHELM, *Unter Drei Gouverneuren* (Korn, Breslau, 1938).

MIRBT, CARL, *Die Evangelische Mission in ihre Geschichte und Eigenart* (Hinrichs, Leipzig, 1917).

—— *Mission und Kolonialpolitik in den deutschen Schutzgebieten* (Mohr, Tübingen, 1910).

MOFFETT, J. P., ed., *Handbook of Tanganyika*, 2nd edn. (Government of Tanganyika, Dar es Salaam, 1958).

MUELLER, FRITZ FERDINAND, *Deutschland–Zanzibar–Ostafrika* (Rütten & Loening, Berlin, 1959).

—— *Kolonien unter der Peitsche* (Rütten & Loening, Berlin, 1962).

MÜLLER, KARL, and SCHULZE, ADOLF, *200 Jahre Brudermission*, 2 vols. (Missionsbuchhandlung, Herrnhut, 1931–2).

MUMFORD, W. BRYANT, 'The Hehe–Bena–Sangu Peoples of East Africa', *The American Anthropologist* xxxvi (1934).

—— 'Malangali School', *Africa* iii (1930).

—— 'Native Schools in Central Africa', *Journal of the African Society* (1926–7).

MURRAY, A. VICTOR, *The School in the Bush* (Longmans, London, 1929).

MWASE, SIMON, *Strike a Blow and Die*, ed. R. Rotberg (Harvard University Press, Cambridge, 1967).

MWASHITETE, MSATULWA, *Ways I Have Trodden*, trans. M. Bryan, ed. E. Kootz-Kretschmer (Sheldon, London, 1932).

—— *Wege, die ich gegangen bin* (Missionsbuchhandlung, Herrnhut, 1936).

NIGMANN, ERNST, *Geschichte der kaiserlichen Schutztruppe* (Mittler, Berlin, 1911).

—— *Die Wahehe* (Mittler, Berlin, 1908).

NITSCH, W., 'Zwischen Nil und Tafelbai: Die evangelische Mission am Scheideweg', *E.M.M.* lxxv (1931).

OLDHAM, J. H., and GIBSON, B. D., *The Remaking of Man in Africa* (Oxford University Press, London, 1931).

OLDHAM, J. H., *The Missionary Situation after the War* (Edinburgh House, London, 1920).

OLIVER, ROLAND, and MATHEW, GERVASE, *The History of East Africa*, vol. 1 (Clarendon Press, Oxford, 1963).

OLIVER, ROLAND, *The Missionary Factor in East Africa*, 2nd edn. (Longmans, London, 1965).

PAUL, D., ed., *Die Leipziger Mission, daheim und draussen* (Evangelisch-lutherischen Mission, Leipzig, 1914).

PERSONN, H., 'Konferenz der evangelisch-lutherischen Missionen von Tanganyika-Territory (Ostafrika) in Daressalam', (1930) *E.M.M.* lxxv (1931).

PETRICH, HERMANN, *Alexander Merensky—Ein Lebensbild* (Berliner Mission, Berlin, 1919).

PRINCE, MAGDELENE VON, *Eine deutsche Frau im Innern Deutsch-Ostafrika* (Mittler, Berlin, 1908).

PRINCE, TOM VON, *Gegen Araber und Wahehe* (Mittler, Berlin, 1914).

RANGER, T. O., 'Christian Independency in Tanzania: The Negative Case', in D. Barrett, ed., *African Initiatives in Religion* (E.A.P.H., Nairobi 1971).

—— 'Primary Resistance and Modern Mass Nationalism', *J.A.H.* ix, 3 (1968).

RAUM, J., '*Educational Problems in Tanganyika Territory*', *I.R.M.* xix (1930).

RAUM, OTTO, 'Dr. Gutmann's work on Kilimanjaro', *I.R.M.* xxvi (1937).

REDMAYNE, ALISON, 'Mkwawa and the Hehe Wars', *J.A.H.* ix, 3 (1968).

RICHARD, T., *Von Katunga nach Makapalile* (Winter, Herrnhut, 1892).

RICHTER, JULIUS, 'Der Berliner Kolonialkongress und die Edinburgh Weltmissionskonferenz', *A.M.Z.* xxxviii (1911).

—— *Der deutsche Krieg und die deutsche evangelische Mission* (Bertelsmann, Gütersloh, 1915).

—— *Geschichte der Berliner Mission* (Berliner Mission, Berlin, 1924).

—— *Tanganyika and its Future* (World Dominion Press, London, 1934).

RICHTER, PAUL, 'Die 13 kontinentale Missionskonferenz', *A.M.Z.* xl (1913).

RONICKE, CURT, *Kleine Erinnerungen an einen grossen Mann; zum Gedenken an Walther Trittlewitz* (Bethel Anstalt, Bethel, 1959).

RUDIN, HARRY R., *Germans in the Cameroons* (Yale University Press, New Haven, 1938).

SCHÄPPI, FRANZ S., *Die Katholische Missionschule im ehemaligen Deutsch-Ostafrika* (Schöningh, Paderborn, 1937).

SCHLATTER, W., *Geschichte der Basler Mission, 1815–1915*, 2 vols. (Basel Missionsbuchhandlung, Basel, 1916).

SCHLUNK, MARTIN, *Die Schulen für Eingeborene in den deutschen Schutzgebieten* (Friederichsen, Hamburg, 1914).

SCHNEE, HEINRICH, *Deutsch-Ostafrika im Weltkrieg: wie wir lebten und kämpften* (Quelle & Meyer, Leipzig, 1919).

—— *German Colonization, Past and Future* (Allen & Unwin, London, 1926).

SCHULZE, ADOLF, and MÜLLER, KARL, *200 Jahre Brudermission*, 2 vols. (Missionsbuchhandlung, Herrnhut, 1931, 1932).

SCHULTZE, ERICH, *Soll Deutsch-Ostafrika christliche oder mohamedanisch werden?* (Berliner Mission, Berlin, 1913).

SCHWEINITZ, HANS HERMANN VON, 'Die Unternehmungen des deutschen Antisklaverei-Komitees, 1891–1893', *Afrika* iv (1897).

SHEPPERSON, GEORGE, and PRICE, THOMAS, *Independent African* (University Press, Edinburgh, 1958).

SHORTER, AYLWARD, 'Nyungu-ya-Mawe and the "Empire of the Ruga-rugas" ', *J.A.H.* ix, 3 (1968).

SMITH, H. MAYNARD, *Frank, Bishop of Zanzibar: Life of Frank Weston D.D., 1871–1924* (Society for Promoting Christian Knowledge, London, 1926).

SMITH, K. W., 'The Fall of the Bapedi of the North-Eastern Transvaal', *J.A.H.* x, 2 (1969).

STEINBORN, ERWIN, *Die Kirchenzucht in der Geschichte der deutschen evangelischen Mission* (Hinrichs, Leipzig, 1928).

TEINONEN, SEPPO, A., *Gustav Warneckin Varhaisen Layetysteorian Theloogiset Perusteet* (Suomen Lähetystieteellisen Seuran Julhaisuja, Helsinki, 1959).

THOMSON, JOSEPH, *To the Central African Lakes and Back: the Narrative of the Royal Geographical Society's East Central African Expedition, 1878–80*, 2 vols. (Low, Marston, Searle & Rivington, London, 1881).

TOWNSEND, MARY E., *The Rise and Fall of Germany's Colonial Empire* (Macmillan, New York, 1930).

TRITTLEWITZ, W., 'Die Bielefelder Ostafrika-Mission', *A.M.Z.* xxxv (1908).

VELTEN, CARL, *Schilderungen der Suaheli* (Vandenhoeck & Ruprecht, Göttingen, 1901).

—— *Sitten und Gebräuche der Suaheli* (Vandenhoeck & Ruprecht, Göttingen, 1903).

Verhandlungen des deutschen Kolonial-Kongresses 1902 (Berlin, 1903).

—— *1905* (Berlin, 1905).

—— *1910* (Berlin, 1910).

VIETSCH, EBERHARD VON, *Wilhelm Solf, Botschafter zwischen den Zeiten* (Wunderlich, Tübingen, 1961).

WANGEMANN, THEODOR, *Motive und Erläuterungen zu der Missions-Ordnung der Berliner Gesellschaft zur Beförderung der Evangelischen Missionen unter den Heiden* (Berliner Mission, Berlin, 1882).

WARNECK, GUSTAV, *Die apostolische und die moderne Mission* (Bertelsmann, Gütersloh, 1876).

—— *Evangelische Missionslehre*, 3 vols. (Perthes, Gotha, 1897–1903).

—— 'Die Aufgabe der Heiden Mission', *A.M.Z.* xviii (1891).

—— 'Kirchen Mission oder Freie Mission?', *A.M.Z.* xv (1888).

—— *Modern Missions and Culture: Their Mutual Relations*, trans. T. Smith, 2nd edn. (Perth, Edinburgh, 1888).

—— *Outline of a History of Protestant Missions*, 2nd Engl. edn. (Oliphant, Edinburgh, 1901); 3rd Engl. edn. (Revell, New York, 1906).

—— *Zur Abwehr und Verständigung. Offener Brief an Herrn Major von Wissmann* (Bertelsmann, Gütersloh, 1890).

—— 'Zur Missionsfrage in unsern Schutzgebieten', *A.M.Z.* xix (1892).

WEICHERT, LUDWIG, *Mayibuye i Africa! Kehre wieder Afrika!* (Heimatdienst, Berlin, 1927).

—— *Das Schulwesen deutscher evangelischen Missionsgesellschaften in den deutschen Kolonien* (Berliner Mission, Berlin, 1914).

—— *Zehn Jahre Berliner Missionsarbeit in Daressalam* (Berliner Mission, Berlin, 1913).

WESTERMANN, DIEDRICH, 'Die Deutsche Gesellschaft für Eingeborenenschutz', *A.M.Z.* xli (1914).

WELBOURN, FREDERICK B., *East African Rebels* (S.C.M. Press, London, 1961).

WILSON, G., *The Constitution of Ngonde*, Rhodes–Livingstone Papers, No. 3 (1930).

—— 'Introduction to Nyakyusa Law', *Africa* x (1937).

WILSON, MONICA, 'An African Christian Morality', *Africa* x (1937).

—— *Communal Rituals of the Nyakyusa* (Oxford University Press, London, 1959).

—— *Good Company: A Study of Nyakyusa Age-Villages* (Oxford University Press, London, 1951).

—— *The Peoples of the Nyasa–Tanganyika Corridor* (University of Cape Town, Cape Town, 1958).

—— *Rituals of Kinship Among the Nyakyusa* (Oxford University Press, London, 1957).

WISSMANN, HERMANN VON, *Afrika, Schilderungen und Ratschläge zur Vorbereitung für den Aufenthalt und den Dienst in den Deutschen Schutzgebieten* (Mittler, Berlin, 1895).

—— *Antwort auf den offenen Brief des Herrn Dr. Warneck* (Walther & Apolant, Berlin, 1890).

—— 'Die Entwicklung Deutsch-Ostafrikas', Lecture, Munich, 11 June 1897. Printed in *Verschiedene über Ostafrika*' (Kolonialgesellschaft Coll., Frankfurt University Library).

—— *My Second Journey Through Equatorial Africa, from the Congo to the Zambezi in the Years 1886 and 1887* (Chatto & Windus, London, 1891).

WRIGHT, MARCIA, 'Chief Merere and the Germans', *T.N.R.* 69 (1968).

—— 'Local Roots of Policy in German East Africa', *J.A.H.* ix, 4 (1968).

—— 'Swahili Language Policy, 1890–1940', *Swahili* xxxv, 1 (1965).

WÜRZ, FRIEDRICH, 'Karl Axenfeld', *E.M.M.* lxviii (1924).

ZACHE, HANS, 'Albrecht von Rechenberg', *Die Zukunft* (March 1912).

—— *Deutsch-Ost-Afrika, Tanganyika Territorium* (Safari-Verlag, Berlin, 1926).

—— 'Die wirtschaftlichen Verhältnisse des Nyassagebiets', in *Verhandlungen des Deutschen Kolonial-Kongresses 1902* (Berlin, 1903).

ZAHN, F. M., 'Selbständige Kirchen, das Ziel evangelischer Missionsarbeit', *A.M.Z.* xvii (1890).

Index